I FOUND NO

PEACE

A Journey through the Age of Extremes

W E B B M I L L E R

deCoubertin
B O O K S

"I have had a grandstand seat at the most momentous show in history. From there I have witnessed the decline and fall of empires, the birth of new nations, the rise of new philosophies of government and the disappearance of old ones. I have seen the map of the world redrawn... I have made friends with presidents, premiers, dictators, generals, soldiers, common workers, murderers, thieves, pimps, panders, and prostitutes."

Webb Miller

Published by deCoubertin Books Ltd in 2011.
deCoubertin Books, PO Box 65170, London, SE18 9HB
www.decoubertin.co.uk

First paperback edition.

Introduction © John Corbett, 2011.
Design and layout © de Coubertin Books, 2011.

Cover photograph: Frank Hurley, The Morning After the First Battle of Passchendaele.
Reproduced courtesy of the National Library of Australia.

ISBN: 0956431313
ISBN-13: 978-0-9564313-1-8

A CIP catalogue record for this book is available from the British Library.

Cover and typeset design by allenmohr.com
Printed and bound in Great Britain by CPI Mackays, Chatham ME5 8TD

WEBB MILLER (1891-1940) was an American journalist and war correspondent. He relocated to Europe during the First World War and lived for many years in London. For more than a quarter of a century he was one of the most brave and ubiquitous chroniclers of world affairs and was twice nominated for a Pulitzer Prize. Nearly half a century after his death, Martin Sheen portrayed a fictionalized version of Miller in the Oscar-winning film, Gandhi.

CONTENTS

INTRODUCTION

Webb Miller's world is reflected in the title—I Found No Peace—he chose for these memoirs in 1936. As a young reporter in Chicago his reputation was established by his enquiries into gangland activity, executions and local disasters. From an elementary school-educated farm boy from Pokagon, Michigan he became a rising star in the field of international journalism by the time he was in his mid-twenties.

Miller's big break from provincial reporter to foreign correspondent came following his accounts of General Pershing's pursuit of the Mexican revolutionary general, Pancho Villa, in 1916. The relatively small US military became involved in a cat and mouse pursuit of the Mexican border raider, who had wreaked havoc in the state of New Mexico. Miller had taken himself into this dangerous area of insurgency largely at his own expense. His stories of random violence, executions by firing squad and a train ambush were serialised in provincial newspapers across the United States through 1916 and 1917. Miller also claimed to have found evidence of German funding for the Mexican raids. While this was not widely accepted at the time, the so-called Zimmerman telegram (thought by some historians to be the work of British agents wanting the Americans in the First World War) seems to support him. The entrance of the United States into the conflict in April 1917 brought an end to Pershing's Mexican embarrassments and the beginnings of Webb Miller's international career.

The next phase in Miller's career—1917-19—coincided with the arrival of the United States as a major world power during a time when the great empires of Europe were disintegrating at the end of a four year war of attrition. Webb Miller offered a new perspective on the First World War and was the eyes and ears of the new world reporting on the death throes of the *ancien regimes*. His style is both descriptive and anecdotal, describing the snap shot of a visit to the British Front at Ypres at the end of the Battle of Passchendaele in November 1917. Reporting on an aircraft attack on a balloon, he brought to his reading public the horror and fascination of modern technological war–a notion far-removed from the heat and dust of the cavalry skirmishes of Mexico. This was the art of a modern war correspondent.

In London he was able to cable reports of Zeppelin and Gotha bomber attacks on a surprised and frightened London public. This gave Miller an insight into the potential destructive power of future wars. Zeppelin Captain Ernst Lehmann was at the helm of his craft the night Miller was sharing drinks and anecdotes with a group of Royal Flying Corps aviators in the Savoy Hotel in September 1917. The bombs missed the American correspondent but blew in the front of the foyer killing Henry ("'Enery'") the doorman. In 1936 Webb Miller flew on the maiden flight of the Hindenburg from Germany to Lakenhurst Field in New York. The helmsman was–unbelievably–Ernst Lehmann, who gave Miller a tour of the ship. A few months later the Hindenburg exploded whilst attempting to dock at Lakenhurst and Lehmann was fatally injured. Miller was by then completing his memoirs. This was one scoop he missed.

Webb Miller shared the tension and climax of the final days of the First World War by locating himself in Paris in August 1918. Having mastered the art of delivering his story via cable stations situated as far away as South America, he was poised to report on either a German breakthrough or an Allied counter attack, either of which would bring the war to a conclusion. By November he had already reported on American action on the Argon where the slaughter of trench warfare had been replaced by carnage across the now opening borderlands. Miller had the unique experience of reporting the Armistice from the Allied front line on 11 November 1918. The American air ace Eddie Rickenbacker flew him over the retreating German troops giving him the kind of viewing advantage unheard of by journalists at that time.

The story Miller tells of his appearance at significant world events over the next eighteen years shows his instinct at being a witness to some of the most important moments of the inter-war years. He was to rub shoulders with Hitler and Mussolini, meet Ghandi and be on nodding terms with Franklin D. Roosevelt. The reputation he had created for incisive reporting in the closing stages of the First World War opened doors into nearly every major crisis up to the start of World War Two. In his own words he claimed, "What the average non combatant civilian fails to comprehend is that modern warfare is essentially a tedious business." Viewed from over the shoulder of Rickenbacker flying in an open cockpit at 10,000 feet across the Western Front, war seemed exciting, dramatic and compulsive reading to the millions who read Miller's articles back in the United States.

Miller witnessed the French re-occupation of Alsace Lorraine and spent months in the American zone of occupation in Coblenz. Like many Americans he was confused by the haggling amongst the Allies over the fate of Germany and the new post-war Europe. His disillusionment with the peace process led him to request a place in the London office of his press agency instead of witnessing the Versailles Treaty on 28 June 1919– a mistake he admits in his memoirs. Miller's stance reflected an attitude prevalent at the time in the United States. American involvement in the war had not been universally popular in 1917 and by 1918 the casualty figures amongst the rookie American forces were high and opposition to the country's continued part in the conflict increased. President Woodrow Wilson lost the support of his Congress and like Webb Miller he was absent from the signing of the Versailles Treaty. This was the beginning of American isolationism, a "Fortress America" mindset that lasted until the Japanese attack on Pearl Harbour twenty-two years later. Miller was to offer the US public a window into world affairs at a time when most never considered owning a passport. With the breakdown of Woodrow Wilson's health shortly afterwards, all hope of the USA joining the League of Nations was gone. The future president, Calvin Coolidge, famously dismissed any international responsibility with the phrase, "the business of the American people is business."

The curiosity of Miller for the unusual led him to the steps of the guillotine in Versailles in February 1922 to witness the execution of Henri Desire, better known as 'Bluebeard'. Timing the demise of the womanising mass murderer with his pocket watch, the almost botched decapitation of France's most famous criminal was reported with the attention to detail he used for describing world events. Miller had just weeks earlier returned from the Cannes Conference where he had shared the press room with an Italian journalist, Benito Mussolini. By the end of 1922 Mussolini was in charge of Italy and Fascism entered the political vocabulary of the twentieth century. Miller would meet Mussolini again in 1932 and would later still accompany Il Duce's son-in-law, Count Ciano in a private air tour of the Italian invasion of Abyssinia in 1935. Truly Webb Miller was the man on the spot.

The British Empire was at a crossroads by the time Miller took up residence in London in 1919. The Irish Question, which had divided political parties since 1886, had boiled over into armed rebellion in 1916 and by 1920 the armed uprising had entered a new phase, with assassinations and attacks on the government and police infrastructure of British rule. In April 1920 Webb Miller went to Ireland to interview the Sinn Fein leadership in hiding. The British Liberal Party, long term advocates of Home Rule, was losing control of the situation. An independent Ireland would mean abandoning a Protestant Loyalist community in the north; worse still it would send the wrong message to other corners of the British Empire, especially India where agitation for self-government was increasing. Miller's Irish adventure allowed him to interview Desmond Fitzgerald, poet and veteran of the Easter Rising and future member of the Irish Free State government. Fitzgerald, whose family were to be involved in the politics of Ireland until the end of the twentieth century, was a skilled propagandist. He recognised that the support of the United States, as the emerging new world power, was important both for recognition of the 'cause', but also for financial and political backing. Miller's interview with Fitzgerald and Arthur Griffiths was conducted in hotel rooms around Dublin, as police and military units hunted the city's streets for the two men. Griffiths, like Michael Collins, was to go on to support the Treaty, a controversial decision that would bring independence. Whilst Collins was assassinated by his former supporters, Griffiths died suddenly in 1922 of ill health. Miller's scoop reached a massive Irish American audience. The United States was to maintain an interest in Irish affairs for rest of the century.

Watching the European empires teeter on the brink was a feature of Webb Miller's career. He travelled to Morocco in 1925 to report on the defeat of the Spanish army at the hands of the Riffs. His description of Alexander Moore the US Ambassador to the Court of King Alfonso is both dramatic and sensational, "I'm just a travelling salesman for the United States and I just slap'em on the back, tell 'em some dirty stories, give 'em a cigar, and sell 'em a bill of goods." Miller may well have unwittingly created a stereotype that would be used by Europeans for the next half century to describe the typical American abroad. Miller also perhaps did not realise that he was witnessing not just the last days of the old Spanish Empire but also the beginning of the end of Spanish royalist government. The King would abdicate in 1931 and Civil War would erupt in 1936. Miller would later report on this as well.

Meeting Gandhi was a highlight of Miller's career. It came at the Dorchester Hotel in London, where the Indian independence campaigner was having talks with the British following his successful non-violent protests over the salt tax. Previously Miller had visited India in 1930 and had reported on clashes between protesters and the British at the salt pans in the suburbs of Bombay and later very dramatically at Dharasana. His witness of the practice of satyagraha, the use of non-violent soul force, in the face of British over zealous police brutality shocked the world. Decades later, Martin Sheen would play a fictionalised version of Miller reporting on these events in Richard Attenborough's Oscar winning film, Gandhi. At the time, Miller's writings helped Gandhi surmount the moral high ground in a way that some historians suggest was a factor in his later successful work towards independence. When Miller eventually met Gandhi in England at the Round Table Conference in 1931 he persuaded the Mahatma to sign his name in his cigarette case, he had agreed as long as Miller promised never to put tobacco in it again. The signature joined those of Clemenceau (French President), Lloyd George (last liberal PM of Britain), Pershing (commander of US Army 1918), Dollfuss (assassinated President of Austria 1934) and bizarrely Adolf Hitler (an aspiring German politician in 1932).

At a period when reporting on foreign news stories meant overcoming the dangers and discomforts of travel, Miller was fearless and relentless in his pursuit of the next scoop. Travelling to Liverpool from New York in 1917 meant dodging the U Boat blockade at a time when unrestricted submarine warfare had already taken 200 American lives on the Lusitania in 1915.

Flying to India and Palestine in 1930 was an expensive and risky adventure at a time when passenger air travel was in its infancy. Miller was one of a handful of journalists able to travel to the remoteness of the Abyssinian frontier in time to get the first reports of the Italian invasion. This was an event he witnessed from General De Bono's observation post. Be it airship, tramp steamer or biplane, Miller was crucially at the right place at the right time.

In an age before television journalism and without the advantage of live radio, the written word, transmitted by cable or telephone, made him the unofficial voice of America in the 1930s. Like William Shirer in Berlin, he saw events unfold with a degree of objectiveness peculiar to American writers at this time. The Second World War was a conflict he had predicted in his memoirs in 1936. He saw the root causes in the failure and violation of the Versailles Treaty, the inability of the League of Nations to stop the Japanese invasion of Manchuria in 1931 and the Italian invasion on Abyssinia in 1935. He stopped short of warning about the dangers of Nazism and Communism but lamented the stance of his own American government as a spectator to world affairs and its pursuit of economic protectionism. Designed to protect the achievements of the New Deal, Miller recognized that this could lead to a new form of mechanized slaughter should the fragile world peace of the 1930s collapse.

His death on the London Underground in May 1940 was both mysterious and untimely. Three days later the German Blitzkrieg was unleashed against France and Belgium, an event he surely would not otherwise have missed.

John Corbett

John Corbett is a history teacher with more than 35 years of experience. He also works as an educator for the Holocaust Educational Trust.

1

FARM BOY

I was born forty-four years ago on a run-down tenant farm near the tiny hamlet of Pokagon, Michigan, five miles from our metropolis, the little town of Dowagiac, with its 5,000 inhabitants. Except that my brother Milo, who was two years my junior, and I had measles, mumps, whooping cough and scarlet fever there, I remember only a few incidents connected with that farm. I recall that we must have been poor because my father and mother worried often over the doctor's bills. My father worked part of the time as a sawyer in the sawmill at Pokagon for a dollar a day, his principal source of income. I remember starting to school in the crossroads hamlet of Sumnerville, trudging two miles over rutty dirt roads, and crying with fright so the first few days that Simon Witwer, the teacher, sent me home.

We lived in a four-room, unpainted frame house, so cold in winter that my father used to bank the foundations with barnyard manure. A cast-iron wood stove provided the only heat, besides the cookstove, in the house; the stovepipe ran through the room in which my brother and I slept but did not furnish enough heat to melt the snow which sifted through the crevices in the windows during blizzards; sometimes we found three or four inches of snow under the windows in the mornings.

We moved to another house on the outskirts of Pokagon so my father could be nearer the sawmill, where he now worked regularly. There we boys had chicken pox, lung fever (as pneumonia was then called), and diphtheria; another younger brother, Paul, died from diphtheria. I recall the anxiety of my parents over the doctor's and undertaker's bills, but remember nothing about the funeral except seeing the little white-satin-lined casket arrive. I went to the Pokagon grade school but fell far behind in my studies because of my frequent long illnesses.

After awhile we lived in another house on the outskirts of the hamlet. The only distinct recollection I retain of that period was of the only fist fight I had in my life. The school bully, Abner Lewis, much older and stronger than I, made my life miserable. He kicked, pinched, and beat me whenever he could catch me, and I was terribly afraid of him. One day he got me in a corner and pinched me until I attacked him in a white fury. He was so astounded by my berserk rage that I whipped him easily–blacked his eye and clawed his face. He never touched me again and I never again had occasion to fight.

From Pokagon we moved to an infertile tenant farm owned by John Phillips about midway between Pokagon and Cassopolis. The fields were sandy, stony, and filled with eroded gullies. My brother and I walked about two miles to the Hampshire School, a one-room rural school. By this time we had a baby sister named Martha. Although the soil was poor and "farmed out"–that is, exhausted from lack of fertilizer–the house was the best we had yet inhabited. It had seven rooms and a large grassy front yard with about a dozen fine maple shade trees and was set back about a quarter of a mile from the road.

It was here that I first conceived the ambition to write and cribbed the nature poem from Pennsylvania Grit; that still makes me uncomfortable when I think about it. I wanted to read but we had no books in the house except half a dozen paper-backed novels and a book on excavations in Nineveh. I teased my father into subscribing to a daily newspaper, the Kalamazoo Gazette, and borrowed books from Lucetta Weller, the wife of our nearest neighbour. One which I remember vividly, a book on life in China, made me long to see far-away places.

As I remember, we were quite happy on the Phillips place until a drought ruined our wheat and oats crops. Notes for our two horses and our farm implements were falling due; my father was greatly worried. He decided to spend the summer working in the harvest fields of South Dakota, where they were paying the high wages of $2.50 a day. It was the first time I recall his being away from home at night. I remember distinctly that he kissed me when he started to Cassopolis to take the train. As our family was unusually undemonstrative it was the only time he had done it, and I can still feel the prickly stubble on his unshaven face.

But I was proud because he let me cultivate the corn that summer; it was the first time I had worked regularly in the fields. I was too small and not strong enough to harness and unharness the horses; my mother had to do that. The corn-plough handles were too high for me and it was sweaty work in the hot, dusty fields, but I had the pleasant feeling that I was helping in our financial crisis.

From the Phillips place we moved in a couple of years to a more fertile farm, the Van Vlear place, five miles south of Dowagiac and owned by my great-uncle, John Van Vicar. He had chopped it out of the woods before Michigan became a state. Uncle John, a patriarchal man with white whiskers, left us his long-barreled flintlock musket, with which he had killed wild turkeys in the woods in his youth. It fascinated us; it was still in fine condition, with powderhorn made from a polished cow's horn, homemade leather bullet pouch, ramrod and bullet mold. We often wondered whether Uncle John had killed any Indians with it.

There were still many Potawatami Indians in the region. A few worked as farm hands on neighbouring farms and the others lived in shacks at Silver Creek, about fifteen miles away, where they hunted, fished, and picked wild berries for a living. In the fields we frequently ploughed up Indian arrowheads, and I made a collection of about a hundred.

I tried to find out from Lawrence Moose and Thomas Winchester, two Potawatamis who worked as farm hands for neighbours, how the Indians made arrowheads. They didn't know and said that none of the Potawatamis remembered how it was done. I asked how they got their names and they said that their ancestors had adopted the names of animals, guns, or anything else that struck their fancy. They told me about their tribe's claim to the land on which Chicago stands, over which there had been litigation in the federal courts for over half a century.

I walked from the Van Vlear place to school at Pokagon, about five miles away, and after I had finished grade school I walked five miles to Dowagiac to high school; in years of covering between four and ten miles daily to and from school I walked at least 15,000 miles, more than the distance around the world the way the around-the-world fliers go.

My father was a hard, diligent worker and was accounted a good farmer. Unlike most of our neighbours he insisted upon regular hours in the fields, seven to noon and one to six; he was meticulous about ploughing straight furrows and planting his corn and potatoes in precise, even rows. But he was always in debt and I remember that the purchase of schoolbooks and clothes for me strained his finances.

As a tenant farmer he furnished labour, implements, and tools and retained half of the produce from the farm. He struggled constantly to get out of debt, which he regarded as a disgrace. But there were always several chattel mortgages hanging over his head for horses, cows, or farm implements. From discussions which I overheard I knew that the interest payments on these notes caused a serious crisis several times a year. They were renewed time after time so that the interest often amounted to a quarter of the principal before the debt was paid.

My father had had only a few years of rural school instruction in the three R's. He wrote seldom and with difficulty, using the old-fashioned "s"; he read very little and when he did moved his lips unconsciously, pronouncing each word under his breath. For him writing was such labour that I never received more than half a dozen one-page letters from him in the years I was away from home before he died.

But in the light of later experience I now know that despite his lack of conventional culture and the literary arts he was an excellent man; he possessed to a remarkable degree the quality of tolerance which I learned later was so rare in this world. I cannot recall a single instance of hearing him speak ill of anyone; he liked everyone upon first contact, was widely liked and respected himself, and even when anyone did him an ill turn never seemed to harbour resentment.

I remember my mother's upbraiding him often for his complaisance when neighbouring farmers borrowed his implements or tools, as they often did, and brought them back broken or rusty. He repaired them and loaned them cheerfully the next time. Although untrained, he was naturally at home with machinery and in constant demand to tinker with broken equipment, which he could always fix. He was traditionally a Democrat for no other reason than that his father had been one; the highest office he ever attained was that of township highway commissioner, which he held for a couple of terms. I had to keep the simple books because they were beyond his abilities.

I never learned much about our ancestry, except that we were of English-Scottish stock which had come to America in the middle seventeen hundreds, and to which a strain of Pennsylvania German was later added. Seven of my forebears were scalped by the Indians in western Pennsylvania in 1790; afterwards others went west to Indiana, settled, and chopped out farms in the wilderness. My maternal great-grandmother Platt went to Oregon, smoked a pipe, cussed like a man, and lived to the age of a hundred and four.

My paternal grandfather, Nicholas W. Miller, occasionally visited us at the Van Vlear farm. He was born at Warren, Indiana, in 1831 and served as a private in the Twelfth Michigan Infantry during the four years of the Civil War. He was captured at Hickory Valley, Tennessee, paroled, and re-enlisted. I remember his stories of the horrors of the Battle of Shiloh and could never understand how men could bring themselves to kill one another in masses.

As I perceived much later, he was a remarkable old gentleman: slender, upstanding, with a finely chiselled face, white hair, sensitive, well-shaped hands, and a tolerant attitude toward life. He had only the rudimentary education available in the days of the Middle Frontier, but he was a man of obvious natural refinement. He always dressed neatly and rather formally: starched shirt and collar, black coat, and striped trousers. He lived in Chicago on his war pension. In his youthful days as a sailor on the Great Lakes he put into Chicago when it was only a small town of a few thousands; often he laughingly told the story of how a man almost sold him a piece of farm land, now worth tens of millions, lying where Jackson Park is nowadays. But he did not want to be burdened and hindered by property. Perhaps I inherited from him my delight in nature, because I well remember his ecstasy over an unusually beautiful sugar-maple tree and his wish that he could own it.

I borrowed books from the whole countryside – any kind, about anything. Mrs. Ruth White, who lived with her husband in a remote log cabin in the woods, was probably indirectly responsible for turning my interests toward nature. She lent me some books, Thoreau's Walden among them. Later, when a Carnegie library was opened at Dowagiac, I began to read widely. The kindly interest of Grace ReShore, the librarian there, directed me to Muir, Burroughs, Audubon, Agassiz, and others, and I started to sketch birds and collect their eggs.

Often during the winter vacations I plodded five miles through the snow, sometimes ankle-deep, to Dowagiac and five miles back to get a book from the library. When Grace ReShore learned that I came in on foot she violated the rules of the library and let me have three books at one time. Sometimes I read half of one while walking home. For many years my reading averaged more than one book a day.

We had no rural free delivery, no telephone, and no automobile; none of the farmers in that region had. My father went to Dowagiac on Saturdays to sell butter, eggs, and other produce and do the week's marketing. Otherwise, he did not leave the farm from one week to another. Eggs sold for eight to twelve cents a dozen; butter for eighteen to twenty cents a pound, and hogs for five cents a pound. Except for occasional trips to the library, I did not get to town often, as I had to stay home and work during the three-month summer vacation and the one-month winter vacation from school.

My father had been to Chicago, a hundred miles away, only once, and that was when he made the trip to South Dakota. Many of the farmers in the region had never visited Chicago. One neighbour had never travelled on a railroad train; he was afraid of them and would not let his two daughters take one either. Lake Michigan was only twenty-five miles away, but I saw it only once during boyhood, and that was when we made a two-day trip there by horse and buggy.

We bathed in the woodshed in the summer time and in the kitchen in winter; there were no bathrooms, running water, or toilets in the whole countryside. I can remember vividly the feel of the sharp wood chips on my bare feet when I bathed in a washtub in the woodshed. In the winter my mother set a washtub full of water on the cast-iron kitchen stove and in it the family bathed on Saturday nights. In summer the frequency of baths depended upon what kind of work you were doing; if I was ploughing or harrowing in dusty, dry weather, my mother insisted upon a bath every night.

Of course, we had the old-fashioned Chic Sale privy in its classic form, and the Montgomery Ward catalogue served its traditional purpose.

The lives of the farmers in those days were intolerably barren by the standards of thirty years later; their activities were mostly confined to working, eating, and sleeping. Only an occasional "pedro" card party, country dances at Pokagon, or, rarely, a barn-raising followed by a barn dance broke the monotony. We children were taken to dances at Pokagon sometimes, where the country people danced square dances and a few waltzes to the music of Murphy and Becker, two farmers who played the violin and banjo. They played from eight o'clock until one for two dollars each. I remember that my father was an excellent dancer, popular with the women, and puzzled over how different he was at dances or card parties from his normal taciturn everyday self.

Just one of the two score farmers I knew in boyhood was a drinker; and he got drunk only once every few months. But old Bill's binges were the talk of the countryside. Once he fell asleep while coming home from town in zero weather and nearly froze. His horses knew the way home and brought him to the barnyard gate. His wife and daughter had a difficult time thawing Bill out enough to get him into the house. Another time he fell out of his sleigh into a snowdrift. His horses didn't know he was gone and continued home. Bill had to stagger several miles in the snow.

Another incident which furnished conversation was the mystery of who "knocked up" the Sneyheimer girl. (These names are fictitious.) Her father, a notorious ne'er-do-well, assisted his daughter's memory in fixing the guilt upon my chum, Harry Benson, because his father owned a horse which Sneyheimer coveted. Harry's father had to surrender the horse as the price of the girl's blemished honour. He and Harry always maintained that the father of the child was one of three or four farm hands who sporadically courted the Sneyheimer girl. He applied a story which was then popular to the case: "If you're hit by a buzz saw, how the hell can you tell which tooth cut you?"

Probably the absence of amusement and diversion was responsible for the strange case of Wes Hartzell, a farmer with stonemasonry as a side line. In his middle age he suddenly announced that he was a spiritualistic medium and started giving seances to which neighbours were invited free of charge. Wes sat behind a curtain in the corner of his darkened parlour and after neighbours had sung hymns for a few minutes "materialization" appeared purporting to be the faces of dead relatives of some of the persons present. They spoke to their friends and relatives in voices which were thought to be recognizable. My aunt Libby thought she saw the face and heard the voice of her long-dead sister and wept copiously.

The news of these remarkable occurrences spread rapidly and soon Wes was "materializing" for crowds of fifty or sixty people from the whole countryside. He charged nothing and never made a cent from it. After dozens of farmers and their wives had "recognized" long-dead relatives, Wes's wife dramatically exposed him. She snatched the curtain aside one night and lighted a lamp. Wes was caught red - or rather white-handed, his hands and face covered with flour. He had a secret niche in the wall in which he concealed flour for whitening his face and hands, as well as bread dough to change the contours of his face, and a few wigs and simple make-up materials and a bed sheet. With this paraphernalia he befooled his neighbours. "I did it for fun," was all they could ever get out of Wes. He resumed the humdrum life of a farmer.

After a couple of years we moved to the Clarence Merwin farm, half a mile away. It included 120 acres with a better than average house, barn, granary, corncrib, and windmill. We were in easier circumstances and my father installed a telephone; they were just being extended into the country in that neighbourhood. This was the first time we had ever talked on the telephone, and I never forgot the thrill of hearing a voice over the wires. We spent evenings talking to neighbours just for the excitement of using the new-fangled instrument, while three or four people always listened in on the party line. It seemed to me that the advent of the telephone was the most important event of our life on the farm. I had seen at that time only one motion picture, a ten-minute film of harvesting in the West. That was exciting but didn't mean as much in our lives as the telephone.

Soon we encountered another setback: the death of John, one of our two horses. He was intelligent, plump, dappled gray with the sweetest disposition I ever encountered in man or beast. When ploughing corn with him, he turned around at the end of the rows ever so carefully and never knocked down a hill of corn with his big feet. His mate, Dan, who resembled him greatly in appearance, was a sardonic misanthrope with a leering eye and a genius for shirking his share of the work. He knew exactly how far to lag so that the doubletree would lock against the farm implements and force John to pull the whole load. Dan managed maliciously to crush every stalk of corn within reach when turning at the end of rows. He and John were as unlike in disposition as two animate beings could be.

The grief and tension in the family, which now included another brother, Alton, the night John fell ill and died is burned in my memory. We stayed up and made frequent anxious trips to the barn, where my father sat in the stall with a lantern watching John, bloated and heaving with pain. Dr. Whalen, the veterinarian, was delayed in arriving. When John died, close to midnight, father came into the house with a set face, shook his head, and sat down heavily. "John's gone," he announced. Nobody said anything and we went to bed.

Next morning I helped my father dig a pit in the back barnyard. We used Dan to drag John's carcass by a chain hitched to its hind-legs from the stall into the pit. Dan sensed he had lost his mate and wouldn't go away from the pit until we pulled him back to his stall. Then my father and I covered John with earth. My eyes were blinded with tears and father swallowed often.

John's death was not only a family tragedy but an economic disaster. Father still owed $65 on the note for John. We sent word to William McGill, the itinerant horse dealer, to bring another mate for Dan and gave a note for $125.

That summer another disaster prevented my father from catching up with his debts. We grew twenty acres of fine potatoes, the principal money crop of the year. But the market was glutted; the best offer was ten cents a bushel, delivered on board cars in Dowagiac, five miles away. After all the work on the potatoes – ploughing, harrowing, buying and cutting seed potatoes, planting, cultivating three times, and spraying with Paris green – it would have been throwing good money after bad to dig them and haul them five miles in farm wagons. We dug only enough for family use and turned in our pigs to eat the rest. Potatoes retailed for ninety cents a bushel in Chicago, less than a hundred miles away, and thousands of people didn't have enough to eat. I remember my father's discouragement and his attacks on the political talk of "prosperity and the full dinner pail."

To bolster our finances that fall before school opened I worked for the highway commission shovelling gravel into wagons on a road-construction job, monotonous, back-breaking labour that earned one dollar for a ten-hour day. We worked in a pit fifty feet deep under a burning sun. No breeze reached us. Everyone stripped to the waist and sweated unbelievably, soaking pants and shoes. We often drank a quart of water an hour and sweated it out. To prevent sunstroke we put green leaves in the top of our hats and fixed wild-grape leaves over the back of our necks. It was the first disciplined day labour I had done and it determined me more than ever to get away from the farm into newspaper work, where there was life and variety. I wondered how men bore the monotony of doing the same thing day after day, month after month.

But most of the men seemed not to mind it; they were conscientious workers who had a certain pride in their work and kept their shovel blades scoured bright and their shovels piled to the handle, though a few shirkers developed the trick of pulling their blades halfway out before lifting, thus diminishing the weight. Some deliberately delayed the physical calls of nature in the morning until after they came to work. That gave them the opportunity of taking ten minutes off. The nonshirkers applied blunt Anglo-Saxon terms to that particular trick.

The noonday lunch period was the only pleasant part of the day. I still remember the grateful sensation of sprawling inert in the shade of a big maple, grass blades cool against my sunburned, naked back and the green timothy and clover tossing in the breeze above my head as I lay resting after lunch.

On another job I worked as slip-scraper filler making a road cut just north of the Pea Vine Creek between Pokagon and Dowagiac. That was less monotonous than shovelling gravel but hard work. You flopped the scraper over, grabbed the handles, and held the scraper at an angle until the straining horses scooped it full of a cubic yard of earth. If you held on too tight and hit a root or stone you'd be thrown into the heels of the horses; if you didn't hold on tight enough you risked a broken arm or jaw.

In after years I conceived a kind of pride in my road cutting and when I came home from Europe went to see my handiwork. It is probably the most permanent and useful mark I shall leave in this world and will last for centuries. Now I know the feeling that impelled the Pharaohs to leave their mark on the world!

With my father I helped to build a bridge over the Dowagiac Creek, six miles away. We left the farm before six o'clock every morning to reach the job by seven; this meant we arose about a quarter to five to do the necessary chores, which took more than an hour. We brought the cows from the pasture, milked them, ran the milk through the separator, carried the skimmed milk to the pigs, fed and curried the horses, cleaned out the cow and horse stables, brought fresh bedding for the animals, harnessed the horses, and ate breakfast. That was the usual routine the year around, even when I was going to school.

For the use of his horses and wagon and for his own labour my father received $3.50 a day and I received $1.00. I noticed that a horse's labour was valued at 25 cents a day more than a man's, which didn't seem fair, and asked the foreman the reason. He said he had never thought of it before but guessed it was because a horse was stronger than a man. When we returned, after seven o'clock at night, there was the same round of chores, and we'd drop into bed about nine dog-tired.

During the winter vacation I helped my father with log-cutting in the woods. We cut down trees with a cross-cut saw, sawed them into logs, loaded the logs on a sleigh, and hauled them to the sawmill at Pokagon. Then we sawed the tree tops and limbs into short lengths and split them for firewood.

My father, who was a competent woodsman, taught me how to notch a tree with the axe and saw it from the other side so that it would fall exactly where you wanted. I always got a thrill of excitement from felling a big tree; when the crack upon which we were sawing commenced to widen it was a matter of sawing frantically in short jerks so that the tree would not split in falling. At the last moment, when the tree was going down, we yanked the saw out, flung it aside, and ran. There was always danger that the top of the tree would lodge momentarily upon another tree and shoot the butt back like a battering ram, or that a large limb of the falling tree would come hurtling through the air.

During my vacations from high school I spent hundreds of days alone in the fields ploughing, harrowing, and cultivating corn and potatoes. I disliked ploughing more than any other field work–plodding hour after hour between the plough handles, guiding the heavy implement; keeping my eyes constantly on the furrow to avoid cutting it too wide or too narrow; working in choking clouds of dust when the soil was dry. The only interruption came when the horses started to lather with sweat; then you had to rest them.

But cultivating corn was often pleasant. The moist, mellow soil was soothing to the bare feet, the earthy smell of the freshly turned loam agreeable. I was happy during those sunny days alone in the cornfield when the green pennons of the corn waved in the breeze while woolly clouds marched across the sky and meadow larks whistled their melancholy-sweet song. And on still, hot summer nights I felt an unnameable sense of satisfaction when I actually heard the corn grow, heard the soft rustle of hundreds of cornstalks unfolding and growing as much as two inches in a night.

The hardest work of the year came in the middle of the summer when it was hottest: haying and harvesting and threshing wheat, oats, or rye. I usually drew the job of loading the hay wagon as the hay was pitched up from the ground and "mowing away" in the hayloft. Under the eaves of the barn it was stifling with the temperature in the nineties and I sweat until my shirt and overalls were soaked through, for we never wore underwear in summer. Sometimes snakes were pitched up with the hay; once I stepped on a blue racer with my bare feet and was frightened half sick. When a rattlesnake bit my father on the finger, a neighbour made him drink a quart of whiskey – which he never touched ordinarily – sucked out the poison, and cauterized the wound with a red-hot nail. Within half an hour his arm had swollen to three times its normal size and he was terribly ill.

We always worked under pressure at haying time; the hay had to be in the barn before any rain fell; otherwise it discoloured and might heat and spoil in the barn, so we sometimes worked from dawn until dark if a storm was looming. That summer on the Merwin farm I fainted in the hayloft from exhaustion and heat prostration and spent two days in a darkened room recovering.

I liked cutting hay because I rode on the mowing machine; and I enjoyed mowing straight, even swaths of clover or timothy and hearing the soothing hum of the machine. But I would always unwittingly cut into nests of young rabbits, horribly mutilating some of the fluffy little creatures. Then I would have to get off and kill them with a club to put them out of their misery, an act that left me feeling faintly sick.

Harvesting and threshing time put an especially severe strain on all of us; often my mother left her housework and came to the fields to help us boys shock wheat and oats when rain threatened. Unless the grain was cut and shocked at the exact moment when ripe it might mold or shell in the head.

The whole community participated in threshing. My father and I helped about a dozen neighbours with their work and they in turn helped us, an unequitable arrangement because some farmers who could afford farm hands grew twice as much acreage as we did. But the hire of the threshing machine, for which we often gave the owner a toll from the crop, was so comparatively expensive that speed was all-important.

Men and boys worked to the verge of collapse because an unwritten code proclaimed it a disgrace to reveal exhaustion. We called it being "bushed." They carried me out of Leslie Wells's loft at threshing time exhausted from work, prostrated by heat and partially suffocated by the smut in his oats.

The threshers' wives accompanied them and helped the woman of the house prepare a huge noonday dinner for the men, taking special pride in preparing the best dinner possible and outdoing their neighbours. The visiting women brought contributions to the feast; oftentimes there were as many as three or four kinds of meat, five or six vegetables, half a dozen varieties of pickles and jellies, stewed fruits, pies, and cakes, all spread out on a big table at one time. The women waited on table while the men ate, and several were always chaffed for the enormous amounts they consumed. I have participated in dozens of these threshing dinners but recall none at which alcoholic drinks were served.

I accomplished this hard manual labour on a strictly vegetarian diet. From earliest childhood the idea of eating the flesh of animals nauseated me. All our family ate meat and regarded my idiosyncrasy without sympathy. My mother made no effort to humour my eccentricity; I ate whatever there was available. I existed principally on bread and butter, potatoes, eggs, vegetables, and fruit. I took no poultry or fish. During the winters on the farm my diet was necessarily extremely simple with little variety; in those days farmers in our neighbourhood lived mostly on their own products and bought few "store victuals."

I found that meat did not seem necessary to health even when I did hard manual labour. I was just as strong as any of the meat-eaters in school. In high school I played football and ran on the track team with a certain amount of success, in addition to my ten-mile daily walk and farm chores. It's true that I caught every childhood disease known in the neighbourhood, but so did my brother Milo, who was a meat-eater, and the neighbours' children. I never knew why the mere thought of eating meat was repellent to me; my mother told me I refused it even as a small child.

I deliberately abandoned vegetarianism after I went into newspaper work in Chicago because I resented the attention that my abstinence attracted. I thought that since a large proportion of the world's inhabitants ate meat there must be some natural reason for it and I gradually came to do likewise without particularly enjoying it. Thus the first part of my life I was a vegetarian and since then I have been a meat-eater. I never detected any difference in my health; meat-eating was merely more convenient and conformable.

In summer the five-mile walk to school in Dowagiac was pleasant; I grew to like it and developed a fondness for walking that has endured ever since. Usually I left the farm about seven-thirty in the morning and studied my lessons while walking; in this way I managed to make up the work I missed in grade school owing to frequent illnesses. But I got little social life at high school because I went home after classes. The roads were so sandy and rutty it was impossible to ride a bicycle. Sometimes in winter when the snow was too deep for my father to work with the horses I drove a horse and cutter to school, but not often.

One unusually severe winter – I think it was my third in high school – I stayed in town, living in the back room of Frederic Howe's insurance office with Herman Rutter, a high-school chum. We slept on cots set up in a dusty room filled with files and stationery. I worked for my meals waiting on table in a little restaurant on Commercial Street. During part of another winter I lived with Attorney Clyde W. Ketcham, doing some secretarial work in his office in return.

That winter one of the older boys suggested one night to four of us that we go to "Old Lil's," the only house of prostitution in the little town. It was a shabby, unpainted, frame building beside the Michigan Central railroad tracks near the stove factory. I didn't want to go but was afraid of being called "yellow" if I backed out. Four girls in gaudy negligees, their faces powdered and rouged (at that time no respectable women used make-up or smoked cigarettes) were in the bare back room. Two of them were dancing the turkey trot to the music of an automatic piano. The girls asked us to buy beers, which we did. Then one of them asked if we "wanted to go upstairs–for only a dollar." The older boy suggested that since none of us had a dollar we each contribute twenty cents to a pool, draw cards, and let the boy who drew the highest card take the dollar and "go upstairs." We drew cards; I got a king, which was high. I was frightened, but more frightened of being called "yellow." One of the girls laughingly grabbed me and pulled me up the stairs. In her room she tried to fondle me but I shrank from her. She seemed to grasp the situation, giggled, and asked me questions about life on the farm and my schoolwork. She took the nickels and dimes, put them in her purse, and after a few minutes we went downstairs. I did not tell the other boys what happened and the girl didn't refer to it when we came down. Thus I got the dubious credit among my chums of being something of a man of the world.

The summer after I graduated from high school I worked as a pilot on a ninety-foot passenger steamboat on Diamond Lake, Michigan, after taking a simple pilot's examination. The only noteworthy incident happened when I ran the boat through the Studebaker pier. It was a black night with rain falling in torrents; under local regulations we were forbidden to use searchlights and I was steering by reckoning and occasional lightning flashes. The pier extended into the lake farther than I estimated and without warning the boat tore through it. The two score passengers going home from a dance were frightened, a lot of paint was scraped off the boat, and it cost Bartlett, the owner, about a hundred dollars to repair the pier. I thought surely I'd lose the job; I didn't, but I had to help repaint the boat.

In the fall I tried without success to get a job as a reporter on the South Bend Tribune. Then I decided to teach school to accumulate a stake to support me while I looked for newspaper work.

I took the rural teacher's examination at Cassopolis, the county seat, passed it, and obtained the appointment to teach the Walnut Grove rural school, five miles south of Dowagiac near the Merwin farm, where we lived then. The salary was $40 a month, most of which I saved because I boarded at home. I taught everything from the first to the eighth grade: reading, writing, spelling, arithmetic, geography, history, physiology, civil government, and grammar. There were twelve pupils, ranging from a little negro girl just learning her alphabet to a gawky farm lad in the eighth grade. The five-year-old negro girl was the brightest and cleanest pupil; the biggest boy, nearly as large as I, came to school stinking from stable filth and lack of bathing. Once when the odour was intolerable I sent him home with a note to his parents, who were furious at me.

The school was a one-room frame building with a cast-iron wood stove in the centre. I split the wood, built the fire in the morning, swept out the room, and cleaned the blackboard. I prevailed upon the school board to buy a dictionary and an atlas; the school had neither when I arrived.

In high school I had acquired the habit of smoking cigarettes. At that time in the country anyone who smoked cigarettes was regarded with disfavour; in fact, cigarettes were known as "pimp sticks." A man who smoked them was presumed to be a rakehell and a woman, beyond the pale. Except at "Old Lil's" I had never seen a woman smoke cigarettes. Men chewed tobacco and occasionally, Saturday afternoons in town, smoked a cigar but never cigarettes.

To conceal my vicious habit I smoked only at recess time, when my pupils were playing in the yard. I would open the stove door and sit beside it so that the draft carried the smoke up the chimney. Once a small boy came in unexpectedly and subsequently reported my smoking to his father, who was on the school board. The board held a meeting, then sent word to me that I must not corrupt the morals of the pupils by smoking during school hours.

After school that summer I went to Indian Lake, a near-by resort, for a vacation, and met Charles Fitzmorris, former city editor of the Chicago American, and at that time private secretary to Mayor Carter Harrison in Chicago. I told him of my ambition to enter newspaper work and he offered to try to get me a job in Chicago that fall.

My savings amounted to $210. I bought from Izzy Oppenheim, in Dowagiac, a complete outfit of clothing including two suits. That was the first time I had ever had more than one suit, and I had $150 left with which to start to Chicago.

I had never been in a town larger than South Bend, Indiana, which I had visited a few times; I never had made a railway journey longer than about twenty-five miles; and I was shy and retiring, diffident in the presence of strangers, commonplace in appearance, with a colourless personality. I was far better read than the average high-school graduate and my English teacher said I wrote better than anyone else in the class.

From every other point of view, I could not have been worse equipped for the hurly-burly of reporting in Chicago.

2

CHICAGO CUB

I arrived in Chicago in the autumn of 1912 to enlist Charles Fitzmorris's aid in getting a job on a newspaper. My mother cut a slit in the inside of my coat and sewed my capital in the lining. I took the boat from Benton Harbor across Lake Michigan; it was the first time I had ever seen so large a vessel.

My grandfather met me at the dock and we went out on the South Side elevated to his apartment on Sixty-third Street near Cottage Grove Avenue. The rush and roar of the city bewildered and frightened me. My room was only about ten feet from the elevated railroad structure, where trains thundered past every few minutes day and night.

At first Fitzmorris could not find me a newspaper job. My money diminished week by week. I paid my grandfather $3.50 a week for my room. After a few weeks I found a job in the traffic correspondence department of Sears, Roebuck & Company, far out on the West Side, at $10 a week. It took me more than an hour to reach the office from the South Side.

Eventually, Fitzmorris got me a job as cub reporter on the Chicago American at $12 a week. He warned me that Jim Bickett, the managing editor, wasn't enthusiastic about adding a raw cub to the staff and that I must tell him I knew Chicago. Although I knew nothing about the city or how to get from place to place, I told Bickett I was familiar with Chicago. At nights I studied maps and street guides and soon learned the physical layout of the city.

Hector Elwell, the city editor, made me a "leg man," which meant that I took assignments, gathered information, and telephoned it to re-write men in the office. For a long time I never wrote a line myself and seldom appeared at the office except on pay days.

From the outset I was thrown into a world vastly different from that which I had known: the Harrison Street police court. That precinct comprised the most disreputable sections of the city, including part of the famous "red light" district, where thousands of women lived in houses of prostitution, and some of the Negro and Chinese quarters. Every morning the court was jammed and the cases dealt with almost every kind of human malfeasance–prostitution, perversion, sluggings, stabbings, shootings, burglary, dope addiction, negro razor fights, and Chinese tong hatchet killings. It was a dreary and disheartening introduction to newspaper work. Nearly every person in the foul, dirty room was vicious and depraved. The place stank with the mingled odours of unwashed bodies, alcoholic breaths, and the cheap perfumery of prostitutes. A jangle of street noises filled the room.

Court proceedings were highly informal. We reporters sat on the platform with the judge or perched on his desk and whispered questions which he relayed to the delinquent on trial to bring out some angle of the story.

What Judge Jacob Hopkins's administration of the court lacked in dignity it made up in forthrightness. When he wearied of the tedious succession of routine shootings, sluggings, knifings, or razorings, he would say: "Hey, bailiff, bring in some whores." Usually about a score of streetwalkers were picked up every night, although hundreds of established houses of prostitution were not molested because the owners paid their protection regularly. But the girls who haunted the streets were "picked up" now and then as a gesture and fined $5 or sentenced to ten days in the Bridewell, a municipal prison. Occasionally the judge chaffed the girls good-naturedly with such sallies as: "Well, girls, how's business?" or "What's the market price in Wabash Avenue these days?" Everyone knew that the whole proceeding was a farce and did nothing to decrease prostitution; it merely served to drive the women into the established houses where they were at the mercy of the keepers. Occasionally a girl pleaded that she did not have the $5 to pay the fine, whereupon the judge would say, "Well, you know where to get it, don't you?" and gave her two days' grace.

My first important story was the "tango murder" which developed into one of the biggest crime stories in the Middle West, I worked exclusively on that one case for many months, from the time the body was discovered until Henry Spencer, the murderer, was caught, tried, and hanged. It was then that I witnessed my first execution.

The body of a girl named Mildred Rexroat was found beside the railroad track near Wheaton, Illinois, where she had been struck by a train. But a post-mortem examination revealed she had been shot dead before her body was placed on the track. No evidence implicated any murderer but the police ascertained she danced the tango frequently at a public dance hall with a man named Henry Spencer who had disappeared. A hue and cry ensued; finally the suspicions of Spencer's rooming-house landlady led to his capture.

He confessed that he had killed Mildred Rexroat, robbed her of some diamonds, and placed the body on the railroad tracks. He had taken her to the country, purchasing one round-trip ticket from Chicago and one one-way ticket.

He also confessed to the murder of half a dozen other women, most of which he never committed. But Spencer revealed sufficient knowledge of two unsolved murders to convince the police that he was probably guilty.

Arraigned at Wheaton, he repudiated all the confessions and feigned insanity. During the trial Spencer shouted, screamed, and cursed the judge and jury.

"Hang me, hang me, I want my necktie party today," Spencer screamed at the jury day after day. Once he leaped up and attacked his own attorney in the courtroom. Often for minutes at a time he would shriek unprintable insults at the judge. But as soon as the daily court session ended, Spencer became his normal self and dropped the role of insanity. He was sentenced to hang.

The Chicago American, for which I was working, played the "tango murder" heavily from the time of the discovery of the body until the execution. My assignment kept me at Wheaton week after week producing a story a day. Spencer was imprisoned in the little county jail and I talked with him daily. We became quite friendly and he often embarrassed me by insisting upon talking about plans for his "necktie party," as he invariably called it. So far as I could detect he was mentally quite normal, except for his cold, glassy gray eyes, which chilled me. Otherwise, he was not unattractive physically; he was a well-formed man of medium size with regular features and light hair. He wore glasses with thick lenses. He told me he was an orphan with no known relatives and had served several terms in prison. I could not reconcile his personality with the fact that he was a brutal murderer.

Spencer decided that he wanted to go to the scaffold dressed entirely in white and the sheriff granted him permission to do so. He therefore began collecting a wardrobe for his hanging and bought white flannel trousers, a white silk shirt, and white sport shoes. He ordered a single red carnation to pin over his heart. He even obtained permission to use a white shroud over his face instead of the traditional black.

One day when I was hard pressed for a story I suggested to Spencer that he might get money by selling his body for scientific purposes. He eagerly agreed to the idea and asked me to publish a story that he would sell his body if the money were paid in advance. We discussed how much he should ask. He wanted $400, but I urged a lower price; he finally agreed to $200.

Several days after publication of the story, I received word that my newspaper had a telegram from a man in New Orleans who wanted to buy the body. He had invented a new embalming fluid and wanted to test it. The embalmer's telegram was turned over to me to submit to Spencer, who immediately accepted the offer and commissioned me to telegraph New Orleans to clinch the deal. The New Orleans man came to Wheaton to make final arrangements, whereupon the sheriff took a hand and forbade the sale. He found a state law provided that the unclaimed body of an executed criminal must be buried in potter's field.

The day set for Spencer's execution drew near. A gang of carpenters built the scaffold and erected a stockade between the rear of the jail and the garage to shut out the public. For the convenience of the newspaper reporters the sheriff had a long temporary desk and benches set up about fifteen feet in front of the scaffold. He sent out neat printed invitation cards to the hanging bordered with heavy black and reading: "You are hereby invited to witness the hanging of Henry Spencer at the county jail, July 31st, 1914." Spencer's cell was only a few yards from the scaffold; he heard the hammering and sawing of the carpenters, but did not lose his coolness.

The afternoon before the execution the sheriff sat in a lawn swing on the jail lawn and rubbed talcum powder into the hangman's rope so that the knot would slip smoothly. That evening he permitted visitors and reporters to view the scaffold. Some walked up the steps and looked down through the yawning trapdoor.

The corps of reporters included men who later became famous: Wallace Smith, Ben Hecht, and Hal O'Flaherty. We established a "death watch" at a garage near the jail and shot craps all night. Toward morning the whiskey ran out; a rescue squad went by automobile to La Grange, where the local marshal obligingly aroused the saloon keeper and ordered him to re-open his bar.

I had never witnessed an execution and was intensely wrought up. Watching with your own eyes the deliberate extinction of a human life is a severe shock to the nervous system. Not infrequently newspaper reporters or other spectators faint.

To dull the impact upon the nerves, reporters often drink heavily the night before an execution. But even alcohol cannot prevent a considerable shock. In Chicago, editors sometimes gave a reporter a day or two off duty after he had covered an execution.

It is horrible and sickening, but there is also something repellently fascinating about watching a man die. I suppose it is because it is one of the two great mysteries of existence. Perhaps you instinctively realize that this same mysterious departure into oblivion is the one certain thing that is going to happen to everyone, including yourself.

Each time I reported an execution – and I later covered eight others in various parts of the world by hanging, shooting, and the guillotine –the same fascinating thought kept crowding into the front of my mind.

I kept thinking: "I shall see a human being at one moment alive and in full possession of his faculties—intelligence, sight, hearing—and the next moment he will be dead, the body inert flesh, the faculties vanished. I shall see the deliberate extinction of a human existence."

Early in the morning about a hundred official invitees and newspaper reporters filled the stockade. Telegraph wires connected directly with our offices in Chicago had been installed, with muffled telegraph instruments on the desk in front of the scaffold. Reporters busily wrote advance descriptive material and the telegraph instruments clicked.

About eight o'clock a hush descended. An official of the jail tested the heavy trapdoor for the last time. It dropped with a crash, leaving a yawning hole in the platform. Then it was pulled back into place, ready to send Spencer to his death.

The door of the stockade opened and Spencer appeared with a deputy sheriff holding him by an arm on each side. He was dressed entirely in white and wore the red carnation pinned over his heart. He was pale but climbed the steps to the platform between the deputies without faltering. Then he stepped to the front of the platform, cleared his throat, and started to speak, For eleven minutes he spoke to the hundred upturned faces below. Reporters scribbled feverishly and telegraph instruments clicked. He spoke in a strained voice that verged on hysteria. Spencer said he never had a fair chance in the world and blamed society for forcing him into a life of crime. He recited the Twenty-Third Psalm, then removed his glasses and handed them to the sheriff. A deputy strapped his legs and arms, adjusted the looped rope around his neck with the knot behind his left ear, covered his face with the white shroud, and stepped back from the trapdoor.

The trapdoor collapsed. The white figure shot down with a sickening thud and dangled, twitching and turning at the end of the rope within fifteen feet of the reporters' desk. Minutes passed. Some of the spectators stirred and turned their heads away. There was a sigh of expelled breaths. Two doctors approached the body, unbuttoned the shirt and applied stethoscopes. Then they stepped back and waited more minutes. Another application of the stethoscopes. The doctors nodded. A deputy cut the rope and the limp figure was carried away.

The reporters continued to write their descriptions of the scene. Ben Hecht was turning out a graphic story when his Chicago editor broke in on the telegraph wire with a message: "Ben, don't make hanging so gruesome."

"Good God," Hecht exploded, "how can you make this pleasant?"

This experience left me unnerved and bewildered, with a shaky sensation at the pit of my stomach and confusion in my mind. Back in Chicago I attempted to sort out my emotions about capital punishment and violence. My friend, Charles Erbstein, the attorney who had defended many murderers, told me that from his long experience with murderers he did not believe that fear of the death penalty ever deterred them. I decided that organized society ought not to assume the right to commit legalized murder – to commit the very crime it sought to prevent. I told Hector Elwell, my editor, that I wanted a transfer to another line of duty; that violence and conflict filled me with nausea; that I felt I was too thin-skinned to be qualified for the work. He was sympathetic but said: "That's the reason you are a good reporter on such things. The more you hate it, the better job you do."

Soon afterward I underwent a bizarre experience, the most notable in its effect upon me of anything that happened during my four years of rough-and-tumble reporting in Chicago. It resulted in considerable notoriety in the Chicago newspapers and gave me prestige among my colleagues.

That was my kidnapping and arrest by the well-known salt millionaire, Mark Morton. His daughter, Helen Morton, a familiar figure in social circles, eloped and disappeared with an employee on one of Morton's country estates. She finally turned up somewhere in Virginia after the newspapers throughout the country had been full of the story for days. The family induced her to return and I was assigned to find and interview Helen. The Morton family owned several homes in the vicinity of Chicago and I succeeded in locating Helen at the estate outside Wheaton.

On arriving in Wheaton, I went to a garage to rent a car, telling the garage attendant where I wanted to go. But he refused to take me unless I permitted him to telephone Morton, give my name and business, and obtain Morton's authorization. He told me Morton had given instructions to both garages in the village not to bring anyone to the estate without his permission.

"If you're a newspaper reporter you'd better not go out there," the garage man said. "Morton has announced he will tar and feather any reporter who comes." I supposed this was an idle threat. I went to the other garage and induced the youthful attendant to take me by telling him I wanted to look at property in the surrounding countryside. After we started I casually suggested we might drive past the Morton estate, which was about five miles away.

As we approached the huge estate I saw three men in the barnyard. I judged from appearances that they were two farm hands and a foreman. I told the youthful chauffeur that I wanted to talk with them, but he refused to go up the driveway and waited outside by the gate.

I went up to a rough-looking, middle-aged man in overalls, who seemed to be in charge, and started to ask him a question about Helen Morton. Without warning he hit me on the jaw and knocked me completely out. When I regained consciousness, he was sitting on my stomach shouting a stream of profanity and ordering the farm hands to bring a rope. They appeared with about thirty feet of rope, trussed me tightly from neck to ankles, binding my arms by my sides, then dragged me into the barn. The leader, who was the famous salt magnate, Mark Morton, himself, ordered the farm hands to build a fire behind the barn and heat a kettleful of tar. This turn of events apparently frightened the farm hands, who did not want to participate. They drew aside in the corner of the barn and called Morton. An angry discussion ensued.

Morton strode over, picked me up in his arms, and carried me into the barnyard, where he threw me into a two-seated open Ford. Still cursing continuously, Morton started off toward Wheaton. When we passed my chauffeur at the gateway, I motioned with my head for him to follow. Morton drove furiously and about halfway to Wheaton he entered a rutty country road. He lost control of the car, which left the road and smashed into a barbed-wire fence. I was catapulted some fifteen feet from the car and knocked unconscious. When I came to, I was lying entangled in broken strands of barbed wire and Morton was standing over me with blood from his injured shoulder dripping into my face. The motor car was completely wrecked.

At this moment, my chauffeur drew up, whereupon Morton picked me out of the barbed wire, carried me over and put me in the back seat of my hired car. Aside from a few barbed-wire cuts and bruises, I was not injured. But I was so frightened I had said nothing since the time Morton first struck me. Morton was bleeding from several cuts.

He ordered my chauffeur to drive to the jail at Wheaton. As we neared Wheaton I began to feel ill. For the first time I spoke to Morton and told him I was sick. I asked him to pry into my hip pocket, get a cigarette, put it in my mouth, and light it for me. He refused with a flow of profanity, whereupon I asked the chauffeur. He pried a squashed package of Fatimas out of my pocket and put one in my mouth.

We proceeded to the jail. When we stopped in the driveway Morton dragged me out of the car and dropped me like a sack of meal on the ground. The sheriff was mowing the lawn and came running over. Although he had known me before, he didn't recognize me in my present plight, roped, bloody, and covered with dirt.

Morton informed him he wanted me arrested. The sheriff protested he couldn't make an arrest without a warrant. Morton replied that he would go to the justice of the peace and obtain a warrant, and he left in my car. When the sheriff started untying me I reminded him of our acquaintance, whereupon he recognized me. I asked him to retain as evidence my stiff collar, which showed the deep imprints of the rope, and my shoes, whose tops showed marks of the tight binding.

The sheriff let me telephone my Chicago editors from the jail. I had great difficulty convincing them that the man who had perpetrated the attack was really Mark Morton. Finally, they said they would rush a lawyer, reporters, and photographers out by car. Meantime, Morton had secured a warrant against me for trespass. I was taken before the justice of the peace and bail was fixed at $500. The man who ran the weekly newspaper in the village offered to go on my bail bond and I was released. It developed later he scooped me on my own story as he was a correspondent of the Chicago Daily News. He telephoned the story and the Daily News front-paged it before my own newspaper dared print it, because they could not believe Mark Morton had attacked me.

Next day I was put on trial. Morton testified fairly accurately as to what he had done. My lawyer brought out in cross-examination that Morton frequently sold blooded stock from that estate, and had a sign on the driveway by which I had entered stating: "Blooded stock for sale." My lawyer maintained there was no trespass because that sign rendered the driveway semi-public. The judge held this was true and threw the case out of court.

The incident had great value to me in my personal development; all the newspapers printed prominently stories about the kidnapping and trial for several days; my newspaper bought me a new suit of clothes and raised my salary $7.50 a week. From the obscure position of a "leg man" known to only a few of my newspaper colleagues and news sources, I suddenly jumped for a few days into the spotlight of attention and my name became known to everyone in the newspaper profession in the Chicago area. This had the definite effect of giving me a greater measure of self-confidence.

I then sued Morton for $50,000, charging kidnaping, false arrest and assault to do great bodily injury. Owing to the congested condition of the courts the case waited six years without coming to trial. There were numerous continuances by Morton's lawyers and by mine because of my absence in Mexico and Europe.

Finally in 1920, while I was in London, my lawyer notified me we had exhausted continuances. I wrote to him that I could not afford to come back for trial on the chance of a favourable verdict, knowing that Morton would carry the case into higher courts. So I asked him to drop the case or take any settlement, no matter how small.

A few months later I received a check for $500. The lawyer, Roy D. Keehn, had succeeded in getting $700 in settlement and retained $200 for expenses. I had quit the Chicago American, which he represented, four years previously but they had carried on the case voluntarily in the general interests of the newspaper profession.

Meanwhile I had moved from my grandfather's home to Oak street, on the North Side, where I roomed with a newspaper colleague. With the $25 a week I was now earning I bought Dr. Eliot's Five-Foot Shelf of Books—forty volumes designed to include the great literature and wisdom of the ages. These were the first books I ever bought; it took me more than a year to pay for them on the instalment plan.

From them I became interested in religion, of which I knew absolutely nothing, since both my father and grandfather were agnostics. For a time I read rather extensively in the Bible, the Koran, the precepts of Confucius, the Zend-Avesta of the Persian Zoroaster, and the Hindu Vedas. But I did not find (and still have not) that any of them afforded me the mental comfort I thought a religion should give. I read Darwin, Huxley, and Robert Ingersoll. I read the Bible often for its simplicity and the majesty of its language and sometimes went to Catholic churches for the beauty and impressiveness of the ritual.

For the first time I came into contact with good music; I had come to Chicago before the days of phonographs and the radio and had heard no real music. With a Czech reporter on the Chicago Abendpost, I often went to hear the Theodore Thomas Orchestra, and sometimes attended opera in gallery seats. The Czech reporter also took me to a few performances at the German theatre on the North Side and although I knew only the German I had learned in high school I appreciated that this was the first competent acting I had seen. On Sundays I often went to the Art Institute and formed my first acquaintance with paintings. I was trying to make up for the lack of a college education.

During 1915 my expense account notations showed that I worked on thirty-three murders – murders of revenge, murders committed in anger, murders during robberies, murders of passion, premeditated murders for insurance, "eternal triangle" murders of husbands by their wives and vice versa. The Albanians on the North Side generally used an axe or hatchet and chopped the victim literally to pieces. Italians, on the other hand, favoured the sawed-off shotgun loaded with a couple of handfuls of bicycle ball bearings which scattered widely and riddled the victim.

Even little children committed murder. I covered the case of a ten-year-old Italian lad who deliberately killed his next-door neighbour. Angered because the neighbour chased him out of his garden, the boy dragged his father's loaded shotgun from under the bed, managed to cock it, levelled it over the backyard fence and killed the neighbour. I heard him, as he sat on the knee of the captain of police, childishly recite the story and proudly show the captain how he cocked the shotgun with his foot since it was too stiff for his tiny hands. The police were perplexed because no law covered the crime of premeditated murder by a child of that age. I cannot recall whether he was sent to the reformatory or escaped punishment.

My assignments frequently took me to the criminal courts, where I saw justice continually thwarted by technicalities of the law, by perjury arranged by crooked criminal lawyers, by "hung" juries in which one or more members were bribed by the defence, by the sympathies of weak juries misled by astute lawyers, by graft, and by political influence.

I saw my friend, Chief of Detectives John J. Halpin, a ruddy, personally attractive, grey-haired officer whom I always respected and liked, and several of his star detectives, tried and convicted of collusion with criminals and sent to prison. One of them committed suicide. The revelations of that trial astounded and disheartened me.

At every turn in my work I encountered strife and violence. I have mentioned in detail only a few of the incidents which seemed important in my personal and professional development.

From the point of view of its intrinsic news value, the biggest story I covered was the Eastland disaster. A big Lake Michigan liner with thousands of excursionists aboard overturned at her dock in the Chicago River in July, 1915. Since I lived on the North Side only a dozen blocks from the river, I was among the first to reach the scene of the disaster. When I arrived hundreds of men, women, and children still clung in the water to the hull and keel of the Eastland. Other hundreds were imprisoned in darkness between the decks of the ship, which lay on her side with the stairways under water. With the police and firemen I clambered to the sloping side of the ship over planks laid from the docks. Beneath our feet we heard the agonized screams of people in the interior of the ship.

During twenty hours (with only occasional interludes in South Water Street) I sat on the side of the ship writing brief descriptions of the limp, discoloured bodies of men, women, and children as they were hauled out of the interior through a hole cut through the steel hull. Telephone wires were strung from South Water Street to the side of the ship and I telephoned the descriptions directly into my office. Sandwiches and coffee were brought aboard so that our work might be uninterrupted. I wrote descriptions of hundreds of bodies that day. The total number of dead amounted to 812; one of the worst marine disasters in history.

I covered the story when an anarchist in the kitchen of a big club put arsenic in the soup at a large dinner given for Archbishop Mundelein. Hundreds became ill at the dinner but none died. And I walked over shifting ice floes three miles out over Lake Michigan to cover the sinking of a ship crushed in the ice. I saw seventy-two persons scuttle off the ship onto the ice and interviewed them while they walked to shore.

By good luck I caught a man sought by the police in connection with the death of his sweetheart, locked him in a room in an undertaker's parlour while I telephoned the story, then turned him over to the police. It developed he was not guilty but I scored an important scoop.

My editor wanted to assign me to cover the criminal courts permanently. The job carried an increase in salary, but I refused. My experiences during that year determined me to shake myself loose from that kind of a life. I was not learning to write because practically everything was telephoned to re-write men in the office. The atmosphere of crime and violence became increasingly distasteful, but I was doing what the editors considered good work; perhaps because, as Hector Elwell said, a good crime reporter is one who hates crime.

Early in 1916, Pancho Villa, the Mexican bandit leader, raided the frontier of Columbus, New Mexico, severely straining relations between the United States and Mexico. I foresaw possibilities of a situation of international importance and after a night of consideration I decided to quit Chicago and go to the Mexican border as a free lance. It was a difficult decision for me; I had what was considered a good job among reporters of my experience; my editor liked me; I was getting $25 a week, a fair salary according to the standards of the time.

To prevent myself from changing my mind I bought a ticket to El Paso, Texas, which was fortunate because otherwise my editor would have influenced me to stay. I had saved $16 and had about $120 left after buying the ticket.

Next morning I telephoned Hector Elwell my decision; he asked me to come into the office to discuss the matter and attempted to convince me that I was making a serious mistake; that my capital was meagre and that it was highly uncertain I would find anything to do on the Mexican border. I weakened and would have changed my mind but had the ticket and did not want to lose the money.

❖ ❖ ❖

Four years of rough-and-tumble reporting in Chicago had altered me in many ways from the shy, awkward country youth with colourless personality and extreme backwardness in human contacts who came to the city almost completely ignorant of the complexities, strife, and conflict in human relations.

I had followed with perceptible success the principles Charles Erbstein had revealed to me: that if I liked people and showed it they would usually like me, and that most people suffered to a certain extent from the same disabilities in human contacts that I did. I had made a number of friends and my colleagues regarded me as "one of the boys" although I did not often carouse with them and liked to be alone whenever possible. Still I was far from unconstrained and self-confident with people and had not succeeded in eradicating my diffidence with women; I "went with" only one girl a few times during my four years in Chicago.

Finding my youthful appearance often disadvantageous in my

work, I grew a moustache to make me look older, although moustaches were uncommon at that time. It made me the butt of frequent chaffing but added several years to my apparent age. I have always retained it, although it is no longer necessary for the original purpose.

I changed my given name because I did not like it and it did not make a good by-line. I was originally named Webster, after Noah Webster, but since I had never been formally christened, I merely arbitrarily changed my name to "Webb," which sounded better to me.

I deliberately altered my signature to a bold, self-confident one. In choosing my clothes I purposely selected suits and accessories which I thought were distinctive and noticeable.

From reading Dr. Eliot's Five-Foot Shelf I gained an interest in foreign countries and formed the ambition to become a foreign correspondent; the story on the Mexican border seemed to offer an opportunity to get experience.

I found the philosophy of Thoreau useful to me during the occasional discouraging periods in Chicago when I was badly scooped. It provided mental comfort, much as religion does to those who have faith. I escaped the gnawing fear, which afflicted many reporters, of losing my job. Unlike them, I was convinced from my reading of Thoreau that the minimum vital necessities of existence–food, shelter, fuel, and clothing– could easily be obtained and that I could be happy, or so I believed, with the bare essentials of life. Perhaps that was a negative philosophy, but it comforted me.

On the night of the day I resigned from the Chicago American I started for El Paso. This was the first of a series of journeys which were to continue for twenty years through forty-one countries on five continents. Up to then, I had never travelled more than one hundred miles in one journey or been in a sleeping car.

3

PURSUIT OF PANCHO

By the time I reached El Paso the United States Government had decided to send a punitive expedition into Mexico in pursuit of Villa, who had invaded the United States, burned part of Columbus, New Mexico, and massacred many of its citizens. Villa's troops had revolted against the de facto Carranza government and held the northernmost part of Mexico. The Carranza government lacked the strength to deal with him, yet naturally resented the invasion of Mexico by a foreign army. Washington decided that no effective action could be expected from Carranza under the circumstances and that the United States must punish Villa.

At the time I knew nothing about the complex and controversial background of relations between the United States and Mexico; to me it seemed simply a question of punishing and dispersing an army which had invaded our territory. Much later I learned that it was not so simple a matter and that powerful American interests owning oil and mining properties and vast ranches were largely responsible for our troubles with Mexico, as they had been for years.

At El Paso I found some of my Chicago newspaper acquaintances, including my closest friend, Wallace Smith; Walter Noble Burns; and Floyd Gibbons. A hundred miles westward on the border General Pershing was massing an expedition to invade Mexico in pursuit of Villa. Correspondents scurried around buying supplies and outfits to accompany the expedition. I turned over $90, the major portion of my remaining capital, to Wallace Smith for safekeeping and went to work without a job.

The regular staff correspondents who flocked in from all over the country were busily occupied with the main story; they had no time to develop feature angles. I picked out human interest stories susceptible of development, covered them, and sold the resulting stories outright to the staff correspondents, who were glad to get them and paid liberally. In the first week I made twice as much money as I had been getting in Chicago. Then E. T. Conkle, in charge of the United Press staff on the border, came and offered me a regular job covering the base of the Punitive Expedition at Columbus at $30 a week. On the strength of my work in Chicago my friends had recommended my name to Conkle. I accepted eagerly and immediately went to Columbus.

Villa had raided a hamlet of one- and two-story frame buildings with some two hundred inhabitants set on the flat, arid, mesquite-covered desert beside the El Paso and Southwestern Railroad, a couple of miles from the border. Scarcely a blade of grass grew within fifty miles; the nearest settlement, Deming, about forty miles distant, resembled a movie cow town. The principal buildings in Columbus were in ashes. The Villistas had burned them in the raid.

A large military encampment had been erected across the railroad tracks, and thousands of tons of supplies had been rushed there to supply the column of 12,000 men in its advance across the sun-baked plateau of Chihuahua. Trainloads of motor trucks arrived to carry supplies across the trackless desert: an air field was established and airplanes were shipped by express from the East. Day and night the camp hummed with activity. War with Mexico threatened if Carranza refused to accept the fait accompli of a foreign military expedition. Villa's troops fled ahead of the American troops through Colonia Dublan and then beyond Parral, more than four hundred miles from the border.

Sumner Blossom, Samuel T. Moore, Jack Harding, Phil Mc-Laughlin, and I borrowed a small tent from the military authorities, and set it up on the bare desert. We also obtained mess kits and ate with the soldiers in the camp. They ate better food than that served by Columbus's sole restaurant, kept by a Chinese. Water was scarce; we paid thirty-five cents for a bath at the local barber shop. Although it was March, the glaring sun made it intensely hot in the daytime and the wind would blow up blinding dust storms. Sometimes for a day or two at a time we couldn't see twenty feet and wore tight-fitting dark goggles to protect our eyes. We obtained cots and army blankets and lived six months in our tent. Every morning we shook out our shoes because snakes, tarantulas, and Gila monsters abounded.

A telegraph office was established in an old box-car on the side track. This we used as our office for writing messages and as shelter from the sun. With a dozen correspondents present, great congestion and delay arose whenever an important story broke, for each of us scrambled frantically to get his messages in first. One day by accident I hit upon a procedure which netted me several "beats" later. Lacking other reading matter, I happened to be perusing the voluminous telegraphic guide book, where I discovered that full-message-rate telegrams took precedence over anything except government priority messages Like my colleagues, I had always telegraphed at the cheaper press rate as a matter of course. When the next big story broke – I think it was the skirmish at Carrizal – my messages beat all my competitors.

To be in the current style, the army appointed a military censor at the expeditionary base, and like most censors he knew nothing about the newspaper business or public opinion. And he left, as I discovered after awhile, a gaping hole in the censorship when he instructed the telegraph office to hold for censorship press messages or any messages addressed to a newspaper or press association. That meant that full-rate messages addressed to private individuals were transmitted without question at the telegraph office—if they were submitted by someone not a correspondent. From time to time I made judicious use of this chink in the censorship.

At first the censor forbade us to use the date line, "Columbus, N. Mex.," in our messages and had us write "Punitive Expeditionary Base" instead. Presumably the location of the base was a big, dark secret from the Villistas and the Carranzistas. Yet everyone (except, apparently, the censor) knew this was ludicrous and when newspapers began arriving, they carried the date line, "Columbus, N. Mex.," in spite of our deletion. The censor was furious. I pointed out to him that under telegraphic regulations each message had to bear the name of the point of origin automatically inserted by the telegraph company, and that all his intervention had accomplished was to save us paying for several words on each message.

I had another run-in with the censor when he refused to pass a story about the weather. During the summer on the border, the temperature sometimes reached as high as 126° in the shade. Silver coins carried in the pocket became so hot it was actually impossible to hold them comfortably in the palm of the hand more than a few seconds. But this was not as intolerable as it sounds because the heat was dry, and constant evaporation of perspiration kept the surface of the skin comparatively comfortable. I wrote a story about the weather conditions, but the censor "killed" it. He insisted that such a story might hinder recruiting for the army and the national guard and worry relatives of the troops already on the border. I pointed out to him that most of the newspapers in the United States had been printing every day for years the official Weather Bureau tables giving the temperature in various cities, including several on the border. Therefore, the temperature was no secret. But he persisted in his refusal.

These were my first contacts with censors, of whom I was to see much in various countries during the next twenty years. I found them almost invariably stupid; they did the nation more harm than good in the long run, and always left many holes which an enterprising correspondent could find sooner or later. It has been my experience that no censorship ever prevented a really important occurrence from becoming known to the public sooner or later. Of course, a properly administered censorship during war time has justification. The American censorship at the front during the World War was in the hands of men who knew their business.

As Pershing's expedition advanced it captured four men who were believed to have been members of the Villa band which raided Columbus. They were brought back to the little town of Deming, New Mexico, tried in the civil court, and sentenced to hang. I went to witness the executions. They were held in the little adobe courtyard of the jail. Since Luna County had never before conducted a legal execution the officials were not familiar with the niceties of killing men by hanging.

They decided to hang the men two at a time and erected a crude twin scaffold. Lacking the proper trapdoors, they constructed a raised platform with two hinged doors which were held shut with a rope threaded from a scantling on either side of the scaffold. Between the trapdoors, the rope ran over a block of wood.

The Mexicans were led from the jail in pairs, escorted up to the scaffold, and stationed on the trapdoors. The rope was put around their necks, and then a sombreroed, bespurred deputy sheriff knelt and cut with a hatchet the rope where it crossed the block of wood.

The two bodies shot down, twisting and squirming. One of the Mexicans wore his shirt open at the throat, showing a crudely coloured picture of the Madonna, evidently torn out of some publication, pinned over his heart. But the knots were badly adjusted, the rope was too long to break the vertebrae effectively, and one of the men was being strangled. Two of the spectators fainted at the spectacle, including one of the two doctors assigned to declare the men dead. Since there was only one regular doctor in town, a veterinary had been pressed into service, and it was he who fainted. The other two Mexicans were hanged as soon as the first two bodies had been cut down. The ropes were replaced and the trapdoors rethreaded. The sight of the executions produced such a nervous shock that one of the newspaper correspondents was sick in bed for two days afterwards.

After a few months more at the Expeditionary Base I went to El Paso and established headquarters for the collection of news along the whole border.

One day in November, 1916, the Mexican consul general told me a firing squad would execute three men near Juarez, across the Rio Grande from El Paso, next day. The killings were to occur at dawn.

He offered to conduct me and two other newspaper men to witness the affair. The men to be shot down were Colonel Rosario Garcia and two companions, captured by the Carranzista army carrying military documents to Pancho Villa.

The consul general fixed the rendezvous for three the next morning, in front of the Paso del Norte, El Paso's principal hotel.

Three of us gathered at the appointed hour. Over the edge of the arid Chihuahua desert the darkness was fading into chilly gray. We paced up and down the silent street. We felt tense and strained, like men in the trenches the last moments before "zero hour." We puffed hastily at our cigarettes and kept flinging them away.

A dim light spread in the East. One of my companions hauled out a bottle of cognac. We drank, wiping the neck of the bottle on the coat sleeve before passing it to the next man. That was drinking etiquette on the border. Finally the consul general drew up in a dusty automobile. He took a long pull at the cognac bottle, and we rattled over the wooden bridge across the Rio Grande. Juarez was asleep and silent except for the howling of dogs.

The rutted road outside town led straight up into the foothills to an unfenced sandy cemetery on the hillside. A few mounds with unpainted wooden crosses marked the graves.

Near the middle of the cemetery was a short wall of sun-dried adobe bricks, pock-marked by the impact of hundreds of bullets. On this squalid stage the ultimate drama of three human lives was to be performed. More than three hundred men had died in front of this wall.

In the East pale rose began to tinge the gray. We puffed cigarettes, spoke in monosyllables, and waited. The cognac bottle went around again. Minutes passed.

"There they are, I guess," said the consul general, indicating a tiny cloud of dust far down the hillside. We stared at the scribble of dust, which resolved itself into a group of fourteen men walking slowly in three uneven ranks. A young Mexican officer in a gorgeous tight-fitting robin's-egg-blue uniform trimmed with black led the party. He carried a gleaming sword and had an automatic strapped to his hip.

His smartness and military carriage contrasted ludicrously with his motley squad and their three charges. The consul general saluted the officer and explained we were American correspondents who had come to witness the executions by permission of the Carranzista government.

Behind the resplendent officer walked Colonel Garcia, a middle-aged man of military bearing, followed by two boys. The colonel had a

heavy inch-thick rope tied around his neck. The first and second boy—
mere children—followed at intervals of three paces, fastened together by
the same piece of rope, looped from neck to neck.

Colonel Garcia wore no hat. His hair fell over a lean, intelligent-
looking face darkened by several days' growth of beard. His drab uniform
was faded and crumpled.

The first boy, who looked about sixteen years old, wore only a dirty
shirt and flimsy cotton trousers. He walked barefooted; his beardless
face, unwashed for days, was stained with tears. At the end of the rope
stumbled a barefooted urchin of about fourteen years, his round, coppery
face revealing his Yaqui Indian origin. His only clothing was a thin, dirty
shirt and blue denim overalls.

On each side of the prisoners walked the firing squad of ten
soldiers, five in each rank, dressed in cheap cotton garments which could
scarcely be called uniforms. They wore crude leather sandals tied to their
toes and ankles by thongs. Their bare feet were caked with dirt. Not one
of them was more than twenty years old.

The squad halted before the adobe wall. With grave politeness,
Colonel Garcia requested permission to write a farewell letter to his wife
and children. The officer bowed and granted permission.

The members of the firing squad were ordered to untie the rope
from the prisoners' necks, and after much tugging finally unfastened the
thick knots. The smaller urchin ruefully rubbed his neck, chafed by the rope.

Colonel Garcia coolly drew some bits of paper and a pencil stub
from his shirt and sat down in the sand to write. The boys shuffled uncertainly for several moments, then sat down. The firing squad stood ill
at ease for a bit, then squatted on the bare earth apart from the prisoners.

As Colonel Garcia finished each page he placed it on the ground
between his legs with a pebble on top to prevent the wind from blowing
it away. Minutes passed and still the colonel wrote. The young officer
joined our group. He said the boys had been in Villa's army.

Three dogs which accompanied the squad chased boisterously
over the sandy graves. One approached the firing squad and sniffed. A
soldier tweaked its tail and laughed at the animal's whine of surprise.

The other youths of the squad joined in the game and cuffed at the dog as it romped among them. The two other dogs, understanding it was a game, joined in and galloped joyously around the group.

The eyes of the Yaqui urchin brightened. A dog approached him with wagging tail, offering to include the boy in the game. The boy suddenly seized the dog and hugged it to his breast. Tears rolled down his cheeks and he wiped his eyes on a dirty sleeve.

Colonel Garcia continued to write page after page. About twenty minutes passed. When he had finished Garcia painstakingly re-read his letter, arose, and handed it to the officer. He asked that it be delivered to his wife.

I made voluminous notes during this scene. John Reed, the famous correspondent who lies buried in the wall of the Kremlin in Moscow, had written a remarkably vivid story of an execution in front of this same wall. Reed made many notes during the execution, and I wanted to try to write an equally graphic story.

"I'm ready now. Let's get started," said Colonel Garcia to the captain of the firing squad. He walked briskly over to the wall and called to the two boys, who arose and came to him. He took the smaller boy by the shoulders and indicated where he was to stand. Two paces to the left he placed the second boy. Garcia chose his own position at the left of the larger boy. The captain of the firing squad sharply ordered the executioners into line, about ten paces in front. They rose from the ground and straggled into position.

Then Colonel Garcia asked the captain if he could make a final statement. "Si, mi colonel," said the captain.

Addressing himself to us, Colonel Garcia made a speech that lasted about five minutes. The consul general translated it to us in an undertone as he spoke.

"I am not a bandit," Colonel Garcia said. "I joined Pancho Villa because I sincerely believed he was fighting for the liberation of my country. I hope whatever government survives will bring peace and liberty to my country. I am not afraid to die. Viva Mexico."

Suddenly, Colonel Garcia sat down with his back to the wall and ordered the two boys to do likewise. They sat down. The captain was visibly perturbed and disconcerted. Nothing like this had ever happened before. Traditionally men stood with their backs to the wall to be shot.

The captain remonstrated with Colonel Garcia. He ordered the boys to stand up. Garcia ordered them to remain sitting. The captain pleaded with Garcia to stand. He shook his head determinedly. "Shoot us sitting down or not at all," he said. Then he placed his hand over his heart and said to the firing squad, "Shoot me right there through the hand, brothers."

The captain walked back beside the squad, and lifted his sword. The squad's ten Mausers rose to the aim. The sword flashed down. An irregular volley crashed. Jets of dust spurted around the sitting figures. The bodies of the boys jumped forward slightly then sagged like half-filled sacks of meal. Both were apparently dead. But Colonel Garcia tipped over on his right side. One of his legs jerked and jerked. He was perfectly conscious.

"Shoot me there . . . there . . . through the hand, brothers," Garcia pleaded to the squad, patting his breast over his heart with his left hand. The squad inserted fresh cartridges. The sword came up – dropped. Another volley. Still Garcia lived. His mouth worked and his leg quivered. His hand still patted the spot over his heart. A third volley. The crumpled figure lay still.

The captain pulled out his automatic, walked over to the body, put the muzzle in the ear, looked away, and pulled the trigger. A muffled explosion. This was the "tiro de gracia," the "mercy shot" which terminates Mexican military executions. Then he performed the ghastly rite for the two boys.

The captain saluted the consul general. At a phrase of command, the firing squad shouldered their Mausers and slouched off down the hill towards Juarez, followed by their dogs.

We walked silently back to our automobiles. The bodies lay huddled against the wall. "God, how I need a drink," said the International News Service correspondent. We finished the cognac. I felt ill, with an empty, paralysed feeling in the pit of my stomach. Mentally I tried to frame the opening paragraphs of my story. I couldn't find words to convey the casual horror of the scene.

"I've seen men die," said one of the reporters, "but never as bravely as that colonel."

"Yes," said the consul general sadly, "Mexicans know how to die." We climbed into the automobile and started back to El Paso. The sun bounded up into a cloudless sky, preparing for another of those brilliant days. It was good to be alive. Back in El Paso, I hurried to the Postal Telegraph office and rapidly wrote my story for the wires, gulping black coffee to steady my jumpy nerves. I felt "cryey" inside.

I wondered what the casual slaughtering of the seven Mexicans whom I had seen put to death by legalized murder accomplished. They were ignorant men who had not the slightest idea what they were fighting for or why; their deaths made not the slightest difference one way or another to the obscure conflicts in progress. I didn't know the answer then and don't know it yet.

As I write this twenty years later, I have before me a yellowed clipping from the Denver Times of the story I wrote that morning. The editor didn't consider the story important or significant; he cut it to two dozen paragraphs. He deleted the names of the youths, simply calling them "two boys, followers of Pancho Villa." And I cannot remember what they were called either.

From several officers of the Aviation Service I obtained a startling story about the dangerous inefficiency of the airplanes sent to the Mexican border and decided to take the chance of ejection from the expedition base by evading the censorship. Concealing as a matter of course the sources of my information, I wrote a detailed story of the critical state of American military aviation on the border and smuggled it out by courier.

Eight airplanes of the type Curtis JN-2, equipped with OX-5 motors, constituted the air service of the expedition. Scientific wind-tunnel tests had previously condemned this type. They were subject to spinning and pitifully underpowered, with only four-horse-power excess power at sea level. In the thin air at the altitude of about a mile where the expeditionary base lay, the planes were terribly dangerous and the pilots had great difficulty in even taking off the ground. Propellers split in flight and other dangerous material defects developed. At times only two airplanes could fly and they rarely covered as much as two or three hundred miles. Pilots frequently could not cross the mountains to reach the front lines in Chihuahua, even at the lowest passes. In a flight to Colonia Dublan, Lieutenant Willis crashed and Lieutenant Edgar S. Gorrell was forced down in the desert. After walking as far as he could, he stole a Mexican's horse at the point of his gun and forced the man to guide him out of the desert. Mind you, this situation existed less than a year before the United States entered the World War.

Publication of my story in hundreds of newspapers throughout the United States caused a furore in Washington. The War Department issued a blanket denial, putting me into hot water with my New York office, and ordered an investigation. Of course, I flatly refused to reveal my sources of information. The inspector general questioned the entire corps of aviation officers at the expeditionary base. All but one denied having given any information. That one man courageously stated that he had given the information because he believed it would result in saving many valuable lives among the few trained pilots we had. He was withdrawn from the border and sent to the Massachusetts Institute of Technology to study aeronautical engineering in a routine capacity. There he remained until the World War gave him his chance.

That man was Lieutenant Edgar S. Gorrell, now "czar" of commercial aviation in the United States in his capacity as President of the Air Transport Association of America. I have always thought that the army air service owes him much for his moral courage and forthrightness. Had it not been for the shake-up which Gorrell and others, including myself, created, our army air corps would have entered the World War more unprepared than it was. As a result of the public revelations of inefficiency Secretary of War Newton D. Baker and General Pershing took immediate action to provide better airplanes and forbade the use of the original equipment. None of the aviators was courtmarshalled and I was not ejected from the expeditionary base.

That was my first encounter with official government denials, of which I was to meet many more later in Europe. It disillusioned me, for somehow I had the idea that official statements by governments must be true. In Europe I found that governments commonly used the dementi, or official denial, for purposes of expediency, lying coldly and deliberately.

In February, 1917, when the Punitive Expedition had been in Mexico nearly a year, President Wilson decided to withdraw it. Villa was in hiding, his troops were scattered and no longer represented a potential danger to the American border, and our invasion of Mexico had enraged the Mexican people. Furthermore, our relations with Germany were becoming daily more critical.

I returned to Columbus to cover the withdrawal of the army from Mexico. The army censorship insisted that the crossing of the border by the Expedition be censored. This was patently ridiculous and I determined to violate the censorship again.

The night before formally crossing the frontier line, the Expedition encamped a few miles from the border. Staff officers gave me a detailed description of exactly how the army planned to cross. I wrote the story that evening in the past tense as though it had already occurred and mailed it special delivery on the night train to the manager of the Postal Telegraph office in El Paso, with instructions to wire it to Denver, then the nearest point on the transcontinental United Press trunk wire system. At the commencement of the message I wrote instructions to the Denver office to hold it until they received a full-rate telegram addressed not to the United Press but to the manager of the bureau, personally, at his office address. The telegram would be an inquiry about the price of cattle signed "Johnson." That would be the signal to release the story of the army crossing the border.

I hired a youth in the village to post himself on top of a building with field glasses. He was to watch the border a few miles away, and send my previously prepared telegram about cattle prices the moment the expedition started to cross. The stratagem worked and I was credited with a considerable "beat" on the story. My competitors had to come up from the border, write their descriptive stories, and pass them through the censorship, which took considerable time. Since the cattle-price inquiry was a private message to a private individual it was not subject to censorship.

I don't want to give the impression that I was never scooped, because I was; sometimes badly, but I'll tell about that later.

After the withdrawal of the Pershing Expedition, I went to Mexico City, entering the country from Laredo, Texas. Repeated revolutions and bandit raids had damaged the railroad from El Paso so badly that trains were not running and only one line connected Mexico City with the north. Furthermore, the trains were frequently attacked or wrecked and the passengers robbed and sometimes killed by bandits. Conditions throughout Mexico were chaotic and especially dangerous to Americans, because the invasion by American troops left a legacy of hatred of all gringos.

My friend Andres Garcia travelled by the same train. The journey took four days because nothing ran at night on account of the bandits, and the tracks were in such a dangerous condition that trains ran slowly. We had no dining car, and ate food bought from vendors at stations. At that time the Carranza government had a rule that bandits killed or executed for raiding the railway be hanged to the telegraph posts beside the line as a warning. Often we saw their desiccated bodies dangling in the air—on one occasion ten at a single place. Fragments of railway trains that had been wrecked during years of revolutions and bandit attacks strewed the line. I suppose we saw several hundred wrecked cars during the trip.

Each train was preceded by an explorador to fight off bandits. The explorador, which was run about half a mile ahead, consisted of an engine and four box cars loaded inside and above with Carranza soldiers. They wore cheap, faded denim uniforms and big straw sombreros. The few who had shoes wore crude native sandals. Many of them were only fifteen to eighteen years old. Their fighting gear consisted of old rifles of various vintages and models.

Shortly after dawn on the fourth morning near Queretaro we heard a grinding crash from the explorador ahead, followed by shouts and shrieks and a flurry of shots. Our train quickly halted. Garcia and I looked out the window and saw men running about wildly and shooting I sat with shaking stomach, knowing if the bandits won we should be robbed and perhaps shot. I carried most of my money in large bills folded lengthwise and strung on my necktie inside the folds of my stiff collar. Bandits often stole passengers' clothing and shoes, but I guessed that Mexican bandits would probably have little use for a linen collar.

Firing continued several minutes then gradually grew fainter in the distance. With Garcia and other passengers, I went forward to the explorador. The engine and box cars lay toppled over in a narrow cut. By removing the spikes from the rails in the cut the bandits had derailed the explorador; but it had been travelling slowly up a grade and suffered little damage. The Carranza soldiers had courageously jumped from the cars on the opposite side of the cut from the bandits. They then surrounded the little hill where the bandits were lying on the lip of the cut and fought them off. Thirteen dead bodies strewed the ground. Several had rolled down into the cut by the side of the track. I saw no wounded. Apparently they had been summarily killed on the ground.

After a while, the Carranzistas returned from pursuing the bandits, bringing with them a cow which they proceeded to slaughter and skin. They built a fire and roasted hunks of meat to celebrate their victory.

Then they commenced to hang the bodies on the telegraph posts. One soldier shinned up a post with a rope which had been attached to the neck of one of the dead bandits. He threw it over the cross-arm and a group of soldiers started hoisting the corpse. When they had it about halfway up, the rope broke and the body tumbled down on the heads of the hanging party. They laughed uproariously, gave it up as a bad job, and did not attempt more hangings as long as we were there.

We had to stay here most of the day until another train was brought up from Queretaro, the nearest station. Except for the hospitality of an old American miner on the train, who carried a basket of food and bottled water, we should have fared badly. We did, however, manage to buy a few eggs from peons who lived near by and to boil them beside the tracks. When a new train arrived to pick us up, we had to step over the body of a bandit officer which lay beside the track below the car steps. Garcia pointed out that his only insignia consisted of a cloth star sewed on his trousers inside the thigh so that it would not show when he was astride a horse. This was to guard against his being recognized as an officer and singled out as a target during raids.

While in Mexico City, I obtained from a reliable source a very important story which I held until I reached the Texas border. According to my information, German emissaries had gone to Villa to offer him money and support if he would resume attacks upon American border towns at widely separated points. Villa was hiding in the mountains beyond Parral with remnants of his band. The German idea, evidently, was to keep the United States immersed in the Mexican situation and force the retention of a large military force on the Mexican border. This occurred a few months before the United States entered the World War and I heard of it a month before.

I left Mexico and telegraphed my story from Laredo, Texas. At that time it sounded fantastic and was generally discredited. Many years after the World War the revelation of documents concerning the activities of the German Secret Service in Mexico confirmed my story.

From the border I returned to Chicago where I worked three days in the offices of the United Press. From there I was sent to the New York office, where I again worked three days. I was then transferred to Washington, in the early spring of 1917.

Washington pitchforked me into a new kind of work. War loomed; the greatest national crisis since the Civil War fermented the Capitol with excitement and confusion. The Senate was debating our entry into the war. My first assignment took me to the Senate, although I protested I knew nothing about politics and had no experience covering legislatures. I did a poor job in the Senate and was soon transferred to assist Carl D. Groat covering the State, War, and Navy Departments. During my brief time in the Senate I conceived a great admiration for Senator Robert LaFollette, who was leading the opposition of the "little group of willful men" to the entry of the United States into the war. I thought then, and still do, that he revealed more moral courage than anyone else in that chamber, and more bravery than a soldier at the front.

On the momentous night of April 6, 1917, I helped cover the tense scene in the House of Representatives in joint session with the Senate when President Wilson declared the United States in a state of war with Germany. I realized I was witnessing one of the most important moments in American history. But unfortunately, my impressions of that night remain jumbled and unclear. I remember President Wilson taking his place at the Speaker's desk, pale and overwrought, and the thunder of frantic applause that greeted him. But I spent most of my time in the press room behind the press gallery helping to put the text of the President's speech on the wires. Hundreds of newspapers throughout the nation held their presses for the news and every second counted.

The text was held back until the President entered the door of the Capitol, when copies were handed to the press associations. We had delegated Tony, our fleetest-footed and most resourceful office boy, to snatch the first copy and run pellmell into the press room. There Robert J. Bender, then manager of the Washington Bureau of the United Press, grabbed a copy, frantically paged through it to the crucial words declaring the United States at war. He shouted a "flash" of half a dozen words to the telegraph operator, who clicked it out to hundreds of newspapers. Bender tore the text apart and gave several of us a page each. We hastily ran through the page, jotted down on slips of paper the most important phrases or sentences and handed them to Bender. He glanced at the slips, collected them in the order of their importance, and dictated dozen-word "flashes" directly to the telegraph operator. That night leased wires linked together hundreds of newspapers in every corner of the country; they received their news instantly and simultaneously. At that time the Morse telegraphic system was used; when the operator in the House press gallery clicked out a word it reached hundreds of telegraph instruments in newspaper offices at the same moment. Thus the first flash, "President declared United States state of war with Germany," went to hundreds of towns and cities within a few seconds; within a few minutes all of the essential points of President Wilson's declaration followed. Meantime, the full text of the speech was clicked out on another wire. The loss of a few seconds was irreparable; the slightest error unforgivable. That night we worked under intense strain and tension.

While at the War Department I obtained from a source which I still do not choose to reveal a story of immense importance. It was so far ahead of its time that the newspapers, with one exception, disregarded it almost completely.

At this moment the American public, the newspapers, and most of the government still lived in a state of almost complete ignorance regarding what our entry into the War would entail in men, money, and munitions. The Allies had deliberately misled us concerning the real state of affairs, and until they gradually began breaking the bad news after our entry on their side, people generally believed that we could loan them a few hundred million dollars, perhaps send one or two divisions to "show the flag," and the war would quickly end.

At this time a competent authority in the War Department gave me the startling news that the United States might have to send as many as half a million men to France; that the Allies were in a critical position; that the war might last more than a year; and that the United States would undoubtedly be forced to furnish vastly more money than anyone anticipated. At the moment the story sounded absurd and few newspapers gave it much attention. I know of only one editor in the United States who sensed he had a story of predominant importance. He ran a paper in Manistee, Michigan, and spread the story with an eight-column banner line across the entire top half of his paper in heavy black-faced type. He gave me a by-line nearly an inch high, the largest I have ever seen. He knew he had a story, but he didn't know, nor did anyone else, that it told only a fraction of what was to be.

When organization of the draft plan began under General Crowder and Captain (now General) Hugh Johnson, I was sent to cover it. Johnson was then a virile, aggressive young captain, one of the handsomest and smartest officers in the army. Even then his great ability attracted attention and I recall other army officers' praising Johnson's brilliance. Through Lieutenant Allen W. Gullion, my good friend of border days and now a member of the draft board staff, I had an inside track throughout on the draft story. This brought me to the attention of United Press executives in New York.

One morning about ten o'clock the telephone rang. "Do you want to go to Europe?" someone asked me abruptly. I said I did. "All right, then, get a passport, catch the four o'clock train to New York. You'll get here at nine and will sail at midnight."

In New York I was taken to a private house where the British consul was dining. He had agreed to interrupt his card game, take his rubber stamp, and visa my passport.

I sailed at midnight for London.

4

"THE BELLS OF HELL GO TING-A-LING-A-LING"

"The bells of Hell go ting-a-ling-a-ling,
For you but not for me,
Oh, Death, where is thy sting-a-ling-a-ling,
And grave, they victoree?"

(A British soldiers' war song)

I sailed on the old American liner New York. This was the first time I had been aboard an ocean liner or seen the Atlantic. The New York was armed with six-inch guns forward and aft, manned by naval gun crews. German submarines sank ships daily; we were prepared to run the submarine gauntlet. We carried only about two dozen passengers bound to Europe on business connected with the war; some brought their own life-saving devices. Two nights out from Liverpool we were ordered to sleep in our clothing ready to debark if we were torpedoed or struck a mine.

My first contact with the World War occurred off Ireland. In the middle of the morning the aft gun crew sighted what they thought was a submarine periscope and opened fire. I grabbed a life preserver and rushed on deck. I saw nothing that resembled a periscope, but the crew fired half a dozen shots; six-inch shells skipped miles over the surface of the sea like flat stones over a pond. We never learned whether a submarine had actually come near us, but for several hours the ship proceeded in sharp zigzags and we reached Liverpool safely.

I found war-time London grim, dreary, and depressing. Street lamps were darkened at night, shop windows went unlighted, and trams and buses ran with dimmed lights because of the danger of air raids. The lake in St. James's Park had been drained to prevent its serving as a landmark for bombing attacks on Downing Street or the Foreign Office. Civilians in the streets wore drab, shabby clothing and patched shoes; their sallow, sunken faces revealed the effects of the rigid food restrictions.

Hundreds of people dotted the streets, waiting in line to purchase their restricted quotas of rationed food: meat, sugar, butter, fats, and tea. The rationing system permitted "butcher's meat" only twice a week. I obtained a ration card from which the waiter clipped a tiny triangle each time I ordered meat. Owing to the scarcity of fats everyone lost weight. In our office we amused ourselves by making a weekly check to determine who lost the most.

At the little Wellington Restaurant in Fleet Street where many American correspondents ate, we discovered that a nearsighted waiter permitted us to detach from our meat card the triangular bit of cardboard entitling us to one meat meal. We found that the corner of a two-penny bus ticket was exactly the same size and colour. Often we deceived old Carlo, the waiter, and thus ate meat four or five times a week. We ate the soggy, gray bread dry and used saccharine tablets in lieu of sugar because restaurants served no butter or sugar. I lived in a cheap hotel in Norfolk Street with cold, clammy rooms, unheated because of the drastic coal restrictions. Warm baths cost twenty-five cents; the rooms had no private baths. The room rent of six shillings and sixpence – about $1.62 a day – included breakfast, which consisted usually of a flabby fish called a bloater served whole, tea, and dry toast. The fish was so soggy and repulsive that usually I could not eat it. Several mornings I noticed that the fish looked familiar; apparently they were bringing back the same one several mornings in succession. I therefore cut my initials on its side each morning, which forced the hotel at least to serve a fresh one.

Women and girls in coarse, drab uniforms acted as bus conductors and subway guards; the man power of the country had gone into the army. Once it took two months to have my watch repaired and two weeks to get a suit cleaned–they sent it to Scotland, more than four hundred miles away. Subways and buses ceased running about midnight to conserve coal and power; there were few taxis on the streets and private cars had either been commandeered for war work or entirely prohibited to save gasoline.

That autumn the Germans repeatedly bombed London from the air. The last week of September, 1917, German "Gothas," the new, huge tri-motored bombers, raided the city five times–on Monday, Tuesday, Friday, Saturday, and Sunday nights, usually early in the evening. That week shops closed at five o'clock to enable workers to get home before the raids started. On the Sunday night raid ten airplanes succeeded in penetrating the outer defences. I was working nights that week.

News of impending air raids always reached us first over the Exchange Telegraph news printer in our office. The machine suddenly stopped, spluttered a few moments, then typed: "Alert. Hostile aircraft have crossed the coast." All lights in the streets were extinguished, buses and trams were abandoned where they stood, and the subway stopped running. Air-raid sirens shrieked and "maroons" – explosive rockets used to give warning – exploded with loud crashes high above the city. Special constables bicycled through the streets blowing shrill police whistles to clear the streets while everyone sought shelter in cellars, basements, or subway stations. Dozens of searchlights crisscrossed the sky.

Within about twenty minutes anti-aircraft guns thundered on the eastern perimeter of the city. Rapidly, the firing came nearer. Fingers of light from the searchlights frantically sought the invaders, ten or twelve thousand feet above us. We heard the heavy drone of the tri-motored Gothas. Bursts of shrapnel, sometimes half a dozen at once, spangled the sky, and we heard the chatter of machine guns from pursuit planes two miles above. Chunks of shrapnel rained down on the roofs and in the streets; once dozens of fragments fell in our little block. Guns mounted on motor trucks rushed through the streets, firing now and then. We heard the heavy explosions of falling bombs, preceded a few seconds by a lightning-like flash.

Usually I witnessed the raids from the doorway of Temple Chambers, where our office was located, sheltered by the stone archway from falling bits of red-hot shrapnel. It was a rule that I formally declare everyone, including the office boys, off duty as soon as the air-raid warning arrived. We could cable nothing about the raid anyhow, until the official announcement afterward, for the censor passed only the official announcement. After the firing ceased in the central area, but still continued to the westward, our office boys ducked out into the streets to pry bits of shrapnel out of the paving blocks and bring them to the doorway to cool.

One night several heavy bombs dropped within a few hundred yards of the office, and the building shook as though in an earthquake. The roar of the explosions and the concussion deafened us and frightened us badly. The marks of one of the bombs can still be seen on the base of Cleopatra's Needle on the Embankment, where the heavy granite was badly chipped by fragments and the bronze lions punctured. Other bombs that night fell near the Charing Cross Hospital.

After the war, at Coblenz, I met the German ace, Hans Christiansen, who had dropped some of those bombs. We compared notes and he told me they were aiming at the Cecil Hotel, which their spies correctly informed them was the headquarters of the Royal Flying Corps. They missed by less than a hundred yards, despite their altitude of over two miles. He told me they located the hotel by counting the Thames bridges, which looked like dark lines from that height. Also he told me they were always ordered not to drop bombs in the vicinity of Buckingham Palace, which explained its immunity.

On another night a toothache confined me to bed in the Norfolk Hotel. I was asleep and did not hear the raid warnings. My first intimation of the raid came when a bomb fell two hundred yards away. The concussion was so great that the window shade over my open window was blown inward as though by a strong wind. The fright stopped my toothache.

With Hal O'Flaherty, now managing editor of the Chicago Daily

News – who proudly hailed from What Cheer, Iowa, in the Skunk River Valley – I was at the Savoy Hotel bar one evening during a raid. An hilarious party of young British aviators on leave from the front filled the room. While the guns roared and bombs dropped one flier leaped to the top of a table, looked upward, raised his glass, and shouted, "Here's to the Jerries" (a war-time nickname for the Germans). They drank the toast and resumed the noisy party heedless of the raid. At that time the average life of an active combat flier was three months; these clean-cut boys devoted every moment of leave to a furious enjoyment of life; they knew that within a few months they'd be shot down, wounded, dead, or burning to death.

After the raid I walked home with O'Flaherty to his hotel in Southampton Row. A crowd filled the street. A bomb had blown in the front of the hotel, killing 'Enery, the night porter, and several guests. Poor 'Enery had been our friend and sole source of whiskey after closing time.

Hundreds of thousands left London for the country to escape the raids. Top-floor apartments were unusually cheap; they were considered less safe, so I managed to rent one in the exclusive Temple for $17.50 a week. In the next raid a big shell fell in the courtyard but failed to explode.

That winter the United Press sent me to the British front in Flanders for some feature stories. I sailed in a troop ship from Dover. As we were entering the harbour of Boulogne that night, German airplanes started bombing the city. Lights were extinguished on the ship, everyone was ordered below deck, all cigarettes were put out, and we turned back into the Channel. We were packed as tightly as matches in a box in the darkness between decks. At my back I heard two men talking with an American accent and fell into conversation with them. They told me they were American air officers en route to the British front to study the organization of the Royal Flying Corps. When the raid ended, and the lights went on, I found the officers were two old friends of the Mexican border, Lieutenant (now Lieutenant Colonel) Edgar Gorrell, who had given me the airplane scandal story on the border, and Captain (now

General) Benjamin Foulois.

In Flanders they assigned me to the so-called "guest chateau," whence an officer took me daily to some point on the front. Although we were about thirty miles behind the front, we heard the low rumble of guns like the beating of surf. At dinner the first night I noticed that whenever the Germans were mentioned an elderly white-moustached colonel mumbled, "The bloody swine." After dinner I mentioned to one of the officers that the colonel didn't seem to care much for the Germans. "No, he doesn't," the officer replied. "He was left for dead on the battlefield among a lot of other wounded. The Germans bayoneted all the wounded; he escaped only because a dead man was lying on top of him."

The next day I caught my first glimpse of the World War in Flanders; the imperturbable officer who was conducting me wore a monocle and spoke in monosyllables. We went by car into the ruined city of Ypres on a brilliantly sunny December morning. As we approached the city between rows of tree stumps shattered by artillery, shells occasionally dropped a few hundred yards from the road, shooting up fountains of earth. My heart was thumping with excitement; involuntarily I jumped at each explosion, but my conducting officer, who later became Lord St. Aubyn, merely adjusted his monocle and refrained from glancing in the direction of the shell. His manipulation of the monocle fascinated me; it was the first time I had seen a man wearing one.

In Ypres, now only a huge heap of rubble, shells plopped down every few seconds, throwing up geysers of dust and stones. We left the car in a ruined courtyard and tramped through a communication trench into a dugout. The casual atmosphere there astonished me; I listened intently for every shell, but the officers and men in the dugout ignored them all, brewed tea, shaved, played cards, and "read shirts"–that is, hunted lice.

I watched two German airplanes trying to shoot down one of about half a dozen British observation balloons anchored to wires and windlasses just beyond Ypres. When the airplanes commenced to dive toward the balloon the observers jumped out in parachutes, the balloon was rapidly hauled down, and British airplanes and artillery drove the

Germans off. Shrapnel burst like popcorn in cottony puffs around the fleeing Germans. Then several German planes flew toward the line, where British machines engaged them. I watched them manoeuvre a couple of miles above us and heard the staccato crackle of machine guns; none were shot down and my companions manifested little interest in the spectacle, which I was following with breathless interest.

As we returned to the château that evening I witnessed a drum-fire bombardment of Kimmel Hill by the Germans. For fifteen minutes shells burst like bundles of firecrackers. From our point of vantage we could see clusters of flashes, accompanied by the continuous roar of explosions. "Just the routine evening hate," St. Aubyn said in bored tones. I thought my first glimpse of the War provided an interesting and exciting story. But the official communiqué that night merely stated: "There is nothing of importance to report on the western front." Next day I went to Vimy Ridge and heard heavy German shells passing continuously overhead, bound miles behind the lines. Try as I might, I could not find words to describe exactly the slithering, rumbling sound made by the shells.

The rest of the winter I spent in London, where the food situation was becoming rapidly more critical. German submarines were sinking hundreds of thousands of tons of ships. We sent three copies of all our mail to New York, each on a different ship. At press conferences the British military and naval spokesmen admitted that the situation was serious. British inventors were racking their brains to discover means to circumvent submarines and mine fields.

Admiral Reginald Hall, Chief of Naval Intelligence at the Admiralty, told us confidentially that the British had installed a huge wire submarine net in the British Channel. He said the British Secret Service knew of the activities of a certain German spy in London but permitted him to continue to operate, indirectly feeding him false information from time to time. This spy was induced to purchase false plans of the submarine net for 1,000 pounds sterling from intermediaries whom he did not suspect. After he had transmitted them to Germany, he was taken to the Tower of London and shot. The net was then stretched across the Channel in a different location from that indicated in the false plan.

Admiral Hall said the net caught several submarines, thus revealing their position so that airplanes or destroyers were able to sink them.

Hall once stated that the Admiralty "knew within twenty minutes" whenever the German fleet commenced to get up steam; naturally he gave no details of the workings of the British Secret Service, but I assumed this feat must have been accomplished by the use of a secret wireless post; no other means existed at that time of communicating so rapidly between England and the Continent.

German submarines cut some of the transatlantic cables, and the congestion of official government cablegrams on the remaining wires became so great that at one time the American press associations were restricted to six hundred words daily. Delays in cable communication with New York, even at the urgent rate, varied between six and ten hours.

Ed L. Keen, a great newspaper man, now dean of American correspondents in Europe, headed the United Press organization in Europe. At this time he worked out a stratagem which resulted in several important "beats" on stories of world-wide significance. The idea was so absurdly simple that our competitors failed to discover it. On stories of exceptional importance we sent a bulletin at urgent rate to our Buenos Aires office, which relayed it over the Andes and up the west coast of South America to New York. Thus the message travelled more than three times the distance across the Atlantic but moved much faster because the cables to and from South America were naturally less congested. Although it cost four dollars per word at the urgent rate, a "beat" of an hour or two was well worth the price.

Occasional air raids on London still occurred, eleven of them while I was there. One was a Zeppelin raid which included an airship commanded by Ernst Lehmann, with whom I was to cross the Atlantic by air nineteen years later on the flight of the Hindenburg.

The United Press required a new manager of the South American service with headquarters in Buenos Aires and offered me the post at a considerable raise in salary. I was in a confused and perplexed state of mind, disgusted by the atmosphere of mud, blood, and the slaughter of Europe.

After anxious consideration, I accepted the offer to go to Buenos Aires. They wanted me to arrive as soon as possible; the quickest way to reach Buenos Aires was to sail to New York and take a boat southward. I bought a Spanish grammar, dictionary, and histories of South American countries, especially Argentina, and again started through the submarine zone.

The ship for Buenos Aires was to leave the same day I arrived in New York. The United Press brought my father east from Michigan to bid me goodbye. But the liner for South America broke a propeller in dock and was delayed. Then my father told me that the registration papers for the army draft, which I had duly filled out in London and mailed to our New York office, had never reached our local draft board in Michigan, and I was in danger of being regarded as a draft dodger.

In the New York office I learned that my papers had inadvertently been pigeonholed. The man responsible made an affidavit that he was to blame and forwarded the papers. But I was so upset by the incident I decided to go out to Michigan and join the army, although the idea was thoroughly obnoxious to me. In Dowagiac I soon found I could not get into the army immediately but must await a summons under the selective draft system. Meanwhile, my papers arrived; the draft board classified me several categories down the list. This meant that a year or two would elapse before my summons arrived. William W. Hawkins, general manager of the United Press, then wired that he wanted me to go back to Europe because meanwhile another man had been chosen for the South American job.

I started for the third time through the submarine gauntlet. With me on the ship were two other correspondents, Adam Breede and Otto Higgins, of whom I was to see much later. By this time the British had evolved the "convoy system," which meant that a dozen ships passed through the submarine zone together guarded by destroyers. Since the speed of the convoy was limited to the speed of the slowest ship, it took us seventeen days to reach Europe. A ludicrous incident occurred during an unexpected drill for abandoning ship in case of being torpedoed. An English woman on board had bought an elaborate life-saving device consisting of a suit which the wearer donned and then inflated by blowing up like a toy balloon. It was fitted with pockets containing food and water. Hearing the signal for the drill, and not knowing but what it was a real disaster, she inflated herself and then could not get through the door of her cabin. Convinced now that the ship was sinking, she screamed frantically for help and snickering stewards had to deflate her to get her out.

I worked in the London office again for a few months, then was sent to Paris in the summer of 1918 as an assistant on the staff.

5

HE WHO GETS SCOOPED

A palpable atmosphere of impending dread enveloped Paris like smoke in the air. You could almost sense it with your eyes shut. More than a million persons had left the city; thousands fought on the platforms at the Gare de Lyons and the Gare d'Orsay to board trains for the south of France; the boulevards were almost emptied of civilian traffic.

Less than forty miles away gray masses of Germans were hammering a triangular salient toward Paris with smashing drives. The famous long-range gun, "Big Bertha," which astounded the world, fired every day or so upon Paris from its secret emplacement forty-five miles distant. Allied airplanes frantically sought the location of the emplacement to bomb it out of existence. But shells continued to plunge into Paris from twenty miles in the stratosphere at intervals of exactly fifteen minutes during daylight hours.

In our office on the Rue Rossini, just off the Boulevard des Italiens, we often heard the dull explosions above the noise of the streets. Sometimes I went to the open window and listened when another shell was due. Since censorship permitted us to send out nothing about the bombardment except the official communiqués and the fact that it was resumed each morning, there was no point in gathering details about where the shells struck or the damage they did. Usually we never knew. Unlikely as it sounds, the bombardment quickly became such a routine matter that one morning while I was busy preparing to cable a dispatch sent in by motorcycle courier from the front, I forgot to add that the bombardment had been resumed that morning.

Soldiers in the uniforms of a dozen nationalities crowded the sunny boulevards and filled the cafe terraces. Laughing soldiers with their temporary sweethearts and a few civilians tranquilly sipped weak war-time beer or read newspapers. Every quarter of an hour pedestrians hesitated in the boulevard, café loungers consulted their watches and leaned forward in a listening attitude; everyone paused expectantly. Above the rumble of motor buses they sometimes heard the muffled thud of the explosion; then they went on with their love-making, drinking, or reading. Once a shell fell on a hotel near the Place Vendome and gave everyone in the vicinity of the boulevard a momentary flutter of excitement but hurt nobody. Our office shook, although it was a quarter of a mile away.

About dawn on the morning of July 18, 1918, the rumble of heavy cannonading awakened me in the little Hotel Louvois. I listened at the open window. Birds twittered in the trees in the leafy Place Louvois and the water of the fountain tinkled musically. Only an occasional cart rattling home from the markets broke the stillness of the sleeping city. But the rumble of thousands of guns continually rose and fell like far-away thunder.

I knew the Germans were at the Marne, less than forty miles from Paris. "They've broken through," I thought; hastily throwing on my clothes, I rushed down to the lobby. Only the night porter was up. "They're coming, they're coming," he said breathlessly. I hurried to the office, passing the huge building of the Crédit Lyonnaise, one of the principal banks. Outside stood a long line of motor trucks into which men were hastily loading bank records and correspondence.

At the office John de Gandt came in shortly; we excitedly discussed plans to cover the entry of the Germans into Paris. We felt certain it was only a question of a day or two and guessed they would enter by the Rue Lafayette and march up the Champs Élysées to the Arc de Triomphe. We arranged that when the Germans approached, de Gandt would go outside the city to some point on the telegraph line to Brest, the cable head of the fastest cable to New York. I would remain in Paris, obtain the use of an American Red Cross automobile, watch the Germans march into Paris, then escape to the nearest town that communicated with Brest.

De Gandt and I spent the morning burning with excitement, tense with impatience, smoking innumerable cigarettes. The Ministry of War could not or would not tell us anything except, "You must await the official communiqué at noon." The hours of that July morning were the longest, most excruciatingly nerve-wracking I ever lived through. I twitched with excitement but could not even release myself with physical activity. We tried to make telephone calls to government departments; the telephone service was disrupted; often five minutes passed before the girls at the central exchange answered. The American Embassy had no news. The American Red Cross agreed to lend us a car flying its insignia. None of our friends on the Paris newspapers knew what was happening. Although one of the greatest events of the war was occurring only forty miles from us, we might as well have been thousands of miles away for all the news we could obtain that morning. Here loomed what might be one of the greatest stories of our lives. And we could do nothing but consume ourselves with anxiety.

Before noon a group of about fifty French and foreign correspondents gathered in a dingy office of the Ministry of War in the Rue Saint-Dominique, paced up and down, puffed cigarettes, and conversed in undertones. At noon a disheveled officer walked rapidly out of an inner office with a sheaf of typed carbon-copy communiqués. The newspaper men tore them from his hands and scattered into the streets to telephone without pausing to read.

I ran pell-mell to a prearranged telephone on which we kept an open line direct to the terminus of a secret leased wire into Brest. So excited and breathless I could scarcely articulate, I dictated the text of one of the most momentous communiqués of the war.

Marshal Foch had started his great counter-offensive; the Germans were fleeing in confusion from the Marne salient with their backs to Paris; Foch was smashing with gigantic triphammer blows on both sides of the salient. Paris was saved; the beginning of the end had commenced, although we did not realize that at the moment.

After I had dictated the text and run to the nearby telegraph office in the Rue de Grenelle to send a duplicate cable by the regular French telegraph lines as a precaution, my knees weakened, I staggered and nearly collapsed from the reaction after the hours of nervous strain.

I remember little of the following days except our furious activity. Long lines of ambulances brought thousands of wounded into hospitals in the Paris area. Foch threw corps after corps upon the retreating Germans. Daily the intervention of the American Army increased. Day and night motorcycle couriers from the American front brought messages from our three staff correspondents. I helped prepare them for transmission on our secret leased wire.

In addition to having the exclusive use of the only private leased wire to Brest, we managed to gain an additional ten or fifteen minutes' advantage over our competitors. Normally the motorcycle courier came down the Rue Lafayette, passed near our office, and reported to the press officer at the Rue Sainte-Anne. Then he started making rounds, delivering the dispatches to the various press associations and newspaper offices. We casually suggested to the couriers that they would save themselves an additional trip by dropping off our messages when they passed near the United Press office before reporting to Rue Sainte-Anne They gladly acceded; thus our messages were actually on the wires before our competitors had even received theirs.

Newspaper men of twenty years ago will recall the series of remarkable "beats" achieved by the United Press during those war days. Our competitors were frantic but for a long time could not ascertain how we did it. There can be no harm now in revealing the secret.

Lowell Mellett and John de Gandt succeeded in locating and making a contract for the exclusive use of the only private leased wire between Paris and Brest, the cable head. Louis Coudurier, owner of the newspaper, Dépêche de Brest, held all rights. The utility of this wire lay in the fact that messages did not have to pass through the Bourse telegraph office and censorship in Paris, where most of the delay en route to New York occurred. Sometimes urgent-rate messages costing seventy-five cents a word were an hour getting through the red tape at the Bourse, while our messages over the leased wire were transmitted instantly, and taken across the street in Brest to the cable office. Thus we gained an enormous advantage on certain classes of news.

De Gandt concluded a private arrangement with the chief censor, who permitted us to telegraph over the leased wire without Paris censorship anything from the American front which had already been censored by the American military censors, anything that appeared in the Paris newspapers, and any official communiqués issued in Paris, but nothing else. We furnished the censor copies of everything sent over the wire afterward. Of course, we did our utmost to keep these arrangements secret.

Probably by engaging private detectives to follow our men to the terminus of the leased wire, one of our competitors ascertained what we were doing. The chief of their bureau went to Brest and offered Coudurier six thousand dollars in cash to violate his contract with us and give them exclusive use of the wire. Also he promised that his organization would defray any expenses Coudurier might be put to as a result of litigation over the broken contract.

Be it said to the honour of Louis Coudurier that he stoutly refused to consider violating the contract under any circumstances, and told us of the machinations. In appreciation of his action, the United Press continued payments to Coudurier long after the wire had ceased to be of any use to us.

During the Battle of the Ourcq, in which the Americans participated heavily, I was suddenly summoned to the front. It should have given me a supreme thrill. But actually it was dust and ashes. I felt like a gnat on a huge whirling flywheel. The war took place on such a stupendous scale that when you were close up to it your mind refused to grasp it. I felt bewildered and obsessed with a sense of futility. I saw only one tiny cog of a vast machine; it seemed almost impossible to integrate it with the thundering roar of the machine which sucked in hundreds of thousands of men, ground tens of thousands of them into bloody fragments, and spewed back tens of thousands broken and bleeding. Again I perceived how rapidly human beings become accustomed to their environment, accept it as though it had existed always; and how casual, impersonal, and machinelike the whole proceeding becomes.

What the average noncombatant civilian fails to comprehend is that modern warfare is essentially a tedious business. Out of a million soldiers, not more than a few hundred thousand ever reach the front lines, and a comparatively small number of them experience more than a few of the heart-clutching thrills of personal combat. The rest spend the greater part of their time in the army doing the labour of a worker in a construction gang or a clerk in an office. My predominant impression of the five campaigns of which I saw something is that war is intrinsically a boring business.

I remained at the American front during the battles of the Ourcq and the Vesle. When the Americans reached the line of the Vesle River, operations in the Marne sector became stabilized and I went back to work in the Paris office until the Battle of the Argonne began. This was the greatest battle in which American arms ever participated, the battle which was terminated by the Armistice.

I have never yet seen in writing the real story of how the war ended in the frontline trenches; how stupendous machine-like organizations constructed for killing ceased operations at a specified moment; what an awkward and grotesque impression a fighting army gave when its functions suddenly ceased at a word in the midst of white-hot combat. The biggest news in the history of newspapers, perhaps in the history of humanity. A scrap of news that two thousand million people–the whole world–awaited breathlessly. News that would mean to tens of millions that their sons, husbands, or sweethearts would come home alive and unmaimed. News that would mean to millions of people life, love, money, food, everything . . . News that had never before and could never again mean so much to so many people. The Armistice!

These thoughts continuously raced through my mind those last exciting days of the war in early November. Our men were sweeping the German army out of hitherto impregnable positions it had held for four years in the Argonne Forest - sweeping so fast that it was difficult to keep the pins that denoted the front lines in the proper places on the big wall map kept by Captain Arthur Hartzell at press headquarters.

All the correspondents were under intense mental strain those last few days of the Battle of the Argonne. We guessed an armistice was imminent. We slept little. I felt terrific responsibility because I was the sole representative of United Press at the front. The other two men had scurried away in preparation for events after the expected armistice. Fred S. Ferguson went to Paris to see Colonel House, and Frank J. Taylor went to Switzerland to rush across the frontier into Germany the moment an armistice went into effect.

Press headquarters now lay some forty miles behind the front. We therefore faced the dismaying prospect of having the Armistice become effective suddenly while we were in Bar-le-Duc, forty miles from the greatest story in the world.

Night and day unending columns of marching infantry, innumerable motor trucks bearing food and ammunition and the thousand-and-one things needed to supply an army of 600,000 men jammed the roads to the front. Often it took hours to get there, even with our Cadillac cars and General Headquarters insignia.

In an effort to devise a scheme to reach the front faster than my competitors, witness the Armistice, and get back to press headquarters first, I visited Eddie Rickenbacker's squadron. Rickenbacker, the premier American ace, maintained his flying field only a few miles outside Bar-le-Duc. If I could get somebody to fly me to the front, watch the Armistice from the air, and fly back near Bar-le-Duc I could score a big "beat" and have an unusual story of the ending of the World War. It would be a violation of regulations, but regulations didn't matter in those last hectic days.

Eddie Rickenbacker helped me arrange it with Lieutenant Jimmy Meissner of Brooklyn, a slim, attractive youngster who had shot down more German planes than any other American flyer except Rickenbacker. He promised to fly me to the front for the Armistice. I was set for a remarkable beat. But as a precaution I charted the roads to the front likely to be least encumbered with traffic and figured that Bras, a ruined village near Verdun, was the place nearest the front which could be reached easily by automobile.

About nine o'clock on the morning of November 11, I was at army headquarters at Souilly, about midway between Bar-le-Duc and the front. The commanding general excitedly rushed out of his office with a slip of paper in his hand. "Boys, it's over. Armistice at eleven o'clock," he shouted. He added that the flash was to be announced in Washington. My story now was to describe the end of the war.

I got Jimmy Meissner on the telephone. Breathlessly I asked if he was ready to start. Jimmy replied, "There's fog all along the Meuse Valley. We couldn't see a thing. It would be useless. I'd go but you wouldn't get a story. I'll take you tomorrow if there's no fog and it's still worth a story."

My car with an ex-racing driver as chauffeur waited outside headquarters. I scrambled in and told the driver to go hell-for-leather through Verdun to Bras. The famous "Sacred Road" to Verdun carried three lines of traffic. We took the middle lane reserved for staff cars. Columns of troops marching up to be thrown into the battle choked the right-hand lane. They didn't know the war would be over in less than two hours. The left-hand lane was jammed with lines of motor trucks going back for ammunition that would never be needed.

As we approached Verdun, that obscene, hellish wilderness where more than a million men were slaughtered, the front was comparatively quiet. Only desultory shelling. But while we threaded the shell-shattered streets the Germans suddenly opened their last bombardment of the ruined town. Apparently news of the Armistice had just reached that sector of the German front, and they decided to give Verdun a final "strafe" before eleven o'clock.

American and French batteries began to open fire in retaliation. Every few minutes a thunderous explosion came from behind Verdun, far heavier than any of the others. Afterwards, I heard that this was Admiral Plunkett's fourteen-inch naval gun. It had been dismounted from a battleship and brought by railway to Verdun, hundreds of miles from the seacoast, at immense labour. As the Americans were saving it for a surprise in connection with a vast new attack toward Metz, it had never been fired. When the gun crew heard about the impending armistice, I was told, they would not be cheated out of a few shots at the Germans. So they opened fire at random without aiming at anything in particular–

just in the general direction of the German army. As the huge shells cost many hundreds of dollars each, it was an expensive demonstration.

"What'll we do?" my driver shouted, hunching down in his seat as big German shells burst near us. "Go on, fast as you can. Get out of town," I replied. We couldn't tell in the fog just where the shells were falling. Now and then we saw the exploding flashes and spouts of earth unpleasantly near. I was badly frightened; my skull crinkled. Just as we emerged from the other side of Verdun two big shells burst about fifty yards away. We heard the zing of the fragments. Several doughboys standing beside the road started to run. Two fell flat in the mud; we thought for a moment they had been hit. But they leaped up, dripping mud, and disappeared in the fog. Within a few minutes we had left the bombardment behind.

Beyond the shattered village of Bras I left the car and proceeded on foot. I had reached the edge of the torn battlefield wastes. I walked and walked. A soldier directed me to a communication trench, which I followed half a mile ankle-deep in mud. I could see only about fifty yards through the fog. Upon reaching the front-line trench I inquired for the commanding officer. A captain emerged from a dugout. Spying my green armband with the "C" denoting war correspondent, he said: "What are you doing up here? There's nothing happening here."

"I've come to cover the end of the war—the Armistice."

"Good God, when is it?" he exclaimed.

"Eleven o'clock. Haven't you heard?"

It was a quarter to eleven, but he had not received the order. Never did I convey more astonishing news to anyone. He seemed stunned. He shouted to some of his men.

"Hey, this correspondent says the war's over at eleven; says its official; right from headquarters."

They gathered around and questioned me eagerly. They seemed incredulous. "Whaddye think of that!" "War's over—guerre fini!" The word flashed up and down the trench by word of mouth. There were exclamations and an excited flurry of talk. But no demonstrations of joy. No cheering. No frenzy of delight. No drama.

Just then, about 10:50, the field telephone in the dugout tinkled. The captain answered. The text of the official armistice order. I copied it over his shoulder as he jotted it down: ". . . fighting to cease at eleven . . . hold lines where they are . . . do not fire unless attacked . . . no crossing of armistice line or communication with the enemy . . ."

The captain began telephoning the order to his outposts. He made no comment, simply read the order mechanically. As the hour of eleven approached, the men kept their eyes on their wrist watches. From the direction of Verdun the fog-muffled rumble of the cannonade gradually died away. In our sector somewhere to the left there had been occasional rat-tat-tat-tats from machine guns. Now they ceased.

Eleven o'clock! The war ended!

It would make a better story if I could tell of men cheering, yelling, laughing, and weeping with joy, throwing their fin hats in the air, embracing one another, dancing with delight. But they didn't. Nothing happened. The war just ended . . .

The men stood talking in groups. The captain let me talk on the telephone to the outposts. No drama there, either. They said they couldn't see anything in the fog or hear anything. Further up the line it was the same. The army's reason for existence had suddenly ceased. The men didn't know what to do next.

Here I was covering the greatest story in the world and nothing was happening. This was the end of the greatest war in the history of the world, the war that killed eight and one-half million men, the war that affected in some way every man, woman, and child on earth. And here in the front line there was less excitement, less emotion, and less delirious joy than you'd find in a lively crap game. Often I had heard bigger demonstrations when a man rolled seven and won five dollars.

"If I could git me some drinkin' likker I'd git drunker'n a hoot owl," said one private.

"Well, where do we go from here?"

"Bet they keep us in these gawdam ditches all winter just the same."

"Wisht I was in Paris tonight with a couple of them French couchez-avec-moi gals, yes, two."

"Wish I was in Cincinnati with my job back."

That was the way the war ended on the few hundred yards of front that I observed personally.

The front was silent. For the first time in four years men ceased trying to kill one another. Two stupendous organizations for slaughter stopped at a word.

You had to flash your imagination up and down that six hundred miles of front and visualize the millions of men facing one another. At 10:59 it was their duty to kill. One minute later it was not. One man on each side of the lines had sent out the words that stopped all this.

You had to flash your imagination over the seven seas, where thousands of ships were on errands of war; to factories all over the world where millions of persons were making munitions; to Germany, where a dynasty was crashing and millions were on the verge of starvation; to Russia, where dynasty and a system had already gone to smash; to Austria-Hungary, where an empire was disintegrating; to thousands of training fields in a dozen countries where more millions of men were preparing for slaughter.

You had to think of all these things before you could begin to grasp the terrific significance of those words I had read over the captain's shoulder. You couldn't get it here in the frontline trenches. You were too close to it. These men were too close to it.

While I was writing this book, eighteen years after the end of the war, I talked with Sir Percival Phillips, the famous British war correspondent. His experience at the British front resembled mine. He showed me a clipping of his story written that day. It said:

"I have no thrillingly dramatic story to tell you of the actual suspension of hostilities. You may have pictured the sudden cessation of a heavy bombardment, silencing of innumerable batteries, the notes of a bugle, the hush which would follow such an abrupt termination of a battle. I did not hear of any such incidents."

I hastened back towards Bras to my car. We raced back through Verdun and swung on to the "Sacred Road." I told the driver to go as fast as he could without risking a smash. He did – the speedometer registered fifty, sixty, seventy. Beyond Verdun the road was alive with troops slogging up to the front. Millions in France, England, America knew by now that the war was over. These men didn't, and they were only a few miles from the front lines. As we passed the head of each column I leaned out and yelled, "War's over. The Armistice. The Armistice." Heads came up, shoulders went back, the news flashed down the columns like an electric current. You could see it travel. Columns halted and cheered. That was my biggest thrill in the war. I conveyed to them the most important news they would ever hear, and the biggest news it will ever be my lot to tell anyone.

In press headquarters in Bar-le-Duc I rushed to the censor. Yes, I was the first man back. I leaped to my typewriter and commenced as fast as my fingers would fly to write the words I'd formulated in my mind during the trip. At urgent rate. Each word of urgent to New York cost seventy-five cents. I wrote my story in separate sections of about fifty words each, and handed each section as soon as it was written to the censor, who rushed it to the army telegraph office. Section after section was whipped out, hundreds of words; I never counted, but I must have run up a cable bill of five hundred dollars. After twenty-three minutes my nearest competitor rushed in. He'd had hard luck with the traffic. Others streamed in later.

As soon as I finished, I started back to the front again, accompanied by Clare Kenamore, correspondent of the St. Louis Post-Dispatch. We went further north along the front lines and gathered additional details that afternoon and evening. Reports came that the armistice order hadn't reached isolated sectors until after eleven; that men were killed after eleven; that the Germans sent word over to some units that the war was ended and "for God's sake stop firing."

When we headed back towards Bar-le-Duc it was night. The fog had lifted. Along the front, mile upon mile as far as the eye reached, the sky flamed with coloured signal rockets, red and green flares and Verey lights. That was the Yanks' armistice celebration. Having no other means of demonstrating their joy, they shot off their supplies of signal lights. Nobody could get fittingly drunk because there was no liquor.

The villages in this region were wrecked and deserted.

During the war open fires near the front were prohibited. But not tonight. In every direction huge bonfires blazed, surrounded by groups of soldiers, some singing. Most houses in this forested region were built of wood. I think the statute of limitations protects the boys now so I can reveal that some saved themselves the trouble of building bonfires by simply setting fire to ruined houses. It was cold that November night in the Argonne, and the houses made fine bonfires. If the French read this, they'll probably want to deduct the cost of those burned villages from their war debt.

As we jolted along over rough roads in the darkness far behind the front we talked of what was probably happening in Paris, London, New York, and a thousand cities that night. Streets jammed with crowds wild with joy, crowds drunk with excitement and liquor, lights, music, dancing, feasting. . . It dawned upon us that we had eaten nothing all day. The soldiers would have finished their mess at this hour and we carried a single can of bully beef in the car. Stopping beside the road, we twisted off the top of the can and ate the cold, greasy meat with our fingers. That was our armistice supper. Thousands of soldiers fared little better.

Next day I hurried up to Rickenbacker's squadron. It was cold, clear, and sunny. Lieutenant Meissner said he was willing to take me up, despite the armistice order prohibiting flying across the line. He told me to get into one of the fur-lined flying suits lying around headquarters. I climbed into the machine-gunner's cockpit, buckled on the safety harness, and we were off.

I scrawled observations in a notebook as best I could with mittened hands in the jolting airplane. Meissner nosed down over the armistice line and we skimmed along at a height of fifty feet. The front presented a strange scene of inactivity. Doughboys strolled idly over the torn fields without equipment or guns. They seemed awkward and ill at ease. Their reason for existence had ceased. In ruined villages groups of soldiers sat in the chill November sunshine, or gathered around bonfires. At one place we glimpsed a big crap game on a blanket. The crap shooters rose and waved. At another place within a few yards of the front lines we saw a game of "one old cat." About two hundred yards away fourteen Germans watched the antics of the Americans from the edge of a wood.

At another point Yanks were digging three graves. Further along a large group had crowded around half a dozen Germans and eagerly craned at them. Apparently the Germans had crossed the line to fraternize in violation of orders. Then we saw a number of dead, mangled horses with their legs sticking up grotesquely, their bodies bloated. Elsewhere Yanks repaired roads, built temporary shelters, or washed their clothes. One unit with equipment neatly laid out in rows prepared for inspection.

Shell fire had torn up the roads. Smashed gun-carriages and motor trucks lay in the ditches. In one forty-acre patch of woodland every limb had been stripped from the trees and the trunks were mangled by shell fire. Three villages had been reduced to heaps of stones and no living thing could be seen in them. Newly dug trenches crisscrossed the whole landscape in this region. Water filled the shell holes almost rim to rim - a scene of unutterable, sickening desolation. Debris of war lay scattered everywhere, trench helmets, bits of clothing, broken rifles, machine guns, tangles of barbed wire, blankets, stretchers.

Meissner wheeled and headed toward Conflans and Briey, far behind the German lines. Within a few minutes we sighted columns of the retreating German army going home from the war. As far as we could see, dense columns of marching men in dirty gray choked the roads. We zoomed down and flew for miles a hundred feet over the heads of one column. They marched in open ranks in good order. They stared up at us, laughed, waved, and pointed. None so far as we knew attempted to fire at us. Many carried no rifles, having flung them into wagons or motor trucks.

Suddenly in the vicinity of Conflans a huge column of fire and smoke shot up to a great height, perhaps a mile. They were blowing up ammunition dumps. After what seemed a long time we felt the concussion of the explosion, which rocked the plane. Other columns shot up, making our plane toss alarmingly. We counted eight great smudges of smoke behind Conflans. Meissner climbed to eight thousand feet. We saw a vast expanse with every road jammed with the army going back to Germany. Tens of thousands of them.

After penetrating thirty miles behind the German lines we turned back and flew over Verdun. Soldiers filled the ruined streets. The French tricolor floating triumphantly from the cathedral provided the only bit of colour in the whole drab landscape.

Back at the airdrome we made a bad landing. We bounced high into the air and hit a mud hole, tearing off our wheels. The plane flipped on her nose, broke off the propeller, damaged one wing, and came within an ace of turning completely over. I clutched underneath the seat to keep from being thrown squarely on my head. Had we gone on over I should probably have broken my neck.

Flyers who heard the crash ran up and surrounded us. They gave Meissner the horse laugh. "Hey, Jimmy, now that there are no German planes you've started crashing American planes, huh?" A French aviator rushed up to me almost speechless with anger. It transpired he was bound a hundred miles up the line with important dispatches for a French general. He had dropped down here for a cup of coffee. Inadvertently I had taken his flying suit, which had the dispatches and his maps in the pockets. He made me get out of the suit there in the mud.

"Hell of a good story," said taciturn Captain Gerald Morgan, the censor, when I turned in my story of the flight. That was praise indeed. I was the only correspondent on the whole western front who flew over the lines and witnessed the spectacle of the German army evacuating the slice of France they had occupied for years. I had seen the last drama of the front.

6

HOW HISTORY IS REPORTED

Like the life of the average soldier, the life of a correspondent in the World War was far less thrilling and eventful than the layman might imagine. The romantic Richard Harding Davis type of adventurous war correspondent disappeared with the advent of modern military censorship and official regulation of the movements and writing of correspondents. Despite the exciting nature of the news itself, the method of gathering it had been regimented, with a few exceptions, into workaday routine.

Correspondents were herded together in charge of Major Bozeman Bulger, of the Military Intelligence Service, at a press headquarters far enough back of the lines to have adequate telegraph facilities. During the battles of the Ourcq and the Vesle, press headquarters were established in the second-rate provincial hotel, Hôtel de la Sirène, at Meaux, about fifty miles from Paris. Captain Gerald Morgan and Captain Arthur Hartzell made their headquarters there and all dispatches were brought or sent to them from the front for censorship. In civilian life both were excellent newspaper men and both knew their business, which was to delete from our messages information which might be useful to the enemy or unduly depress the morale of the people at home. Within these bounds the military censorship at the American front operated far more liberally than at the Allied fronts, and correspondents were permitted entire liberty of movement within the American Army area. They had no conducting officers to restrict their goings or comings.

The War Department furnished cars and drivers for which our organizations made the nominal payment of $10 a day. Skilful drivers, often ex-racing drivers, were assigned from the army. We usually left

Meaux about six in the morning after a French breakfast of coffee and rolls, carried a mess kit in the car, and, if we were not invited to lunch at an officers' mess, fell in with the first mess line of soldiers and ate with them.

Army or corps headquarters was usually the first objective; here reports came in from the various division headquarters which furnished an indication where the most important activities were occurring or were likely to occur. Normally corps headquarters was established far enough behind the lines to be out of range of shell fire. We sometimes obtained sufficient general information at corps headquarters for a preliminary message, if fighting of considerable importance was in progress. On the basis of the information available there we then chose one or two divisions in the sector where activities were hottest. Division headquarters, three or four miles behind the front lines, were often difficult to find, hidden away in dugouts, sandbagged cellars of ruined buildings, or abandoned underground quarries.

At division headquarters we usually obtained all the information necessary for newspaper purposes concerning the front covered by that division. These headquarters kept in constant touch by telephone with regimental headquarters in the front line, unless shell fire cut the field wires strung over the ground. Occasionally runners arrived with messages if barrages had severed the wires, and from them we obtained descriptive details and colourful features. We were permitted to talk with officers in the front-line trenches by telephone. Commanding generals outlined the situation on their maps and frequently permitted us to read their reports.

Visits to the front-line trenches were seldom necessary or advisable; they consumed considerable time because they entailed several miles of walking through communication trenches; furthermore, descriptions of the front line were old stuff. Occasionally correspondents spent the night in the front line for a feature story. But press association correspondents served many hundreds of newspapers; their preponderant duty was to find out what was happening and get the news back to the telegraph wires. This left little opportunity for sight-seeing.

Our editors impressed upon us the desirability of incurring no more danger than was absolutely necessary. Roy W. Howard, then president of United Press, told me: "A dead correspondent is no good to anyone." Yet there remained a considerable element of danger. Floyd Gibbons lost an eye and suffered several other wounds from machine-gun bullets; a fragment of shrapnel struck the car occupied by George Seldes and several other correspondents; one night while Wilbur Forrest was sleeping in a cave in the Soissons sector a shell fell in the entrance a few yards away, killing and wounding many German prisoners and their American guards who were sheltered there. The explosion extinguished the lights in the cave and when the rock dust from the explosion drifted inside, the occupants of the cave thought it was gas and scrambled panic-stricken in the darkness to don gas masks.

Edwin L. James, of the New York Times, together with several other correspondents, including myself, ran through some gas. Gas shells had struck beside the road while we were motoring down a steep hill a few miles from the front. We shouted to the driver to go through it as we were travelling too fast to halt. We saw the gas drifting across the road. Our gas masks, which army regulations required us to carry, were tangled together in the bottom of the car with mess kits, cameras, and other impedimenta. We all dived for our masks but could not get them untangled in the confusion. Only James, in the front seat, managed to get his on. I shut my eyes and held my breath to the bursting point; we were through it in a few seconds without ill effects.

In accordance with army regulations correspondents wore the uniform of an officer without collar tabs denoting rank and without side arms. We were instructed to return salutes but not to initiate them. We wore on our sleeves a green brassard with a large red letter "C." Our dress, duties, and privileges were described in General Orders, but some officers evidently were not familiar with them. That resulted in misunderstandings over the matter of saluting.

Once I was talking with a couple of privates when a lieutenant colonel passed. They saluted him smartly but I did not. He turned brusquely and barked: "Why don't you salute me?" "I'm a newspaper correspondent; I'm not required to salute," I countered. "By God, you're in the uniform of an officer and you'll salute me," he shouted angrily. "If you knew your General Orders you'd know that a correspondent should not initiate salutes, only return them," I said. "All right, God damn it, salute me then!" He drew himself up and saluted me punctiliously. I saluted; he stalked off. The two privates said they hadn't enjoyed anything so much since the war started; the lieutenant colonel was a well known martinet.

Among all the correspondents at the American front Fred S. Ferguson, general news manager of United Press, in charge of the staff of United Press war correspondents, achieved the most remarkable record of beats and scoops. On the night of February 25, 1918, he slept in a field hospital just back of the lines instead of returning to the press headquarters at Neufchateau as the other correspondents did. In the early morning of the 26th the Germans inflicted their first gas attack upon the Americans. Ferguson gathered details of the horrors that ensued, dashed back to NeufchAteau, and cabled the story. None of the other correspondents learned of the gas attack until noon and by the time they reached press headquarters their cables, due to the normal delay in transmission across the Atlantic, did not reach the United States in time for afternoon newspapers. This gave Ferguson a one-day beat.

At that time correspondents could mention casualties, so Ferguson indicated that the gassed men came from Ohio, Indiana, Illinois, Wisconsin, and other Middle Western states, which happened to be the area from which the famous Rainbow Division was drawn. The story caused a storm in the Middle West and relatives of men in the Rainbow Division bombarded Washington for information. General Pershing was placed in the difficult position of having to reveal important military information regarding which division was in the front line. Actually the gassed men were not part of the Rainbow Division, which was still back in the training area.

As a result of that incident, General Headquarters issued an order that thenceforth names or origins of casualties must not be mentioned by correspondents; the only instance in which names of individuals could be used was when soldiers were decorated with the Croix de Guerre. This combination of circumstances fortuitously enabled Ferguson to achieve another important beat. He learned that Archie Roosevelt, son of ex-President Theodore Roosevelt, had been wounded in an early morning trench raid, and went to see him at the base hospital. Just as he arrived a party of French officers left the hospital. They had just bestowed the Croix de Guerre upon Archie Roosevelt on the operating table in the hospital. Ferguson faced a dilemma. Under the new rules he could cable that Archie had received the Croix de Guerre, but he couldn't mention the wound and hence could not say that the decoration was awarded on the operating table. Ferguson knew that the next of kin of wounded or dead were notified before the War Department in Washington published the casualty. Therefore, he hit upon the expedient of cabling his New York office: "Archie Roosevelt awarded Croix de Guerre under most extraordinary circumstances stop phone Oyster Bay." When the New York office of United Press telephoned Theodore Roosevelt at Oyster Bay he had not yet received news of his son's wounds. The moment the news came he telephoned back and told United Press.

On the Battle of Saint-Mihiel, the first great military operation planned and executed exclusively by the American army and at that time the greatest American battle since the Civil War, Ferguson achieved what was widely regarded as the greatest newspaper scoop during American participation in the World War. He managed to get his story of the commencement of the battle, the occupation of the first lines of objectives, and the names of many captured towns to the United States one day ahead of any other correspondent. Even the War Department at Washington had no information most of that day, and Ferguson's messages constituted the only information in the world concerning a battle of overwhelming importance, a battle which drove the Germans out of the Saint-Mihiel salient which they had held since the beginning of the war.

Although the long preparations for the Battle of Saint-Mihiel had been completed and the operations on the Marne and around Soissons were over, General Headquarters ordered the correspondents to remain on the

Marne front and cover their usual routine trips. They did this deliberately to fool German spies. If the 'correspondents had been permitted to go to the Saint-Mihiel salient before the operations commenced German spies might have warned Hindenburg of the imminence of the Saint-Mihiel attack.

At dawn on the day before the attack the correspondents were ordered to leave press headquarters every fifteen minutes in automobiles for Nancy, which was to be press headquarters for the Saint-Mihiel operations. Arriving in Nancy late at night, they were taken to a closely guarded room in a hotel ; the shades were drawn and every precaution taken to prevent German spies from learning of the meeting. Colonel - now General - Dennis Nolan, Chief of Intelligence, placed a detailed map of the sector on the wall and explained every phase of the operation in advance; told of American tanks being used for the first time, of American airplanes and of American artillery support. About midnight, before Colonel Nolan finished, the tremendous artillery preparation for the attack commenced. The flashes of hundreds of heavy guns shimmered like heat lightning on the horizon and thunderous roars shook the buildings in Nancy. The artillery preparation was to continue until the "zero hour" of five, when the troops were to push forward.

While the other correspondents prepared to start to witness the commencement of the attack, Ferguson wrote in advance the entire story of the attack as sketched by Colonel Nolan. The story was written in "takes," that is, short sections, each complete in itself. Because of unforeseeable delays in transmission and the disorganization of the cable lines, Ferguson marked his messages for transmission by four different routes. Some were addressed direct to United Press in New York, others to United Press in Paris for relay to New York, others to London, and some to Buenos Aires for relay across the Andes and up the west coast of South America to New York. Each of the many messages carried the salient facts but each contained additional new facts.

He deposited all the messages in the hands of the censor with instructions to release them in his absence at the front one by one if and when official reports indicated that the events described in them had actually occurred. If the attack were not successful or if events altered what he had written, the censor had the privilege of deleting sections which did not apply. Then Ferguson started to the front. Within a few hours official reports confirmed that everything was going "according to plan" and while all the correspondents, including Ferguson, were many miles away, his messages were transmitted.

Another circumstance rendered his scoop even more impressive. The American command had decided some time before to have special telegraph lines across France to the cable head; operated exclusively by American telegraph operators for the American army, instead of using the French government land lines operated by French personnel. This American-operated telegraph system was to be used for the first time during the battle of Saint-Mihiel. Ferguson wisely concluded that the American lines would be subject to considerable confusion on the first day, because few of the operators spoke French and the switchboards at relay points were handled by Frenchmen. Therefore, he specifically marked all his messages to be transmitted to the seaboard by the ordinary French land lines. As he foresaw, the American lines were jammed and confused; more than eight hours passed before the telegraphic snarl was untangled and official dispatches from American headquarters to Washington and all other correspondents' messages were hopelessly delayed.

In the autumn the vast Battle of the Argonne commenced, the greatest battle in American history, in which 631,405 Americans and 138,000 French fought 610,000 Germans, broke through the great Hindenburg line, and ended the war. It was the most difficult battle of the war, from the war correspondent's point of view. The weather that autumn was atrocious: driving rain, fog, bone-chilling cold, and deep mud day after day. Few roads existed in the Argonne Forest area; the occasional villages lay in ruins.

Press headquarters were established at Bar-le-Duc, an unlovely, dirty, run-down provincial town, but the only point near the battle area with adequate telegraphic facilities. The front receded daily under the impact of smashing American drives; it took nearly all day to get up there, hastily gather news, and return to press headquarters. Roads, ankle-deep in liquid mud, were extremely congested. We often stood an hour at a time in traffic jams or when shells smashed trucks. Those weeks were unadulterated misery for everyone. As always, we worked from dawn until late at night, Sundays included, without a break. The final crisis of the war was at hand; everyone was keyed to an almost intolerable pitch.

We lodged for a few nights in the great citadel of Verdun, one hundred and fifty feet underground in the labyrinths of the fortress. Verdun was under shell fire most of the time, but down there we did not hear or feel it. The citadel, a congeries of concreted passages, sheltered hundreds of thousands of French soldiers during the months of the butchery of the Battle of Verdun. This citadel, and the safety it provided for large numbers underground, contributed to save Verdun from the furious onslaughts of the Germans.

Tiers of wooden bunks, five or six high, one above another, filled the corridors. They were bedded with straw and alive with vermin. After the first night in a bunk I crawled with lice and did not get rid of them for weeks. During the day out in the cold the lice lay dormant, but in the fetid air of the citadel their bites and crawling were infuriating. At night the depths of the citadel resembled a side show of Dante's Inferno. About ten thousand French soldiers were billeted in the passages; many suffered from light shell shock and made the night hideous with their screams, mutters, or hysterical laughs. Some got drunk on the strong red wine called "pinard"; others coughed their lungs out from touches of gas.

One gray early November day, while motoring to the front in chill, driving rain, I witnessed the only incident during the war that brought tears to my eyes. A division was hastily moving into the front line, marching under forced draft. Obviously they had slogged all day in the rain. Seldom have I seen men so physically exhausted; they lurched along in a daze of fatigue, with glazed eyes and faces deeply lined under stubbles of beard. They marched beside the one-way road, which was jammed by an unceasing line of jolting, roaring motor trucks, for supplies and ammunition must go through. As every motor truck passed, its wheels shot two squirts of liquid mud over the marchers; they literally dripped mud. One of the soldiers had adopted somewhere a little black and white mongrel dog and tied him with a piece of cord to his rifle. The little fellow was so tired that he could scarcely lift his feet. Each squirt of mud half drowned him; he blinked his mud-filled eyes with a pathetic expression of helplessness.

Why tears came to my eyes at the sight of that dog, and not when I saw mangled wrecks of human beings lying patiently on the ground awaiting their turn at the dressing stations, I don't know.

Perhaps this tired, bewildered little dog symbolized to me all these men; he didn't know what it was all about, where he was going, or what would happen to him either.

7

RHINELAND HANGOVER

After the Armistice I went to witness the formal entry of French troops into Alsace-Lorraine, the "lost provinces" which Germany annexed after the war of 1870, thus keeping France simmering with hatred for more than half a century. The return of Alsace-Lorraine to France was the first tangible fruit of victory and gave rise to national rejoicing. The French prepared a great demonstration at Metz for the ceremonial entry of their troops. Arriving in the city, we found it in a ferment of excitement and alive with the fluttering tricolour of France. The statue of Kaiser Wilhelm had been thrown from its pedestal and the windows of a few shops had been smashed.

More than a hundred thousand people jammed the great square of Metz. Two mishaps marked the ceremony. As the parade started Marshal Petain, who led the troops into Metz, was thrown from his horse. Then, later, French military airplanes zoomed low over the tightly packed crowd in the square. While two hundred thousand eyes watched their evolutions, one of the planes struck a wire and hurtled into the square, cutting a wide swath through the packed crowd. Propellers and wings cut off heads. Like everyone else, I saw the plane plunge. For a long moment dead silence reigned, as a hundred thousand horror-stricken people drew in their breath, then came the shrieks and screams of the injured. A wave of panic ran through the massed square as wind ripples growing wheat. For concentrated horror I never saw such a spectacle. Military police instantly took charge and quelled the panic. We correspondents never knew how many were killed or injured. The number must have been very large, but nobody would give us any details and the censorship forbade us to mention the incident.

From Metz we went to Mayence in Lorraine and lunched off the Kaiser's plate with the one-armed General Gouraud at the palace the Kaiser used.

Then the American army began its march into the portion of the Rhineland assigned to it under the Armistice terms. For a time we made our headquarters in the picturesque city of Luxembourg, capital of the Grand Duchy of Luxembourg. The place was honeycombed with intrigue by the French, who were trying to take over this little independent principality.

In Luxembourg we encountered the first of those bitter disagreements between the American and French armies which broke out almost the moment the war ended. One day I obtained from a press officer a copy of an order formulated by Marshal Foch, generalissimo of the Allied and American armies, designed to govern the conduct of German civilians in the regions occupied by all the armies, including the American. These rules were extraordinarily harsh and repressive.

Learning that the telegraph line between Luxembourg and Paris had been restored, I decided to telegraph my message about Foch's regulations by that route. An hour later a press officer appeared in a state of agitation demanding the return of the document. I told him I had already telegraphed it.

He confided that Marshal Foch had issued the order without consulting General Pershing, and its severely repressive nature made Pershing furious. He refused to accede, thus forcing the orders to be withdrawn and revised into milder form. The press officer told me Pershing regarded the regulations as "more Prussian than the Prussians" and would have none of them as originally cast. I was the only correspondent who telegraphed the orders, because all my competitors planned to follow the normal procedure and send their messages by motorcycle courier to Nancy, back in France. A hullabaloo ensued as attempts were made to intercept my message before it reached New York. Urgent official messages went to Paris and to Brest to "kill" my dispatch if it had not yet been transmitted. Others went to Washington asking the government to intercede with my New York office to cancel the message if they had received it already; still others implored my New York office to withhold the message from publication. Actually the message was stopped before it left Paris, and the military censorships prevented the dissension between Foch and Pershing from becoming public. Many other rifts occurred between the American and French commands, but none became generally known until after the Peace Conference.

Crossing the frontiers of Luxembourg, we reached German soil. Defying army regulations, another correspondent and I slipped through the American lines and motored into Trier, the nearest important German city, to catch a visual impression of the effects of the Allied blockade on the German populace. Despite the fact that we wore American uniforms and were the first of the former enemy to reach the city, we encountered no demonstrations of enmity. Many pedestrians turned their heads away and refused to look at us, but others gathered around our luxurious Cadillac, the like of which they had never seen. A glance at the people in the streets instantly revealed how cruelly the Allied food blockade had starved the German people. They had haggard faces and looked listless and sallow. We saw no representatives of the pre-war pot-bellied German. The people wore shabby, threadbare clothing of poor quality and broken, patched shoes. Stocks in shop windows were meagre and depleted, and the city had a generally run-down appearance.

We paid the equivalent of a dollar and a half for an unappetizing luncheon of insipid cabbage soup, a piece of meat, soggy potatoes and turnips, coffee made from an unpronounceable vegetable compound, and a glass of weak, watered beer. The same conditions existed in other Rhineland towns, although this was one of the richest parts of Germany.

At Ems, to the disgust of German onlookers, a detachment of French soldiers urinated on the spot where Bismarck is supposed to have composed the famous "Ems telegram" which helped start the Franco-Prussian War of 1870. At Neiderlahnstein I obtained some local paper money into which a clever artist had worked pictures of turnips and cabbages with the legend, "So we live, so we live, 1917." When the burgomaster discovered the wry joke he withdrew the notes from circulation.

At Trier we encountered for the first time evidences of the now famous schism between Foch and Clemenceau. Marshal Foch summoned the American correspondents to his private railway car, the same one in which the Armistice was signed and which was exhibited later in the Invalides in Paris. There he greeted us briefly and gravely. He then rose to his feet and read in rapid, incisive tones the text of a declaration he had prepared and signed to the general effect that the Rhine must henceforth be the French frontier. That would have meant the annexation of one of the richest German provinces, inhabited by millions of Germans, and would have constituted a flat, unjustifiable violation of President Wilson's Fourteen Points.

This declaration, coming from the generalissimo, constituted big news for us. After reading it Foch handed us the original typed copy bearing his signature which, I believe, Captain Gerald Morgan retained. The whole corps of correspondents hurried over to a room in a nearby hotel to prepare their cables.

The next day the French Ministry of Foreign Affairs at the instance of Clemenceau issued a flat denial and repudiation of Foch's statement. That was not the first time or by any means the last that I had such an experience.

The correspondents corps entered Coblenz a couple of days ahead of the main body of the army to witness the formal crossing of the Rhine. Coblenz, a handsome city at the confluence of the Moselle and the Rhine, lay in a picturesque landscape opposite the towering fortress of Ehrenbreitstein. It was the most important city in the American area of occupation. The inhabitants greeted us coldly but with curiosity, often turning their backs to us as in Trier.

We began to perceive some of the pin pricks which later caused disagreeable incidents. A French liaison officer assigned to the press section by the French High Command told me he had sent down to Paris for the bright-red pants of his pre-war uniform "because the color infuriates the Germans." One afternoon sitting with me in a tea-room he thought his tea was unduly delayed. He called the waiter, stormed at him, drew his revolver and laid it on the table with a threat that he would shoot unless his tea arrived within three minutes, thus terrifying the waiter and the German customers.

We scurried about looking for living quarters in Coblenz. The Coblenzerhof, at the foot of the bridge of boats across the Rhine, was the town's finest hotel and we knew that when the army officers arrived they would requisition the whole building and all the best rooms in other hotels. Damon Runyon and I therefore went to the manager and told him that he would get only six marks a day for his requisitioned rooms (the normal requisition price), but that we would pay him double for a good room with bath. We suggested that he pry the brass numbers off the door and fail to report that room in his report of available space, thus concealing our presence. He agreed. In that way Damon and I enjoyed for the first time in many weeks the luxury of a clean modern room, a spotless bath, fresh sheets, and soft beds. Fortunately our windows overlooked the river exactly at the end of the bridge of boats.

Came the day when the American troops were to cross the Rhine early in the morning, and that was the story we were there for. We left a call for five in the morning, but since our room had been scratched off the list nobody roused us. The first I knew of the historic crossing of the Rhine was when I heard the tramp of feet, jumped to the window, then shook Runyon awake. "The troops are starting to cross the Rhine, they're marching down the street. Get up!" "I'll be damned if I'll get up," Runyon grumbled. I argued with him that it was the biggest story since the Armistice but he was obstinate. I sat in the open window, shivering and only half awake, describing the crossing in staccato phrases while he lay in bed. "There goes General Parker; he has walked out to the middle of the bridge; now he has commanded the troops to march; they are crossing the Rhine . . ."

That was the way I covered the crossing of the Rhine. But Runyon wrote by far the best story of any correspondent. He told how he stayed in bed within a few feet of the ceremony while I described to him the happenings, and he quoted from my verbally relayed description.

Our idyll in a clean room with clean sheets soon ended. Although we always reconnoitred the corridor before going to our quarters, somehow the army authorities discovered we were living in a hotel sacred to generals and colonels, and ejected us upon short notice. We had to go to an older hotel, the Riesenfürstenhof, the headquarters of the other correspondents.

We established a correspondents' club in a suite of rooms once used by the Kaiser; it looked as though we should remain on the Rhine for a long time. We named it the Razzberry Club and our motto, adopted for the benefit of the censors, read: "Let us tell the truth." But we couldn't even yet, for the continual incidents between the American and French armies would have made unpleasant if instructive reading. Indeed, the friction increased daily and the powers-that-were undoubtedly made no mistake in deciding that if the state of feeling between the two armies were generally known it would add difficulties to the Peace Conference. General Pershing came to Coblenz in his private car and invited the correspondents to dinner with him. He told us frankly about the disagreeable incidents, explained the reason it was unwise to permit their publication, and asked the correspondents who were soon returning to America not to write about them, at least not until after the Peace Conference. I think his request was faithfully observed. The German civilians in the occupied area gave practically no trouble, although a few petty incidents of friction occurred between Coblenz and American Army authorities.

My first momentary peeps behind international scenes in the Foch-Pershing and Clemenceau-Foch imbroglios disillusioned me. For the first time I commenced to realize that the men to whom the world looked up often allowed petty personal considerations, private dislikes, hatreds, jealousy, and amour propre to sway their conduct of momentous affairs. I began to perceive that the same motives that inspired the ward heelers I met in Chicago often also inspired these great figures. Somehow I was not prepared for that discovery. Unconsciously I felt that great men involved in great affairs were inspired – or should be – by loftier sentiments and motives than little men in little affairs. But this seldom happens, as I learned rapidly after the war.

I discovered that Clemenceau and Foch were at loggerheads because the old Tiger bitterly resented the Marshal's incursions into the field of international politics and wanted Foch to keep in his place as a military man. I found that the Allies tried to prevent the formation of an American Army; that they wanted the American troops thrown into the Allied armies as replacements under the command of Allied generals; that they had fought General Pershing bitterly on this point, sometimes resorting to tactics not unlike those I saw used in the "Bloody Nineteenth" ward in Chicago.

At Christmas time the thoughtfulness of our humble little German chambermaid touched Runyon's heart and mine. As a surprise she obtained and decorated for us a little Christmas tree, sparkling with cheap tinsel and artificial snow. We saw to it that she carried home loaves of white bread, chocolate bars, and coffee – a priceless treasure to her. She hadn't tasted white bread or real coffee for three years. It was a rather melancholy Christmas for some of us – though I have since spent many like it in far countries – and we drowned our sorrows by getting roaring drunk.

Early in 1919 I went down to Paris for what I thought would be an agreeable break in the routine of the Rhineland, only to undergo the most excruciating physical ordeal I had ever experienced. For a long time after the war the railway systems of France were in a state of chaos, with depleted rolling stock, worn-out tracks, and a disorganized, inefficient personnel. Wrecks occurred frequently. Hundreds of thousands of people uprooted by the war, which had laid eastern France in ruins, were trying to go somewhere. The railways could not possibly cope with the hordes that wanted to travel. At Metz, where I had motored to catch the Paris train, I received the first intimation of the almost unbelievable congestion. A shrill, excited mob packed the station and charged upon the train the moment the gates were opened. The current carried me along and I managed to fight my way into a compartment. The seats were all occupied and men were climbing through the windows. In a few moments every inch of space – compartments, aisles, and vestibules –was jammed with humanity. Ignorant of the situation, I tried to get out but could not do so before the train started. There were eleven in our compartment, five of us standing, with no straps to hold to.

I stood in that compartment nineteen hours without food or water. I could not sit down or shift my position, except to move a few inches to the window to answer the calls of nature. An American officer beside me had a flask of cognac, which probably saved us from collapse. After a few hours the closed windows made the atmosphere unbearable. The American officer, who was close to one of them, asked a Frenchman who was leaning against it to lower it for ventilation. The French all shouted out in protest and it stayed closed. Finally the air became intolerable and the American managed to get his elbow against the window. Amidst execrations from the other passengers he smashed it in, but they could do nothing because we were so tightly crowded no one could swing a fist. From then on we had too much ventilation.

At every station stop swarms of people tried to board the train. This was humanly impossible and the passengers had to fight off the would-be travellers. At one station where, I was told, crowds had been waiting two days they became so infuriated that some of them ran up to attack the engineer and fireman, who started the train before the yelling group reached them. By the time we reached Paris those who, like ourselves, had stood nineteen hours were in a state of collapse. The American officer and I sat on the platform at the Gare de l'Est for half an hour before we could summon sufficient strength to walk out for a taxicab. I went to bed immediately and remained there two days recovering from the ordeal. I had lost many pounds in weight.

On my return to Metz I again could not get a seat and had to spend sixteen hours in a corridor sitting on top of an upended suitcase. That was not so bad because there were only about twenty people in the corridor. I could move a few feet, and took the precaution of bringing sandwiches and bottled water.

All that winter in Coblenz we covered petty episodes, wrote inconsequential mail stories, and lounged at the Razzberry Club. The sudden moral let-down, the hectic, frantic search for pleasure - any kind of pleasure or diversion - that succeeded the war infected us. We drank and gambled far too much. Although few of us in the press section received more than $75 a week, we gambled heavily. I seldom gambled, but once I won $800 in a crap game and lost it in four rolls of the dice. This was more money than I had ever possessed at one time in my life. All over Europe the moral reaction from the war set in; millions went to any lengths to obtain a momentary titillation of excitement from dancing, drinking, gambling, or love-making.

In Coblenz we dwelt on an island surrounded by a sea of misery. The Allied food blockade had accomplished its object of starving the German nation. The haggard, paper-colored faces, the listless movements of the people in the streets emphasized its success. Tens of millions of Germans were not far from the verge of starvation. We caught a glimpse of the results in our own mess.

We discovered that our mess sergeant sold or traded off a good proportion of our supplies. White bread, which the Germans had not eaten for years, chocolate, sugar, real coffee, and canned goods fetched unbelievable prices. German civilians would give almost anything to get them. Our mess sergeant took advantage of the situation and amassed a small fortune marketing the food issued to us by the army. And he had a harem of mistresses baited with chocolate bars. There was a saying: "You can get any woman in the Rhineland for two bars of chocolate." He was later court-martialed. Many American soldiers, touched by the misery, often gave the German civilians part of their liberal rations. Although fraternization with the ex-enemy was forbidden, I'll wager there are any number of youths in the Rhineland now with American ancestors.

At the Razzberry Club I caught another glimpse behind the scenes of great affairs. Charles Schwab, the multi-millionaire steel-maker, once sat through an all-night poker game with us. Incidentally, the money all gravitated to him, despite his obvious efforts to lose. He told a remarkable story of his bet with Lord Kitchener on the production of submarines. Kitchener wanted Schwab's firm to build a certain number of submarines in the shortest possible time. Schwab asked how long it would take to manufacture them in England; Kitchener told him and Schwab named a period of time, months shorter, in which he thought he could construct them. Kitchener offered to bet him a huge sum, totalling several hundred thousand dollars, that it was impossible. They recorded the bet in the form of a bonus of so many thousand dollars per submarine per month for those completed under the British time, and vice versa. Schwab won. He told us he distributed the money in the form of bonuses to the workers who built the submarines.

Dynasties and empires crashed; new nations were born. Revolutions broke out all over Europe and the continent seethed in an uproar, adjusting itself to the sudden cessation of four years of war. Meanwhile I tranquilly wrote a detailed history of the war activities of the foremost American divisions. Somehow the history-making events occurring all around meant nothing to me then. I had spent months in the midst of the greatest events in recorded history. The reaction of those last weeks of strain set in; I couldn't interest myself in the aftermath. It seemed at that time that nothing again would ever matter much. Many others underwent the same reaction, as I perceived later from the irresponsible actions of some of my friends who "went to hell" after the war. They could not apply their minds to their work, lost their jobs, drank to excess, and died prematurely.

Eighteen months in war-time Europe had altered me more than any previous phase of my work. They had made me harder, more cynical, and had destroyed many illusions. The fact that I had covered some of the war, the greatest story in the history of newspapers, increased my personal and professional self-confidence. I learned gradually to be less constrained in human contacts. As my self-confidence grew, I unconsciously developed a less colourless personality In the rush and excitement of the war I had no time for solitude and introspection; for the first time I lost my hold on the philosophy of Thoreau and did not carry a copy of Walden. My backwardness in contacts with women persisted. I had had no opportunity for normal social contacts since I left Chicago.

By reading biographies, memoirs, and histories of the principal countries, I learned something of the background of European affairs. Beginning with Leavitt's Europe since Napoleon, I gradually educated myself in the diplomatic background of Europe.

I detested the idea of going to the forthcoming Peace Conference to watch the haggling over the ruins of Europe and the war loot, and notified my office that I preferred not to go. Afterward, I knew that I had made a mistake; that I should have been on the ground to witness the formulation of what was to be the diplomatic charter of Europe for nearly a generation.

In March, 1919, I took charge of the London office while Ed L. Keen gathered the Peace Conference staff in Paris.

8

IRELAND FOR THE IRISH

Throughout the Peace Conference I remained in London in a peaceful backwater eddy of the news which suited my mood at the time. The United Press informed me that I was to be appointed manager of the Paris Bureau later; therefore, I commenced to attend night school regularly, studying French.

During this period I found more opportunity for normal social contacts, met and became engaged to Mary Alston, an English girl. She went to night school with me, studying French in preparation for living in Paris. With the $500 I received from Mark Morton, I bought an engagement ring. We were married just before I was transferred to France.

About this time I encountered a classic illustration – I was to see others later – of spying by European governments upon communications between European countries and Europe and America.

Bela Kun, the Hungarian Communist, had staged a coup d'état in Hungary. This first attempt to extend the Communist system into Central Europe drenched the country in blood and another blood bath ensued when the Whites overthrew the Communists. While Bela Kun controlled Budapest, our correspondent there, Edward J. Bing, conceived the idea of interviewing Lenin and Trotsky in Moscow, more than a thousand miles away, by using the Budapest wireless station to transmit the exchange of questions and answers. He staged a remarkable interview with the two Communist chiefs, who gave an extensive statement of their opinions on current affairs in answer to Bing's wirelessed questions. Bing then transmitted the interview, which an to about 2,000 words, by land wire from Budapest to London. It took two days to reach us and arrived somewhat mangled. From London we relayed the text by wireless to New York, and three days after sending it I received from the Soviet Foreign Office the first direct telegram that had reached us from Moscow since the revolution. It had taken three days to transmit and it drew my attention to the fact that three words in the interview, as we wirelessed it to New York, were incorrect, having been distorted in transmission from Budapest. They asked us to make the necessary correction, but the interview had been published days before and anyhow the corrections had no significance. What had happened was that the Moscow wireless station picked up the text of the interview from the air while it was being flashed from London to New York, and compared it word for word with the original text of Lenin's and Trotsky's statement.

In the spring of 1920 the Sinn Fein terrorist movement broke out anew in Ireland. Two officials of Dublin Castle – Alan Bell and Commissioner Redmond – were assassinated. Sinn Feiners sporadically attacked outlying police stations, thus forcing the British government to evacuate more than three hundred of them and leaving the countryside without police protection. Sir John Taylor, Under-secretary for Ireland, was virtually imprisoned in Dublin Castle; on his visits to the Viceregal Lodge he travelled in a military armoured car. Occasionally Sinn Feiners fired shots into Dublin Castle, the headquarters of the British government. Another bloody phase of the seven hundred years of strife between Ireland and Britain had begun.

I went to Ireland in April. Arthur Griffith, the founder of Sinn Fein and Vice President of the "Irish Republic," and Desmond Fitzgerald, Minister of Propaganda, the principal leaders of the movement, were in hiding from the British police.

A few hours after my arrival at the Gresham Hotel the Sinn Fein secret service informed its organization I was in town and an unknown voice over the telephone said: "Mr. Desmond Fitzgerald will come to see you Sunday at your hotel if you care to talk with him."

But Fitzgerald failed to appear. On Monday the messenger telephoned again to explain his absence: "You see, the police nearly got him early Sunday morning. He got out about two jumps ahead of them;

we don't know where he is now. But he will drop in as soon as the coast is clear."

The next afternoon a bell boy brought the message that "a man" was waiting to see me. He came to my room and introduced himself as Desmond Fitzgerald – a slender man of about thirty-five, with sandy hair and complexion and a slow drawl. He was wounded in the Easter Rebellion of 1916 and served nearly two years in prison. The police now "wanted" him badly.

"Yes, they nearly had me Sunday morning," Fitzgerald said, grinning.

"I got out dressed only in underwear, slippers, and a raincoat. I usually change my sleeping place about three times a week. We who are 'on the run' have the freedom of the homes of hundreds of sympathizers and merely move from place to place.

"I usually sleep clothed on a sofa or couch, wrapped in a quilt or comforter. In case of an alarm, the quilt can be hidden, leaving no traces of an extra lodger.

"My office is likewise migratory. I have several typists and type-writers and a mimeographing machine for getting out our publication. We've moved the office as often as four times in one week.

"About three o'clock Sunday morning I heard a motor lorry draw up in front of where I was staying. Someone had tipped the British military. I slipped out the back way and hid in the hills all night because there was a cordon of troops around Dublin."

I asked Fitzgerald how he dared come to see me at the principal hotel.

"The hearts of the ordinary police aren't in their work. Unless they have explicit orders for the arrest of a man they seldom interfere. The men we have to fear are the military raiding parties or plain-clothes detectives with explicit orders for our arrest."

A tap at the door of my room interrupted Fitzgerald's story. A Sinn Fein look-out man in the corridor asked me to tell Fitzgerald, "There are two 'deks' in front of the hotel."

"Apparently I must be going," Fitzgerald laughed. "If I don't see you again here tomorrow afternoon, you'll know that my new address is Wormwood Scrubs Prison. I understand they are saving a cell with southern exposure for me."

Two minutes after Fitzgerald left the bell boy brought a message that a "little girl" was waiting with a note for Mr. Fitzgerald. Whether it was a ruse of the detectives to ascertain Fitzgerald's whereabouts and how the bell boy knew where to bring the message remained a mystery.

But the next afternoon Fitzgerald blithely appeared to take me to interview Arthur Griffith, Acting President of Sinn Fein. We walked down the back stairs, through an alley, and entered a car which took us to a house on the outskirts of Dublin.

The next time I saw Desmond Fitzgerald, years later, he held the office of Foreign Minister of the Irish Free State.

Griffith, short, sandy, methodical, and unimpressive in appearance, spoke eloquently and vehemently.

"If the English refuse to grant us independence they will have to extirpate the Irish nation; they will have to accomplish this extirpation in the face of the world. We have made this question of the independence of Ireland an international question and we intend to keep it so. The Irish have lost all care for their lives and property and are steeled to every sacrifice. Ireland has done forever with subservient bargaining and will keep up the struggle until she is free and equal."

For days I tried to obtain an interview with the Viceroy of Ireland, Lord French, formerly Commander in Chief of the British armies in France. At last an appointment was fixed for two days later; I was assured that mine would be the first interview. The next morning to my astonishment the London Daily Express published a long interview with Lord French. That afternoon he issued an official statement flatly denying the interview.

I went to the Viceregal Lodge at the appointed hour. Lord French, short, portly, and rubicund, greeted me with military gruffness. "You know I never give interviews and this is not an interview," he opened. "But I was clearly informed, Lord French, that you were giving me an interview," I said. "But I never give interviews. I'll talk with you and whatever you write about is your own affair, but I never give interviews."

I talked with him for half an hour, during which he outlined the British viewpoint at that time. "

"We cannot grant Ireland self-determination," he said emphatically. "They're too close to us. Self-determination has its limits. It must be applied within reason, otherwise the nations of the world would break up and revert to the ancient feudal system. Ireland can't have Dominion Home Rule. They are a part of the United Kingdom. We cannot give them a government like that of Canada because they are too close to us. It's largely a geographical question."

I asked him how he dared ride horseback around the Viceregal grounds in the midst of a campaign of assassination.

"I wouldn't dare walk," he smiled. "But the Irish are softhearted; I'm safe on horseback because they wouldn't want to chance hitting my horse. They love horses."

I puzzled over how to handle the material he gave me in view of his stipulation that it was not an interview. Finally I evolved a scheme and started my story as follows: "This is not an interview. Lord French insists that he never gives interviews. But to the best of my knowledge and belief this is what he said during a half hour's talk today at the Viceregal Lodge. And Lord French is hereby relieved of responsibility for whatever appears in this report of our talk."

He never denied the interview.

I picked up the insistent rumour of a plot to assassinate Lord French and included it in one of my dispatches, properly qualified, as a rumour. In New York the cable editor lifted those few lines out of the context of the story and made them the opening paragraph, which naturally drew the headlines. Two days later some terrorists attempted to assassinate Lord French by shoving a farm cart across the road ahead of his car and firing upon it from ambush. He escaped unhurt. I was credited with a "beat." Apparently Irish conspirators were extraordinarily loose-mouthed.

About a year before, on the second anniversary of the Easter

Rebellion, I had witnessed another phase of the Irish troubles. At that time the Four Courts and the Post Office buildings still lay in ruins from shells of British warships. The British feared another outbreak on the anniversary; the town was jammed with troops.

The front of a large crowd in O'Connell Street, the main thoroughfare, caught me up and began to mob a small detachment of British troops. Unable to escape, I was shoved in the front line closer and closer to the cordon of troops standing with fixed bayonets. As the mob edged forward, shouting curses, I saw them nervously fingering the triggers of their rifles. A machine gun was set up on the cobblestones behind the first line of troops. When it seemed inevitable that we would be pushed onto the bayonets, the machine gun suddenly opened fire. The mob broke with shrieks and ran helter-skelter. I ran with them (passing many of them!) and heard the whistle of bullets. Men fell. I thought the mob was being mowed down. After I reached the O'Connell Street bridge I found that the troops had fired over the heads of the mob; that the men who fell had slipped and were not injured. Similar incidents occurred every day or two.

On Easter, Sinn Fein bloodlessly demonstrated its strength by simultaneously burning about one hundred and fifty abandoned police posts throughout the south of Ireland. From twenty to fifty men participated in each attack. This constituted the first definite indication of the strength of the organization.

History has related how Sinn Fein, after years of struggle and much bloodshed, finally won for Ireland the status of a Free State within the British Empire.

9

FRENCHMEN CAN BE WRONG

In January 1921 I was transferred to France as manager of the Paris Bureau. From the first, for what reason I never knew, the Press Department of the French Ministry of Foreign Affairs on the Quai d'Orsay disliked me, which rendered my work difficult.

After France made the momentous decision to occupy the Ruhr, the richest industrial and mining section in Germany, as a "sanction" for the non-fulfillment of the Treaty of Versailles, I went to the Ruhr to observe the French experiment of "digging coal with bayonets."

The Quai d'Orsay objected bitterly to the series of articles I wrote on the Ruhr, particularly when I stated that the rusted network of railway lines crisscrossing the region clearly revealed a lack of success in producing coal, an undeniable fact which no one could fail to perceive. When I went to the Ruhr I realized that I faced an intensely controversial situation, and since our organization made factual, objective reporting its fundamental rule I was careful to write impartially and objectively. Yet my stories displeased the French Minister of Foreign Affairs.

Count Charles de Chambrun, a descendant of Lafayette – and thus by act of Congress an honorary citizen of the United States – was a charming gentleman, an astute diplomat, and an amusing raconteur. He also headed the Press Department and he didn't like me, even holding me responsible for the headlines which papers put over my dispatches. One day during one of my sessions "on the carpet" I tried to convince him of my personal neutrality and objectivity in what I wrote. "But you cannot be neutral about France," he said. "Either you are with us or you are against us; there is no such thing as neutrality toward France." These words accurately described the attitude of his department at that time.

The Press Department keeps a dossier on each foreign correspondent which contains a record of his antecedents, clippings of his writings, and so on. De Chambrun once showed me mine. It was about four inches thick and apparently consisted mostly of clippings, but he would not permit me to examine it.

During the period of wild fluctuations in the exchange rate of the French franc, de Chambrun summoned me. His face was purple and he was almost speechless with anger. "Now I have you. I've always known you were hostile to France. Now I have the evidence. I'm going to have you deported from France. I'm going to inform the American ambassador." When he calmed down I asked him what it was all about.

"You telegraphed a false quotation of the franc; a quotation lower than the franc was at that moment. Our legation at Rio de Janeiro reported that when your false quotation was published in the newspapers in South America it precipitated a further fall of the franc, which spread all over the world. Also you said there was a panic on the Bourse. That was false. You are going to be deported from France immediately as an undesirable alien."

"Do I get any opportunity to submit evidence to prove that your statements are incorrect," I asked, "or are you going to deport me without a hearing? I can produce irrefutable evidence that these charges are unfounded. An official record of the various fluctuations of the exchange is kept at the Bourse, and I can get a certified copy of my message from the cable company proving exactly at what minute my telegram was filed and the minute it was transmitted. These will prove that the franc had reached the point mentioned in my message before the message was written. As for the question of panic, I did not say it was a panic but described it as a near panic, and I think I can produce evidence on that point." De Chambrun agreed to give me an opportunity to furnish evidence.

I obtained an official certified copy of the fluctuations of the franc on the day in question, specifying the times the franc had reached certain points in its fall. I also produced certified copies of my messages proving that I sent the cablegram referred to fourteen minutes after the franc had reached the quotation given in the message. Finally I obtained clippings from the semi-official newspaper, Le Temps, which had referred editorially to the scene on the Bourse as " Une panique," and a clipping of an article by Leon Bailby, a staunch supporter of the government, in the newspaper L'Intransigeant, referring to the happenings in the Bourse as "a disgraceful panic."

Armed with these I went to de Chambrun. He sulkily admitted that apparently there had been an error and said he would not proceed with the plans for deportation. As I was departing he aimed a Parthian shot. "Anyhow, I know that your organization is hostile to France. Listen to this. It was sent by one of your offices; not from France. But it was published by your organization." He read from a paper: "If France is out to cause trouble in Europe she is going about it in the right way." "That," he said, "is the first sentence of a story published by your organization. It clearly shows deliberate hostility to France."

"But that is impossible," I replied. "That sentence contains an expression of opinion and of bias, what we call an editorial statement. None of the men writing for our press association would dare start a message like that, unless it were a clearly stipulated quotation from someone worth quoting. If any of our men wrote such a statement it would be cancelled before it was ever put upon the wires. In what paper was it published and what was its origin?"

De Chambrun made a mystery of it and refused to tell me where it originated. I soon learned the cause of his reluctance to reveal the source.

On my way back to the office I had an inspiration. The sentence de Chambrun had read sounded vaguely familiar. At that time Lloyd George, Poincare, and other prominent statesmen were writing fortnightly articles for the United Feature Syndicate, expressing their personal opinions of European affairs under their own signatures. These articles were marketed to newspapers separately and not issued in the service of the United Press. The United Feature Syndicate had arranged for our European offices to cable the articles for them to our New York office, where they were turned over to the United Feature Syndicate. For my information, the London office always sent me copies of Lloyd George's articles, which I read or glanced at and then filed away. I consulted my files; behold, that was the first sentence of the last Lloyd George article.

To my astonishment I perceived that the article was not to be released for publication for several days, since the statesmen furnished their copy many days in advance to give time for transmission and distribution all over the world. This meant the Quai d'Orsay possessed a copy of a private message which was still confidential and had been published nowhere in the world. I immediately realized I had stumbled upon a fact of great importance.

I telephoned to our London office and learned that the Lloyd George article had been transmitted by wireless to New York two days before and that it did not bear his name but was preceded by a code word, "Seal," which stood for the former British premier. Then I obtained a copy of the International Telegraphic Convention, subscribed to by all nations. This made all private communications secret, and carried penalties for infringement.

Armed with the copy of the Lloyd George article showing its specific release date, and the International Telegraphic Convention, I revisited Count de Chambrun at the Quai d'Orsay. "Apropos the matter of that message you mentioned, Count de Chambrun, can't you give me any details as to where it was obtained?" I asked. "No, I told you it was reported by one of our embassies and obviously was published in your newspapers. I will tell you no more."

"Wouldn't you be surprised, Count de Chambrun, to learn that message has never been published anywhere; that it is still confidential between the man who wrote it, our London office, and our New York office, that anyone else in possession of it obtained it by illegal means, that it was never issued and never will be by the United Press, which only transmitted it on behalf of United Feature Syndicate?

"Moreover, it is an article by David Lloyd George expressing his own opinion under his own name, just as your former premier Poincare expresses himself for United Feature Syndicate every fortnight and often says things which are highly objectionable to other countries.

This message was transmitted from London by wireless and, as you will see, bears the release date of the day after tomorrow. Now how did the Quai d'Orsay come into possession of a copy of that message under those circumstances? I have hit upon a good mystery story of France spying on international wireless communications, France spying on private communications between England and America. It's a good story."

De Chambrun's face went livid and he sputtered Finally he admitted that the message had been picked out of the air by the Eiffel Tower wireless station and delivered to the Quai d'Orsay. He maintained that it was picked up by accident, "par hasard."

Then I produced the copy of the International Telegraphic Convention and pointed out to him the provisions for secrecy of private communications. He pleaded with me to "drop the entire matter, which was a regrettable misunderstanding" and thought we could get along amicably in future.

"No, you have unjustly harassed me for a long time. You threatened to notify the American ambassador and have me deported. Now I am going to the American ambassador and tell him this entire story and ask his advice. I am going to notify my New York office and give them full details of the incident."

I went to Ambassador Myron T. Herrick. Although he was a staunch friend of France he readily agreed that the Quai d'Orsay was in a tight spot and said he would invite Peretti della Rocca, then permanent head of the Ministry of Foreign Affairs, to lunch and tell him the story, which he did. Herrick pointed out that the story would be perhaps more valuable unpublished, with which my New York office agreed. We held the story and I was never bothered again by the Quai d'Orsay during the years I remained in France!

Shortly afterward, Count de Chambrun was transferred from the Press Department and sent as minister to Greece. Later he became ambassador to Turkey and is now ambassador to Italy.

10

THE CAPTAINS
AND THE KINGS REMAIN

As chief of the Paris Bureau I met and occasionally made friends with some of the men who bulked large in world events during and after the World War. Undoubtedly the greatest of them in many respects I encountered first when he was a newspaper man himself, a reporter for Popolo d'Italia of Milan. He was destined later to impose upon his people a new philosophy of government and to alter the current of European affairs.

At the abortive Cannes Conference in January, 1922, which broke down when Poincare torpedoed the Briand government in the midst of the negotiations, I worked with one Benito Mussolini. He was covering the conference for Popolo d'Italia, of which he was then editor.

At that time the world knew little or nothing about him. I had never heard of Fascism or Mussolini, and I am certain the words meant nothing to nearly everyone attending the Conference. But within nine months Mussolini was to be master of Italy and confront the delegates at that Conference with a situation which no more fitted into their scheme of things than a cube fits into a bag of marbles.

As far as I know, only one of the foreigners attending the Conference knew anything about Mussolini; that was my friend George Slocombe, correspondent of the London Daily Herald, who talked with Mussolini and afterwards described him as watching the collapse of the Conference "with sardonic eyes and a smile of derision on his harsh, enigmatic features."

Mussolini trotted around with the rest of us, carrying his notebook and pencil; nobody paid any attention to him at all. For my part I would never have known of his presence among the two hundred correspondents of a dozen nationalities but for an incident in the lobby of the Carlton Hotel, the Delegations' headquarters.

A group of correspondents had gathered around Lord Riddell, who was acting as press officer for the British Delegation, asking desultory questions. "What is this thing called Fascism?" inquired one correspondent who had just heard the word. "I don't know anything about it," Riddell replied, "but what little I've heard indicates they are just a gang of hooligans."

Another correspondent, familiar with Italy and standing near Riddell, nudged him: "Careful, that man's the head of it. It's Mussolini." He indicated a stubby Italian correspondent with a massive dark face, heavy jowls, and remarkable exophthalmic eyes, who edged forward, listening intently. Few of the group heard the dialogue. I don't know whether Mussolini did. In any case, he knew little English at the time. That first glimpse of Benito Mussolini was also my last for ten years. But nine months after the incident the obscure Popolo d'Italia editor became master of Italy and the dominant personality in Europe.

Exactly ten years later I visited Rome and obtained an audience with Mussolini. He received me in the Palazzo Venezia. A gaudily uniformed flunky ushered me into the famous huge room where Mussolini received visitors. I walked across sixty feet of polished marble towards the sole piece of furniture, his desk, in the far corner of the room. Often Mussolini abashes visitors by staring fixedly at them as they walk across the great room; sometimes he proceeds with his work without looking up.

In my case he rose, came around his desk, and met me part way. "Ten years ago this week we were reporters together at Cannes on the same story. Well, I am still a reporter," I said, as we shook hands. He laughed, put his hand on my shoulder, and said, "Maybe I shall be a reporter again, too."

In the ten years that had elapsed he had learned to speak English with little difficulty. The man I now saw was outwardly, and inwardly too, no doubt, a different man from the unknown reporter at Cannes. At Cannes he had none of the aura of wilfulness, decisiveness, authority, and power which he now radiated. My fleeting impression there had been of a furtive man, uncertain of himself. Even had I not known what had happened in the intervening ten years, the merest glimpse would have sufficed to reveal that they were two different men. Mussolini once said: "There is no revolution that can change the nature of man." Nevertheless he had changed.

His sombre, suspicious eyes had become softer and more serene, his manner easy and almost genial. The lines of his jaws and lips revealed a powerful, aggressive will in a man absolutely certain of himself. I saw him at the end of the afternoon, when a faint stubble of beard darkened his outthrust jaw.

I wrote the story of our meeting again after ten years. Later I learned that an underling in the Italian Press Department strongly objected to my saying that "Mussolini needed a second shave, his clothes were rumpled, and he seemed fatigued." The principal objection had to do with the "second shave."

Most of my dealings with Raymond Poincare were of a business nature. After his cabinet fell, I contracted with him on behalf of United Feature Syndicate for a fortnightly article on international affairs – or so we thought.

In my contacts with him I found him a precise, punctilious, pedantic little man with a one-track, narrow-gauge mind but with extraordinary alertness. Every morning he used to give his chauffeur a hand-written memorandum of the day's program for his car, accounting for every minute of the day. He insisted upon furnishing his articles to us in his minute handwriting, which was so difficult to decipher that it occasioned ardent profanity around our office. He demanded that an English translation of the article be delivered to him for correction before it was cabled. Although he learned English grammar perfectly during the war, he refused to speak the language. But he could spot a split infinitive as far as you could throw the Treaty of Versailles. He struggled over the translations so long and made so many insignificant alterations that we often had to cable the article before his corrections arrived – and unless the corrections were really consequential we never bothered to cable them. Had he known this I'm sure he would have been horrified.

The Treaty of Versailles was his Bible; it was his mono-mania and I believe he literally knew it word for word by heart. Sometimes in conversation he would refer to a paragraph of the treaty and with his characteristic exclamation, "Tiens!" he would seize the leather-bound copy of that document which he kept always at his right hand and without paging through it would unerringly put his finger on the exact line.

But the editors publishing the articles became fed up with the steady diet of Treaty of Versailles in every article and I was charged with the delicate mission, executed with less than moderate success, of sidetracking Poincare from the Treaty of Versailles. As gently as possible I intimated that the editors wanted his opinion on something other than the Treaty, prohibition, for instance, and that I should like from time to time to suggest subjects in which his American readers would be more interested. The little man readily agreed to accept my suggestions. But it didn't work out in practice, because after the first few paragraphs, he invariably managed to find some connection with the Treaty of Versailles, even in the prohibition article. But despite his narrowness and rigidity of mind – or perhaps because of it – his genius, such as it was, came to the aid of France years later in her financial crisis. To me his characteristic phrase, "Je tiens a preciser," delivered in a rasping, tight-lipped voice, always exactly epitomized the man.

Quite another person was Georges Clemenceau, the old buccaneer. I saw a great deal of him and came to be on terms of friendship with him. Of all the European statesmen I encountered, he had the most vivid personality. Had he lived in the days of the Spanish Main I am sure he would have been a pirate; as it was, he made plenty of his colleagues walk the plank.

For years I tried repeatedly to get him to write his war memoirs for us. Once I almost had him, but his henchman, André Tardieu, blocked me. I visited him frequently in his shabby little apartment in the Rue

Franklin, with its dark, stuffy rooms, worn carpets, and undusted curios. Here his faithful valet, Albert, attended him. He wore a loose, shaggy coat in his littered study and sat in the middle of a horseshoe table which extended halfway around him on both sides. The idea of the U-shaped table he had adopted from American newspaper copy desks which he had seen when he lived in the United States as a young man, teaching French in a girls' school and writing articles for Le Temps on the Reconstruction Period. Invariably he wore gray silk gloves to hide – as Albert confided to us after his death – his unsightly, eczema-covered hands. Once Albert ushered me into his study while the "Tiger" had one glove off. He sharply turned his back on me and did not greet me until he had pulled on the glove.

In the course of our conversations we often talked of political personalities, but he always warned me I could make no use of what he said. He expressed freely pungent, profane opinions of European statesmen and military men. He possessed an excellent command of American English and cursed fluently with imagination, using imagery from both languages.

Once when he gave expression to a particularly forceful opinion of Wilson and Lloyd George, I said: "But, Monsieur le president, unfortunately you will not always be with us. What is to prevent me from publishing what you have said after you are gone?" He grinned maliciously. "By God, I'll come back and haunt you if you do." He composed a rather risque limerick about President Wilson, which he often gleefully recited. The "punch line" concerned Wilson's fondness for feminine society. After the "Tiger's" trip to the United States, he said to me: "What do you think that old fool Poincare is saying around town? He is telling everyone that I went to the United States to increase my prestige so that I could come back and try to get his job – the goddamned old goose!"

On his eighty-second birthday, September 28, 1924, he invited me to spend the day with him in his wooden shack on the Atlantic Coast in the Vendee. He lived in Spartan simplicity in a one-story cabin that overlooked a bleak stretch of the coast, a few steps from the thundering surf. He visited the markets at Sables-d'Olonne daily with a basket on his arm and bought his own food.

He was trying to grow vegetation on the sandy waste surrounding the cabin, no doubt because he had to dominate something. Upon my arrival he walked me around his garden to exhibit his effort to grow tomatoes. The vines had withered and could never mature in that infertile soil. "I've tended these goddamned tomatoes all summer and now they are dying. But I'll raise tomatoes here if it takes all my life." He had packed seaweed around the stems for fertilizer, seaweed which he gathered himself on the beach. There were a few straggling flowers and dejected vegetables. Around the outside of the shack, on the seaward side, the old "Tiger" had piled bundles of twigs to keep sand from blowing into the living room; nevertheless a film of sand covered everything in the house.

We lunched together in the kitchen on a table within a few feet of the stove. His old Breton peasant cook took the frugal luncheon of sole, mutton, and cauliflower from the stove and placed it directly on the table. During luncheon Clemenceau told me he was through with politics, that he intended to spend the remainder of his days completing a philosophical book to be published after his death as his "literary legacy to posterity." He showed me the manuscript of the first volume, hundreds of interlined pages in his own handwriting, but said little about the nature of the book, except that it embodied his philosophy and ideals.

"I shall spend two years redrafting the first volume, then work eight or ten years on two other volumes. After that I shall rest and grow old," he chuckled. He vigorously refused to talk politics. "I am through. My talking would only do harm. I can see how things are going, but they will go that way anyhow.

"I am in bed every night before eight o'clock. I wake up about three or four in the morning, do some light gymnastic exercises, such as I have done all my life, then go to work by the light of a kerosene lamp. This morning I got up at one o'clock and worked until half past four, then went back to bed again.

"How do I keep so well? I eat little and exercise moderately. I sleep as much as I need, work no more than I want to, and, above all, I don't worry. I am one of the few men in the world who is free – absolutely free. I see only the people I want to see. I don't read newspapers any more and pay little attention to the world.

"I have my own thoughts. When a man has gone through what I have, he has plenty to think about."

That afternoon I renewed my attempts to persuade Clemenceau to give me a quotable interview on his opinions of international affairs. He still refused good-naturedly, but said: "I'll tell you what I'll do. Come to see me on my hundredth birthday; I promise you I'll give you a sensational interview for publication then, but not before. That's a definite promise. And I am going to live that long too. I am too tough to die."

Every year until Clemenceau's death I sent him a telegram of congratulations on his birthday and added: "Only – more years until that big interview on your hundredth birthday."

After luncheon we sat talking in a brushwood lean-to by the sea. The conversation lagged. I asked him a question and found he was sound asleep, snoring peacefully.

He died an embittered old man with a canker in his breast because his enemies had snatched from him the presidency of the republic, upon which he had set his heart. Among all the figures produced by the war, Clemenceau was to me the most colourful and picturesque. His whole life had been stormy, and the tranquillity of his last years did not suit him. There was none of the post-war, mealy-mouthed hypocrisy in him. He knew there were no morals in international relations and did not pretend that there were. A grand character, but one I should not like to have had for an enemy.

When David Lloyd George went to the United States after the war I accompanied him – the only American correspondent in the party. On board the Mauretania we played shuffleboard and I managed to win every time. He was not amused; he wanted to win at everything, even shuffleboard. During the war Lloyd George had undergone years of the most terrific mental strain and frightful responsibility, perhaps more than any other man in history. Every day he had faced vital decisions of overwhelming consequence to his country and the British Empire. Nearly every other statesman who underwent even a fraction of his responsibilities cracked physically under the strain. But Lloyd George came through the ordeal with all his mental and physical health and resiliency, with clear eyes, a face unworn by care, and his native good humour. On board the ship I asked him his secret.

"I slept a quarter of an hour any time during the day when I began to feel fatigued, and sang Welsh hymns whenever I began to feel worried," he said. "I gradually trained myself so that I could lie down at any time, go to sleep almost immediately, and sleep fifteen or twenty minutes. When I awakened I was refreshed.

"I think anyone can train himself to sleep at will. At first it is not easy. It's something like training a horse to leap a barrier. At first he shies off and cannot do it. But with persistence it can be done. After experimenting I found I could will myself to sleep at any moment of the day within a few minutes after I lay down. I often interrupted work of great importance to snatch a few minutes' sleep and always awakened with a clear mind.

"I found that singing was a great aid in banishing worry. I like to sing Welsh hymns, and whenever I found that I was becoming troubled by my responsibilities I ceased work and sang hymns for a few minutes. Sometimes I've kept important callers or delegations waiting while I sang. Whenever I felt badly exhausted or feared I was catching cold I immediately went to bed and stayed there till I felt better." Even today the little Welsh wizard shows no marks of the years of war-time strain. I talked with him a year ago; his eyes were clear and untroubled, his chubby face rosy and smooth, his mind alert and quick.

For several years Lloyd George wrote a fortnightly article, which we handled, for United Feature Syndicate. I often had the assignment of suggesting an appropriate subject. He was a consummately skilful journalist; he wrote more simply and clearly than any other war-time statesman in Europe. I would choose some aspect of international affairs likely to interest American readers and submit it. No matter what the subject, Lloyd George would produce a vivid, clear-cut article within a few days. His secretaries gathered the information he needed and he dashed off the article in pencil. I saw some of the manuscripts, which revealed that he did very little revision or editing of the first draft. His articles, which were published in more than a score of countries, were more in demand all over the world than those of any other European statesman. Lloyd George had little money when he left the government, and for years the considerable royalties from his writing provided his principal source of income. He is now at work on the fifth volume of his monumental war memoirs.

For months I covered in Paris the intricate confabulations of the so-called Dawes Committee, which was deciding how much the Allies could extract from Germany in reparations. This was the first considerable modification of the Treaty of Versailles, which was later to be increasingly attenuated by agreement and deliberate violation by Germany.

At a press conference General Dawes, chairman of the Committee, accurately described his own role. We had asked him about some detail of the negotiations. He replied: "Oh, I don't know. Better ask Owen D. Young about that. I'm like the man at the old-fashioned turkey shoot. They put the tied turkey behind a log with only his head showing and handed the fellow a rifle. He had never fired a rifle and anyhow was afraid of it. He pointed the rifle in the general direction of the turkey, shut his eyes, and pulled the trigger and shot the damn turkey's head right off. He gained a great reputation as a marksman. And I have a reputation as a reparations expert!"

In conjunction with the Associated Press we cabled to the United States the entire text of the final report of the Dawes Committee. It constituted the longest cable message ever transmitted across the Atlantic, for the text of the Treaty of Versailles had been cabled in sections over a period of months. The message comprising the Dawes Committee report totalled 49,972 words. At the press rate of ten cents a word this cost nearly $5,000. The United Press cabled the entire text from New York to Buenos Aires for that great Argentine newspaper, La Prensa, the only newspaper in South America to publish it. With combined staffs totalling ten men, we worked sixteen hours continuously preparing the text for cable transmission and dividing it into "takes" of about two hundred words each. It took the continuous use of four transatlantic cables for nearly sixteen hours to transmit the text.

Altogether I covered about a dozen conferences on the reparations problem, which embittered international relations for more than a decade after the war. Hundreds of millions of words described these interminable wrangles. All that I learned from these conferences can be told briefly; the statesmen and economic experts knew pitifully little about the mysterious forces of international economics and finance, and some of them held fantastic notions concerning the ability of the defeated powers to pay for the war damages and concerning the Allies' ability to repay war debts to the United States.

My first contact with these remarkably erroneous ideas occurred in New York, before I went to Europe. I was assigned to interview an important figure in Wall Street, partner in one of the greatest financial houses in the world, and obtain from him an estimate of the largest amount the United States might conceivably loan the Allies to prosecute the war. This happened just as we entered hostilities.

After consulting his partners, this authority, who requested that his name be withheld, estimated that America might possibly loan the Allies one billion dollars. He, if anyone, was in a position to make a reliable guess. My story created a sensation because of the immense figure. But before war-lending finished, we had loaned eleven billion dollars. The expert was just eleven times wrong. And after the war the United States sent abroad in commercial loans another eleven billion dollars. We shall get very little of those twenty-two billions back.

I saw a British committee headed by Lord Cunliffe, Governor of the Bank of England, appointed to estimate how much might be extracted from Germany as war indemnity. That committee fixed upon the fabulous figure of twenty-four billion pounds sterling; they actually reported Germany might pay that amount without disturbing the forces of international trade.

When the Dawes Committee finally fixed a global amount it was just 1/3,636 of the Cunliffe committee figure, or 132 billion gold marks. But even that was never paid; at the time of the world financial crisis Germany was given a moratorium and 142 reparations were whittled down to an infinitesimal token payment.

Those conferences badly shook my faith in the wisdom of international economists.

It was further shaken as time went on. One incident stands out particularly. Sir Josiah Stamp, one of the principal authors of the Dawes Plan, a director of the Bank of England, and one of the foremost economic authorities in Europe, spoke before the Association of American Correspondents in London on "Black Monday," the day after England found herself forced off the Gold Standard. England viewed departure from the Gold Standard as a major catastrophe. The country had never been so gloomy and depressed since the day in March, 1918, when the Germans broke through the Fifth British Army in France. Sir Josiah told us that in his considered judgment the pound sterling would automatically stabilize somewhere around $4.60, the normal quotation being $4.86 to the pound sterling. Stamp stated that the intrinsic value of the pound, taking into consideration all the financial, economic, and political factors, was not less than $4.60. Fortunately, none of us speculated financially on Sir Josiah's estimate. The pound sterling's value sank until it was below $3.20 at one time, and for a considerable period oscillated around $3.50.

On the other hand, John Maynard Keynes, the famous British economist, clearly foresaw far ahead of others the disastrous economic consequences of the Treaty of Versailles and the war-debt settlements.

Also Sir George Paish, another British economist, forecast with uncanny accuracy the world financial crash of 1929. In an interview given to the United Press in London more than a year before the crash, he forecast in detail the forthcoming world financial crisis and correctly analysed the causes of it. But he was too far ahead of his time and no attention was given to his prediction.

In London I gained the dubious distinction of being the only person to turn his back on King George. I hasten to add that it was done unwittingly. I often took a morning walk in Hyde Park. One morning as I walked beside the railings along Rotten Row with my hat removed, as it was warm, I looked up and found myself unexpectedly facing King George riding horseback about five feet away. He bowed gravely. Automatically I turned to see to whom he had bowed, and found he had bowed to me. The next time I encountered him in the Park, he smiled, evidently remembering my faux pas. After that I saw him frequently in Rotten Row about eight-thirty on fine mornings. He usually rode with a friend, and was otherwise accompanied only by an equerry, apparently unarmed, about twenty yards behind. It was significant that the ruler of the world's greatest empire rode in a public park without fuss or obvious measures for his personal protection. At that time of the morning there were few pedestrians in Rotten Row and the dozen or two riders studiously refrained from staring at the King or manifesting consciousness of his presence.

In Paris I suffered the worst scooping of my newspaper career. Some Communists had staged anti-American demonstrations, and an unknown person sent to Ambassador Herrick a bomb concealed in what was apparently a box of chocolates. Herrick's valet opened the box, which exploded and injured him. The Ambassador rushed down to the Hotel Crillon to warn General Pershing, then in Paris, whom he thought might be the object of an attack. As he hurried into the lobby of the Crillon he was seen by J. Carlisle McDonald, a correspondent of the Associated Press, who was there on another story. McDonald perceived Herrick's obvious excitement, asked what had happened, and obtained the full story. I did not hear of the story until frantic cables started arriving from my New York office. The embassy did not answer the telephone, police would permit no one to enter, and I could not find Herrick.

Hours passed before I could get even confirmation of the fact of the bombing. About every quarter of an hour another frantic cable arrived from New York, thirteen in all. When I finally obtained the story it was too late for the afternoon papers in the United States and I had been completely scooped. Only a newspaper man can realize the misery and humiliation of such an episode. My standing with the New

York office was low for months, and even now when I recall the incident I am unhappy.

In Paris I was offered the only two direct bribes which I ever encountered. An influential publicity man who was temporarily representing a syndicate of American corset manufacturers came to my office and offered me $50 a week with an advance payment covering six months to help him bring corsets back into fashion. American women had ceased wearing the old-fashioned corset and many manufacturers were being ruined. They conceived the idea that if an occasional news dispatch from Paris mentioned that corsets were coming back into style, American women would follow like sheep what they thought was the trend. They had retained the publicity man to visit several European capitals and tried to arrange with an American correspondent in each city to send fabricated dispatches about corsets. I refused the offer but later discovered by reading certain American newspapers that the columnist had succeeded in finding a man to do the job in Paris and Berlin. I never knew whether the scheme succeeded in putting American women back into "stays."

The other instance of attempted bribery occurred after I received a message from our Riviera correspondent concerning an automobile accident in which the young scion of a well-known socialite family struck and injured someone with his car. As the news was not important enough to cable I ignored it and filed it among the unused messages. A few hours later I received a message from the young man, who had learned that we had the story and offered "to make things all right financially" if I refrained from publishing anything about his accident. I immediately drew the message out of the file and cabled it to the United States, as a lesson to the young man. Then I telegraphed him exactly what had happened. These were the only two cases of attempted bribery I encountered in twenty-four years of newspaper experience. I think such instances are comparatively rare, as I have heard of very few from colleagues.

In Paris I encountered an unusual illustration of the necessity of checking carefully even insignificant stories. My friend Bartley Grierson (this name is fictitious) obtained from a source he thought to be reliable a story about remarkable house parties given by a British millionaire on the French Riviera. According to information Grierson received, a new synthetic fabric had been discovered which instantly dissolved upon contact with salt water. The millionaire had a number of women's bathing suits made from the fabric. When he gave a party, he always suggested a swim in the Mediterranean and provided the suits for his women guests. The moment they entered the water, according to the story, their suits disappeared.

A few days after Grierson cabled the story, he received a cablegram from his managing editor asking that several of the suits be shipped to him. He said a prominent official of a bathing-suit manufacturing company, which advertised in his newspaper, wanted the suits.

When Grierson checked the story, to his chagrin he found that no such fabric existed and that the story was a hoax. He hated to admit to his editor that he had been lax in checking the story. Therefore, he hit upon the expedient of cabling to his editor: "Cannot ship suits because would dissolve in salt sea air."

The editor immediately cabled back: "Put them in tin box have it hermetically sealed." Grierson was on the spot.

He obtained a tin box and put into it a couple of handfuls of finely pulverized breakfast food. He then had it hermetically sealed and shipped it to his editor, who was thereupon convinced that the suits could not be shipped across the Atlantic.

11

L'AFFAIRE LANDRU

Tʜᴇ most grotesque crime story I encountered in any country occurred in France. It was "l'affaire Landru." The career of Henri Désiré Landru, the "Bluebeard of Villa Gambais," whose head I saw chopped off into a wicker basket by the guillotine at Versailles, France, at dawn on February 25, 1922, reads like a tale from the Middle Ages. He was perhaps the most monstrous criminal character in modern annals.

He was convicted of the cold-blooded murder of ten women and one boy. He had been the lover of two hundred and eighty-three women and operated a wholesale business of seduction and murder. The evidence at his trial revealed that he had hacked to pieces and burned piecemeal in his cookstove at Villa Gambais near Versailles the bodies of ten of his thirteen "fiancées."

The bizarre drama of the crimes of Landru extended over five years. Year after year he pursued the grim business of systematic love-making and slaughter. One by one his "fiancées" vanished forever. Relations duly reported the mysterious disappearances to the police but each time the circumstances and the name of the "man in the case" were different. The police failed to find a single clue or to connect the disappearances as the crimes of one man. The general disorganization of civilian life during the war favoured Landru's schemes. The husbands of many of the women were at the front. Others, whose husbands had been killed, were only too anxious to listen to offers of marriage.

By pure chance in April, 1919, the sister of one of the missing "fiancées" caught a glimpse of Landru in the Rue de Rivoli in Paris. She recognized him, followed him to his apartment, and informed the police. Without realizing they had made one of the greatest catches in Parisian criminal history, the police took him in custody.

On the way to the station the detectives caught Landru surreptitiously attempting to throw away a little notebook. This was the beginning of the whole fantastic story. It was the famous carnet containing the key to the entire series of astounding crimes. Without the carnet it is unlikely that the police would ever have fastened the crimes on Landru, yet at first it remained a mystery as it looked like a series of notations of business transactions. But they held him on an old theft charge.

Finally in puzzling over the meaning of the cryptic entries in the book of which he was so anxious to rid himself, the police compared the names of women in the carnet with the names of scores of missing women. To their astonishment they found that ten of the names in the notebook tallied with those of ten women who had disappeared during the four years since 1915.

From that moment the mystery was unravelled, strand by strand. The investigations lasted two years. Because Landru had lived in eleven different places in Paris, under at least fifteen different names, the police faced great difficulties. Landru maintained an attitude of sarcastic and humorous defiance and the police could get nothing from him. But gradually they pieced together the strange story of the operations and crimes of the modern "Bluebeard" and furnished Paris with the greatest "cause célebre" since the Dreyfus case.

They learned that Landru was the son of a respectable Parisian business man who had become insane in later life and committed suicide. In his youth Landru was studious, bright, and normal. He was an altar boy and became a subdeacon. Then, as he attained manhood, criminal tendencies asserted themselves. In the six years before the outbreak of war, Landru was convicted six times of petty frauds and served two brief terms in prison.

About the time of the outbreak of war, Landru hit upon the unique idea of wholesale love-making as a business. By matrimonial advertisements and want advertisements offering to purchase furniture he came into contact with hundreds of women. He made violent love to every one of them. The entries in his carnet showed that he was successful with two hundred and eighty-three.

Henri Désiré always proposed marriage at the second or third meeting and made violent and skillful love during the brief courtships. His diary revealed him on some occasions courting as many as seven women simultaneously, maintaining a passionate correspondence and turning out love letters by the score. When his murder villa was searched it yielded a bundle of such letters prepared ready for use. At first Landru seems to have confined his operations merely to swindling his enamored victims.

During this time Landru maintained a separate home for his wife and son; by the usual standards was a good husband and family man. Unknowingly his wife and son often helped him dispose of the property of his victims. He explained his frequent absences at the murder villa by telling his wife he was out of Paris on "business trips." Neither his wife nor son knew the nature of his business.

The unforgettable Landru trial occurred during twenty-three days in October and November, 1921, in a bare court room in Versailles. Tout Paris stormed the doors of the court and many gained entrance. Mistinguette was there and Van Dongen. Sir William Orpen sketched the remarkable skull of Henri Désiré. The front rows were liberally sprinkled with the befurred and perfumed demimonde of Paris. Landru maintained an imperturbable dignity. Under questioning about his affairs with innumerable women he smiled deprecatingly and said, "It's an affair of honour. I do not kiss and tell." When his lawyer intimated that the missing women had entered "an unmentionable profession" and dared not show themselves Landru looked slightly surprised and relieved. And when the judge sharply questioned Landru, "But what about the youth, André Cuchet? Did he enter an unmentionable profession?" Landru arched his heavy eyebrows and retorted: "He joined the Belgian army – probably he's the Belgian Unknown Soldier." The audience roared. It was better than anything the Folies Bergeres had ever put on.

Then one day Landru sent for the judge, saying he was remorseful and wanted to talk. At last, buzzed the prosecution, Landru is going to break down and confess. But when the judge went Landru sighed and said: "I am remorseful. I must tell you. I am remorseful about all the two hundred and eighty-three infidelities to my wife." That story ricocheted around the court room to renewed roars of laughter.

But day by day the prosecution unravelled the fantastic story of the "death carnet." The first of the cryptic entries in the book was the name of the respectable middle-aged widow Cuchet. Investigation showed that he met her through a matrimonial advertisement. After a whirlwind courtship she went to live with him at the fateful Gambais Villa at Vernouillet, under promises of marriage. Then came the stark inscription, "One round-trip, two single tickets to Vernouillet," with the cost. Mme. Cuchet and her seventeen-year-old son, Andre Cuchet, disappeared from the face of the earth from that day forth. Some of Mme. Cuchet's furniture turned up in the apartment of Landru's wife. She and her son's sweetheart were wearing Mme. Cuchet's jewellery when Landru was arrested.

The entries in the carnet recurred with monotonous regularity –each marking the final disappearance of one more victim. The second entry was the widow, Mme. Labord-Line, with the date June 15, 1915, and the usual grim, "One single, one round-trip ticket Vernouillet." She had announced her engagement to M. Cuchet – he sometimes adopted the name of his previous victim – a few days after meeting Landru. Nobody ever saw Mme. Labord-Line again after her fatal trip to Vernouillet.

Next on the list was Mme. Guillin. Landru met her August 15 and twelve days later she informed friends she was preparing for her wedding. Her blond wig and lingerie were found in Landru's garage at Villa Gambais.

The fourth was Mme. Heon, a widow past middle age. Little could be learned about her except that she went to Vernouillet with Landru and was never seen again.

"Mme. Collomb–December 27, 1916 – one single, one round-trip Vernouillet – 4 A.M., 5,087 francs." After the usual promises of marriage Mme. Collomb had gone with Landru to Villa Gambais on December 26. The prosecution charged that 4 A.M. was the hour of the murder and

5,087 francs the amount of money Landru obtained. Articles of Mme. Collomb's clothing were found in the villa.

The sixth "fiancée" was nineteen-year-old Madeleine Babelay. Landru met her in the subway. She was weeping, following a quarrel with her mother, and had determined to leave home. She told relatives that Landru in a fatherly way offered to aid her. He enticed her to Villa Gambais on March 29, 1917. The entry "Babelay – April 12–4 A.M." appeared in his carnet. Nobody ever heard of her from the day she told relatives she was going to the country with her "protector." Her wartime identity card and some of her lingerie were found in a box at Villa Gambais. Landru claimed she had left them as security for money he advanced to her.

The next entry concerned "Widow Buisson – September 1, 1917–10:15 A.M." Landru had been making love to her more than two years and had written her dozens of love letters before she succumbed to his importunities. They spent the day before the fatal date selecting her wedding dress. The police inquiries showed that Landru came back to Paris the same day alone to begin his courtship of Mlle. Segret.

"Mme. Jaume – October 26, 1917 – 3 A.M." represented the eighth "fiancée" in the carnet. She was intensely religious and had scruples about living with Landru without the sanction of the church. He went with her to Sacré Coeur church on Montmartre and prayed with her. Her scruples overcome, they made the fatal trip to Villa Gambais.

The ninth was Mme. Pascal. The police discovered that Landru sold her false teeth for fifteen francs. At the trial Landru asserted that the teeth he sold were his father's and that "Mme. Pascal's teeth were gold-filled and would have brought at least sixty francs."

Mme. Pascal had told friends of the strange fascination of her "fiancé's" eyes and related to relatives how he once tried to hypnotize her. She took her favourite cat to Villa Gambais. Its body was found buried in the garden, strangled with a waxed cord.

The tenth and last of the missing "fiancées" was 'Thérèse Marchandier. She told friends that Landru had proposed to her the second time they met. After borrowing twenty francs from his wife for car fare to Villa Gambais, Landru returned next day and paid debts totalling 950 francs. Mme. Marchandier's three pet dogs were found buried in the garden, strangled with waxed cords.

At the time of his arrest Henri Désiré was assiduously courting Fernande Segret, an attractive girl of twenty-nine, who had broken her troth with her fiancé at the front. She was wearing the "death ring" – the engagement ring that Landru had used for nine other "fiancées." During the trial she fixed her attention upon a newspaper colleague of mine, the Paris correspondent of a New York newspaper, and later haunted his office. She used to tell him, "Henri Désiré was so good, so gentle to me, and at the same time such a passionate lover."

At the trial she carefully avoided Landru's gaze during most of the testimony. When she finally looked at him she swooned in the witness box. Despite her knowledge that she had apparently narrowly escaped the fate of the ten preceding "fiancées" she refused to testify directly against him. She said: "He was always affectionate and respectful to me, and quite normal. I loved him and would have married him. He showed delicate attentions to my mother and used to bring her flowers."

But the prosecution revealed that Henri Désiré was simultaneously engaged to Jeanne Falque, from whom he had borrowed 2,000 francs.

To climax the crushing array of circumstantial evidence, Dr. Paul, the celebrated criminologist, produced two hundred and fifty-six fragments of human bones from the ashes of the cook-stove in Villa Gambais. One hundred and forty-seven of these he declared were fragments of human skulls. Dr. Paul testified that these fragments came from at least three human bodies. Another expert testified that the soot in the chimney contained a high content of fat. An ash heap yielded up bits of half-melted corset stays and buttons from women's clothing. One closet contained scores of small bottles and vials that had, according to the experts, contained tissue-destroying fluids. Neighbours testified they had often seen dense clouds of nauseating smoke coming from the mysterious villa. Experiments with the Villa Gambais cookstove showed that quantities of flesh could be burned there in small pieces.

The alienists and scientists who examined Landru many times

during the investigations confessed they could not fathom the mystery of his uncanny attraction for women.

Except for his extraordinary eyes, he had no outward feature to account for his success with women. He was fifty-five years of age, of medium build, sallow complexion, and wore ordinary clothes. At first glance his only unusual features included his remarkably shaped bald head and his Assyrian-like beard, which he was inordinately proud of and kept carefully trimmed and soigné.

But Landru's eyes compelled attention. They were large and serpentlike in their fixity and brilliance. Several of his two hundred and eighty-three women who escaped death told the police that his eyes fascinated and terrorized them but held them charmed.

They described his tender attentiveness and consideration – how he sent flowers and candy to their relatives and how in almost every instance the attentions of Henri Désiré favourably impressed their relatives.

The alienists testified that many tests had revealed that Landru was sane and possessed of an unusually brilliant mentality. One of the alienists who testified at the trial said: "Landru has a remarkably keen mentality. He is a charming talker and has a prepossessing manner which might have a hypnotic influence over women who are hysterically inclined."

The bundles of love letters found indicated that his method consisted of the broadest flattery. In writing to middle-aged widows whose hands were wrinkled and reddened by family washing, Landru would say: "Your hands are beautiful and delicate and full of expression." He would refer to their "wonderful hair" and "seductive eyes." Parisian men about town tried to elicit Landru's system of winning women. But he smiled mysteriously and said: "Our relations were mostly of a business nature and those of a private nature are a matter between them and myself."

Landru's attorney, the famous Maitre Moro Giafferi, later a cabinet member, eloquently and steadfastly maintained that the evidence was only circumstantial, but Henri Désiré Landru was sentenced to have his head cut off in front of the Versailles jail at dawn on February 25, 1922.

As manager of the Paris Bureau of United Press I had written the stories of the investigation and trial and I felt impelled to cover the case to the end.

On the night of February 24, together with half a dozen French reporters, I caught the electric train to Versailles. We went to the courthouse, obtained crudely mimeographed green laissez-passers for the execution, and retired to the Hôtel des Réservoirs with five bottles of cognac to await dawn.

At four A.M. word came that M. Deibler, the famous executioner who performed all the executions throughout France, had arrived with his apparatus. Anatole Deibler, shy, wistful, goat-bearded, had performed more than three hundred executions. His salary was 8,000 francs per year (a little over $1,000 at the present rate of exchange). He suffered from a weak heart and could not walk upstairs, but this did not seem to interfere with his gruesome vocation. He lived in a small house near Versailles under the name of M. Anatole, consorted very little with his neighbours, and led a retiring existence. He kept the guillotine in a shed outside his house. When performing an execution he wore white gloves and a long white "duster."

We hurried to the prison. Four hundred troops had drawn cordons at each end of the street and permitted only the possessors of the little green mimeographed tickets to pass. According to the French law, executions must occur in the open street in front of the prison door. On the damp, slippery cobblestones beside the street-car tracks workmen were rapidly erecting the guillotine a dozen feet outside the towering gate of Versailles prison. It was still quite dark. The only light came from the workmen's old-fashioned lanterns with flickering candles and the few electric street lights. The workmen bolted the grisly machine together and adjusted its balance with a carpenter's level. Deibler hauled the heavy knife to the top of the uprights.

Nearly one hundred officials and newspaper men gathered in a circle around the guillotine; I stood fifteen feet away. News '54 arrived from inside the prison that Landru, whose long black beard had been cut off previously, asked that he be shaved.

"It will please the ladies," he said to his jailers.

His lawyer and a priest went into his cell. He refused the traditional cigarette and glass of rum always offered just before executions.

Landru wore a shirt from which the neck had been cut away, and a pair of cheap dark trousers. That was all – no shoes or socks. He would walk to the guillotine barefooted.

As his arms were strapped behind him his lawyer whispered, "Courage, Landru." "Thanks, Maitre, I've always had that," he replied calmly.

Just as the first streaks of the chilly February dawn appeared, a large closed van drawn by horses arrived and backed up within a few feet of the right side of the guillotine. Deibler's assistants, wearing long smocks, pulled two wicker baskets from the van. They placed the small round basket carefully in front of the machine where the head would fall. Two assistants placed another basket about the size and shape of a coffin close beside the guillotine. Into that the headless body would roll.

The cordon of troops halted a street-car full of workmen on their way to work. They decided to open the cordon to permit the car to proceed and it slowly rumbled past within a few feet of the grim machine. Staring faces filled the windows.

The guillotine underwent a final test. Deibler raised the lunette, the half-moon-shaped wooden block which was to clamp down upon Landru's neck. Then he lowered it and the heavy knife shot down from the top of the uprights with a crash which shook the machine. The lunette and knife were raised again. All was ready.

Suddenly the huge wooden gates of the prison swung open. The spectators became silent and tense. Three figures appeared, walking rapidly. On each side a jailer held Landru by his arms, which were strapped behind him. They supported and pulled him forward as fast as they could walk. His bare feet pattered on the cold cobblestones and his knees seemed not to be functioning. His face was pale and waxen, and as he caught sight of the ghastly machine, he went livid.

The two jailers hastily pushed Landru face foremost against the upright board of the machine. It collapsed and his body crumpled with it as they shoved him forward under the wooden block, which dropped down and clamped his neck beneath the suspended knife. In a split second the knife flicked down, and the head fell with a thud into the small basket. As an assistant lifted the hinged board and rolled the headless body into the big wicker basket, a hideous spurt of blood gushed out.

An attendant standing in front of the machine seized the basket containing the head, rolled it like a cabbage into the larger basket, and helped shove it hastily into the waiting van. The van doors slammed and the horses were whipped into a gallop.

When Landru first appeared in the prison courtyard I had glanced at my wrist watch. Now I looked again. Only twenty-six seconds had elapsed.

We newspaper men scattered at a dead run to prearranged telephones on which we held open lines. Down in our Paris offices men waited to flash the news by cable all over the world.

Despite the peculiarly horrible features of execution by guillotine I found the shock to my nervous system less severe than that caused by watching executions by hanging. In one case the writhing body had hung seventeen minutes before it was declared dead. The Landru execution occurred so quickly that I, like the other correspondents, was so absorbed in my work of making notes that I had no time to consider the horrid spectacle. A young attaché of the Argentine Embassy, who had somehow obtained a ticket, rode back to Paris with us by automobile. His hands shook and he looked ill. He drank a swig of cognac every few minutes and emptied a bottle before we reached the city.

12

ROUGH ON RIFFS

In November 1925, Abd el-Krim, the Riff chieftain, defeated the Spanish army in Morocco, captured the holy city of Xauen, and was driving the demoralized Spaniards northward toward the Strait of Gibraltar. I went to Madrid to make an effort to interview King Alfonso and visit the Spanish front.

There I renewed my acquaintance with Alexander Moore, that successful exponent of "shirt-sleeve diplomacy" and the most picturesque personality among American ambassadors since George Harvey. Moore, a Pittsburgh newspaper owner with no previous experience in international diplomacy, had conceived the idea that an ambassador was a salesman for his country. As he told me, "I'm just a travelling salesman for the United States and I slap 'em on the back, tell 'em some dirty stories, give 'em a cigar, and sell 'em a bill of goods." He lived up to his word, and his antics horrified the more staid career diplomats. But they proved highly successful in Spain, delighting King Alfonso and General Primo de Rivera, whom he called "Mike"- his name was Miguel - after meeting him once, and when he arranged a favourable commercial treaty and an American telephone monopoly in Spain, Moore "sold a bill of goods."

Moore dressed flamboyantly, dripped diamonds, wore a fuzzy hat tilted over one eye, and invariably smoked a cigar at a forty five degree upward angle. Arriving in Paris once, he telephoned me and said: "I don't speak French and if you have time I wish you'd help me do some shopping." I went to the Ritz hotel. "I want to buy some bath salts and bath perfume for the Queen. This is confidential and, of course, you won't write anything about it. I don't want to ship the stuff direct to the

Palace, so we'd better have it sent to the American Embassy in Madrid."
We went to the Rue de la Paix, where he spent $350 for expensive bath
salts and perfume. One bottle of bath perfumery, I remember, cost $70.
It will be recalled that Moore in his will left $100,000 to the Queen of
Spain, but as I recall it there was the possibility of litigation and she
finally compromised on $50,000.

Moore told me he advised the King on his investments in the United
States and gave him some good tips on the stock market. The King was
speculating in United States Steel. On a visit to one of the King's estates
Moore had discovered that whenever a Ford car on the estate broke down
the foreman simply ordered a new car, instead of obtaining spare parts to
repair the old machines. The ambassador tipped off the King to this and
Alfonso was grateful.

What Moore told me in confidence at the time left no doubt
that King Alfonso himself had secretly arranged the Primo de Rivera
coup d'état to extricate himself from the disagreeable possibilities of a
parliamentary investigation into the terrible military disaster of Annual
in Morocco. Alfonso previously warned Primo de Rivera that if the coup
d'etat failed he would be repudiated and have to take the consequences,
whatever they were, but if it were successful he would have Alfonso's
support. Primo accepted the risk. Then the King went to the north coast
to await developments. When the coup succeeded he rushed back and
gave his support to Primo's dictatorship.

The ambassador did what he could to aid me in my attempt to
interview Alfonso. He sent a warm endorsement of me to the King's
private secretary and lent me his Rolls-Royce, complete with uniformed
chauffeur and footman and American Embassy insignia, to go to the Royal
Palace. As I went through the city, the police, seeing the Embassy insignia,
halted all traffic, the guards at the government buildings presented arms,
and the Palace guards presented arms as for an ambassador. But I didn't
get the interview.

I did secure what was supposed to be an interview with Admiral
Magaz, a thin, aristocratic, cultured gentleman who was acting as vice
dictator in the absence of Primo de Rivera at the Moroccan front. About

all I could get from Magaz was that affairs were "going according to plan"; but he must have meant Abd el-Krim's plan. I determined to go to Morocco to witness the retreat of the Spanish army from Xauen.

Moore was helpful. He interceded with the Department of War to obtain permission for me, telegraphed Primo de Rivera, asking him to give me assistance, and gave me a letter for the General written in English – which Primo did not understand – addressed to "My dear Mike."

I crossed the Strait from Algeciras, near the Rock of Gibraltar, to Ceuta on the northwestern tip of the African continent. Crossing the Strait of Gibraltar, that narrow gateway between two worlds, and catching my first glimpse of the Dark Continent, with successive ranges of mysterious mountains rising one behind the other under lowering, lead-colored clouds, gave me a never-to-be-forgotten thrill. From Ceuta I went by narrow-gauge railway to Tetuan, the principal city of Spanish Morocco and the Spanish general headquarters.

The late Martin Donohue, bluff, testy, red-faced British war correspondent, who had covered every war since the Balkan wars, accompanied me from Algeciras. We were the only foreign correspondents in Spanish Morocco at the time and installed ourselves in the little Alfonso Trece hotel, which had a tiled Moorish courtyard and tinkling fountain. Tetuan consisted mostly of a typical Arab town with narrow, winding streets and a small European quarter. When Primo de Rivera learned of our arrival he invited us to luncheon with his staff and his two youthful sons at his headquarters. Primo received us warmly; I found him a big, genial man in his middle fifties, with a simplitico nature, friendly hazel eyes, and easy-going ways. He had a pronounced fondness for the pleasures of the flesh.

In the course of the luncheon Martin Donohue, who plumed himself on his knowledge of military strategy, undertook to show Primo his errors and even drew with a pencil on the tablecloth his ideas of the tactics Primo should adopt. Primo laughed and revealed not the slightest irritation at this gratuitous criticism. Next day I noticed there was a clean tablecloth.

On the strength of my personal letter from Ambassador Moore,

Primo granted me a private interview. Stipulating that I treat his views as confidential, Primo talked with amazing frankness, more frankly, in fact, than any other military commander I ever encountered.

"Abd el-Krim has defeated us," he said. "He has the immense advantages of the terrain and a fanatical following. Our troops are sick of the war and have been for years. They don't see why they should fight and die for this strip of worthless territory. I am withdrawing to this line [he drew a line on the map for me] and will hold only the tip of this territory. I, personally, am in favour of withdrawing entirely from Africa and letting Abd el-Krim have it. We have spent untold millions of pesetas in this enterprise and never made a centimo from it. We have had tens of thousands of men killed for territory which is not worth having.

"But we cannot entirely withdraw because England doesn't want us to. England has great influence over the King and, as you know, the Queen was an English princess. England fears that if we withdraw the territory will be taken by France, which might nullify the command the British have of the Strait of Gibraltar with their great fortress on the Rock of Gibraltar. Command of the Strait is vital to England's imperial interests; it is the gateway to her Empire – India and Australia. England wants a weak power like Spain in possession of the territory opposite Gibraltar. They don't want a strong power like France there."

Then Primo bitterly arraigned France, charging that French munition makers were selling Abd el-Krim cartridges smuggled through French Morocco. He thrust his hand into his desk, pulled out a handful of cartridges taken from dead Riffs, and showed me that they were of French manufacture. He claimed that the French authorities were not exercising sufficient vigilance to prevent French cartridges from reaching the Riffs. "Mark my word, when Abd el-Krim is finished with us he will attack the French, using their own ammunition against them."

That is exactly what happened later; France became involved in a war which cost hundreds of millions of francs and innumerable lives. Eventually, despite the personal opinion he had expressed to me, Primo de Rivera joined the French in attacking Abd el-Krim on two fronts.

The two powerful European nations with tens of thousands of

men, with airplanes, armoured cars, artillery, machine guns - all the paraphernalia of "civilized" warfare then managed by much bloodshed to crush the little handful of a few thousand tribesmen, armed almost entirely with rifles. They exiled Abd el-Krim to Reunion Island, a tiny speck of land in the Indian Ocean, where he still lives with four of his wives on a small annual pension.

After our first talk Primo took me with him to visit a military hospital in Tetuan, where we saw about six hundred wounded Spanish soldiers, every one wounded by rifle bullets, which proved that the Riffs had no artillery or machine guns. "Most of these men," Primo said, "were wounded with bullets of French manufacture."

Primo lent me one of his personal cars, a luxurious blue Hispano-Suiza limousine, and sent one of his own aides, a spick-and-span Barcelona count in a smart, expensive uniform with beautifully polished boots, to escort me to the so-called front. Before proceeding far we smashed two mudguards of Primo's car by side-swiping mule carts and plastered the limousine and ourselves with liquid mud. Repeatedly the car bogged down in mud holes; we had to get out to push, or tear branches from bushes and carry stones to give the rear wheels traction. I asked the young aristocrat why they didn't use chains, but he had never heard of them. I then suggested binding the rear wheels with rope but we couldn't find any rope.

The road, inches deep in reddish mud, twisted between frowning, semi-arid mountains. They were trying to run two lines of traffic on the one-track road with practically no places for passing. "Why don't you build turn-out places, and establish signallers on the hills, let the traffic run one way for awhile, then upon signals from the outposts release the traffic in the other direction?" I asked. "Oh, the Riffs would shoot the signallers," my conducting officer replied. This was the main road between Tetuan and Xauen, and I never understood why the Spaniards after all the years they had been in the country had not constructed a passable road. The transport of a defeated, demoralized army in full retreat clogged the winding trail. Heavy mule carts drawn by four mules hitched in single file slowed the retreat to less than a walking pace. Often the mules turned every which way, completely blocking the trail until they were straightened out by dint of much cursing and beating. Riff snipers concealed behind rocks on the mountainside shot down men at will. Being crack shots they nearly always got their man. That morning a general was killed by a sniper, and another general going forward in a Ford to take over his command was killed before he arrived. The army of 40,000 men retreating down that single mountain road bordered on mutiny and panic. Thousands had eaten practically nothing for two days, due to the difficulty of bringing up supplies against the current of a retiring army. Every now and then we heard the sharp crack of the rifle of a Riff sniper.

At Suk el-Arbaa I talked with an officer who commanded a little detachment encamped on a rocky shelf of a few acres on the mountainside. His face, unshaven for days, showed deep lines of anxiety, his uniform was muddy and in tatters; he nearly broke into tears as he showed me the ramshackle huts with leaky roofs under which his men had slept, literally in an inch of mud, for days. He pointed out one but which I would have sworn could not hold more than fifty men; he said 160 men slept there, covering the bare ground like a carpet, with not an inch between them.

"These poor men have had nothing to eat except a few sardines each in the last two days. They sleep on the bare ground in that mud. We can't get any ground coverings or food up here, and we have to stay here to fight off the snipers and protect the flank of the withdrawal," he said, and his voice broke.

Three or four snipers on the mountainside fired at intervals of a few minutes. The officer summoned a detail of about twenty men to drive them off. Never had I seen soldiers in such a state of exhaustion, dejection, and filth; several were barefooted, the soles of their shoes worn off. None saluted their officer and they reluctantly fell into line, mumbling curses. I thought I was about to witness a mutiny, but the detail formed slowly and cautiously ascended the mountainside in skirmish formation. Sniping ceased immediately; the Riffs followed their usual tactics in such circumstances and faded away into the mountains, to appear later at another point. When the officer took me through the camp not a single private soldier saluted him, only the noncoms; sometimes he had literally to shove soldiers out of his way so that we could pass.

Toward sunset an officer took me to an emplacement of several field guns which overlooked a little village in the valley below. "We are going to bombard that village for you," the officer said. I protested that I did not want any bombarding for my benefit. "Well, we'll bombard it anyhow because at sunset the people who are left in the village come in for their evening prayers. We catch them all together then." At sunset Muslims always kneel, repeat their prayers, and bow toward Mecca. I was scarcely in a position to tell the officer what I thought about shelling defenceless old men, women, and children at their prayers. The guns opened fire and methodically threw a few score shells into the village. Through glasses we saw people running wildly about, fleeing into the hills. Although I had witnessed many unpleasant things in the World War, this heartless exhibition sickened me. And I was to see more of the same thing in India and again in Africa.

Every night while I was in Tetuan the Riffs sniped on the outskirts of the city within a mile or two of Spanish general headquarters. Opening the hotel window, we heard splatters of rifle shots every few minutes. Often snipers fired on the Spanish wireless station, which was surrounded by electrified barbed wire.

After a few trips southward to watch the progress of the disorganized withdrawal to the shortened line which Primo de Rivera had resolved to defend, Donohue and I decided to go to the international city of Tangier to file our dispatches without benefit of Spanish censorship. We notified Primo of our intention to depart for Tangier early the next morning and bade him farewell. He assured us that the road was in good condition and quite safe, since all of it lay within the Spanish lines.

Next morning before dawn one of Primo's aides came to our room. He appeared embarrassed, but finally came to the point: "The General thinks you would be more comfortable if you took the railway out to Ceuta. The bus to Tangier really isn't very comfortable." Donohue and I insisted that we didn't care particularly about comfort but wanted to see Tangier, and besides we had already bought our bus tickets. He hastily offered to refund us the money and turn in the tickets. We argued that we really wanted to see the beautiful city of Tangier. Finally he was forced into a corner and admitted that the General had ordered us to take the train, that the route to Tangier was "unsafe."

We had to accede and learned at Ceuta that the Anj era tribe had risen and dominated the road to Tangier far behind the Spanish lines. While we were waiting for the train to start from the Tetuan station we heard a crackle of rifle fire a mile away. A member of the Spanish Foreign Legion told us that the whole area was alive with snipers and they never could tell who were their enemies. During the day the inhabitants were peaceful farmers, but at night they unearthed their hidden rifles and became snipers. The Spanish army was caught in a highly uncomfortable position at that time; probably only the entry of France into the war saved it from gradual attrition.

After arriving in Gibraltar I wrote steadily all night and telegraphed an uncensored story.

The friendship with Primo de Rivera which I formed at Tetuan proved useful in later years. After he returned to Spain he imposed a drastic censorship whenever anything untoward happened, and it often took a day or two for fragmentary news to leak across the frontiers. The government had complete control of the communications and, moreover, no telephone service connected Spain with the outer world at that time.

After I returned to London a rumour reached us from Perpignan, on the Franco-Spanish frontier, that someone had attempted to assassinate Primo in Barcelona. Of course, our regular correspondents in Barcelona and Madrid could send nothing about it abroad through the censorship.

I sent a telegram addressed directly to "General Primo de Rivera, Barcelona," asking him the truth of the rumour. Within a few hours I received an eight-hundred-word urgent-rate telegram from him giving a vivid first-person description of the attempted assassination. The censors had not dared to stop an official telegram written by the Dictator himself. We published the story under his own name: "By General Primo de Rivera, written for United Press."

I utilized the same method five or six times when the censorship prevented important news from being sent out. Invariably Primo responded promptly–and the government always paid the telegraph tolls, which were fifteen cents a word for urgent-rate to London. Once I cabled him from Buenos Aires when I happened to be in South America and he replied at urgent-rate costing $2.50 a word.

13

VERDUN AFTER 1,050,000 DIED

Strangely enough, the cataclysmic horror of the war did not strike me with all its overwhelming obscenity and futility until exactly eight years after it was over. On the eighth anniversary of the Armistice I conceived the idea of visiting the old front to describe the appearance of the battlefields at that time. What I wrote apparently conveyed some of the emotion I felt, because it attracted more attention than anything I had ever done before. Hundreds of newspapers splashed the articles on their front pages and scores of editors telegraphed or wrote congratulations.

During the war I had been deluded, along with millions of others, by ignorance and propaganda into believing that it really meant something, that it was a crusade to crush militarism, smash autocracy, and end war forever. But after eight years had passed, militarism was obviously stronger than ever; greater and more powerful autocracies were rising on all sides. The World War had succeeded only in breeding new wars. Eight and one-half million men had died in vain, tens of millions had suffered unutterable horrors, and hundreds of millions had undergone grief, deprivation, and unhappiness. And all this had happened under a stupendous delusion.

The spectacle of the devastation wrought by the war, seen eight years later, focused these ideas in my mind more sharply and poignantly than ever before. A sense of deep depression and nauseated rage obsessed me after the trip to the battlefields.

I went to the battlefields around Verdun, scene of the greatest battle in the history of the world, where 1,050,000 men were killed. The hills were unutterably desolate at that time of year. A thick growth of weeds and thistles covered the ghastly debris left by the slaughter of a million men. Even after eight years, a few steps off the beaten path anywhere revealed pieces of skulls, bones protruding from rotted shoes, bits of rusted rifles and machine guns, shrapnel-punctured steel helmets, sodden scraps of uniform . . .

I visited the grizzled French priest who lived on the summit near Fort Vaux. He had dedicated his life to gathering bones, which he placed in a temporary mortuary. There I saw piles of skulls with great jagged shrapnel holes, shattered arm and leg bones, and bits of skeletons, all of which he had collected. They were to be placed in fifteen huge caskets, one for each of the fifteen sectors of the battlefield. Each casket in turn would represent thousands of unknown soldiers. The caskets were to be placed in a huge memorial which the French were constructing on the hills. It staggered the imagination to think that more than 300,000 French bodies were never identified and thousands upon thousands never found; that the greater part of the 600,000 German dead also remained unidentified.

I visited the famous Trench of Bayonets, where 170 French soldiers were buried alive by shell fire while waiting in a trench to attack. Their long bayonets protruded in a row from the earth, just as they stood when the hurricane of shells engulfed them instantaneously. A massive memorial donated by an American, George F. Rand, protected the bayonets and tops of the two score rifles still protruding. Many had been stolen by ghoulish souvenir hunters during the years the trench had remained unprotected, and the remainder were slowly rusting away.

At the exact point where the Germans had advanced nearest Verdun at Fort Souville stood an affecting monument of the figure of a dead lion twisted in the agonies of death. The little village of Fleury, once a peaceful spot where the peasants grew fine fruit, was still a pile of weed-grown rubbish. It will probably never be rebuilt.

While leaving Verdun in the grimy train I caught a brief glimpse of what this place meant to sorrowing millions. To military men it signified the greatest battlefield in the history of humanity, where men exhibited unbelievable powers of endurance and bravery, where the German invasion was halted as against a stone wall and the current of history was turned. But for two or three million living persons it meant something else.

In one corner of the shabby compartment huddled a thin, careworn old German woman, poorly dressed in obviously homemade clothing. As the train drew up the slopes she nervously brushed the moisture from the rain-swept window for a last look at the desolate hills where more than 600,000 of her countrymen had been slaughtered. Then she subsided into the corner, weeping quietly; furtively dabbing her eyes with a sodden handkerchief.

In broken French she timidly asked me where she must change trains for Reims. I asked if she had lost relatives in the battle of Verdun. She broke into tears. "Yes, my two sons and my husband. Nobody knows where they fell. I could only walk over the terrible fields. I have been saving eight years to make this trip. I can never do it again. Everything is gone. Oh, this horrible war!"

At the next station a stout French peasant woman in faded black entered the compartment. She took the other corner and stared silently through the window. At the junction I helped the German with her cane suitcase; she thanked me haltingly and stood uncertainly in the rain until the train left. Then I fell into conversation with the French woman, who said she was Mme. Laval of Besancon. I told her about the German woman. The French woman kept silent for a few moments, then tears filled her eyes.

"The poor old woman," she said. "Our countries were enemies, but I can't help pitying that poor German woman. It must be terrible to come all this way and not to know where her dead lie. I come every year at this time. My husband, my son, and my brother are up on those hills. We know where their bodies lie; that is some consolation."

From Verdun I traversed the terrible wound that the Meuse-Argonne battle tore deep into the smiling countryside of France. Eight years had changed it from a wound to a ghastly, disfiguring scar. The desolation caused by that titanic struggle will disfigure France for many years.

At such historic points as Vauquois, Avocourt, and Montfaucon the battlefield had become a wilderness of dead weeds rustling in the chill autumn rains and winds. On the tops of the hills, where thousands of shells tore up the chalky subsoil, nothing will grow and you could see the scar for miles across the country. The trench lines had fallen in, and the heavy winter rains washed soil over the grim relics of the killing.

The Argonne Forest was doing its best to efface the memories of eight years before. Trees which had not been utterly killed had grown new branches to replace those torn away by steel and lead, and a new forest was appearing. The trunks of new saplings were as thick as a man's arm. There were still thousands of stark, shell-torn boles of dead trees which would stand for many years. The smoke and gas of battle seemed to have left a permanent blight. Far fewer villages had been rebuilt than in other sectors.

Only a crudely painted signboard marked the little ravine where the "Lost Battalion" made history. The thicket had grown so dense that it was impossible to penetrate to the position where 564 Americans marched in but only 194 came out.

In Vienne-le-Chateau, where the Seventy-seventh Division from New York established headquarters in a cellar, only about 600 of the 2,000 pre-war inhabitants had returned. The building where General Alexander made his headquarters had been repaired and made into a little restaurant for tourists. The manager, M. Piot, had gathered many souvenirs of the Seventy-seventh. He had nailed a piece of glass over the hastily blue-pencilled sign which indicated the headquarters of the "Lost Battalion." The cook's indignant pencil scrawl on a door, "Kitchen, you keep out," was still legible. If John F. Newman, of New Haven, Connecticut, still survives, he will be interested to know that his pencilled name on the door was still visible. The machine-gun positions behind the house had caved in.

Not far away the Four de Paris still lay in ruins, apparently untouched since the battle. Naked stumps of shell-shattered trees and tangles of barbed wire studded the Bois de Rossignol. The village of Varennes was nearly unrecognizable. Rubbish choked the stream where the villagers' ducks swam. Evidences of the American occupation still existed – faded divisional signs painted on crumbling walls; a peasant woman wheeling her baby in a cart made of an old American candy box.

The crests of Vauquois and Montfaucon were visible from miles away and looked as though they had suffered a bad attack of smallpox. Thousands of shell holes, rim touching rim, had not been filled; gas had killed all vegetation.

Back toward the Champagne battlefield the desolation was profoundly depressing. Mile upon mile of ruined country without a human habitation within eyeshot. Many of the villages will never exist again. Perthes-les-Hurlus, near where the Second Division went in, used to be a pleasant village with five hundred inhabitants; it has ceased to be. Only a heap of weed-grown rubbish not as high as a man's head remained. Hurlus presented the same aspect except that the shattered walls of the church remained standing. Les-Mesnil-les-Hurlus has gone forever; only a mound of rubbish marked its site.

It will take a generation to wipe out the traces of that great battle which lasted only forty-six days but in which 1,379,405 men tried to kill one another.

Château-Thierry, which will forever figure in American school books, was a poky little provincial town, nestling in the fertile valley beside the placid Marne and shouldered by rolling hills. In the pale autumn sunlight laborious peasants and slow-moving animals worked the fields on the hillside; peasant women were digging sugar beets; yellow wheat stacks dotted the fields on the slopes.

The town had reverted to its sleepy pre-war peace. Occasionally the clatter of a dusty automobile over the rough cobbled streets or the rattle of a heavy farm cart broke the silence. Old men drowsed in the sun on a little cafe terrace twenty yards from where Lieutenant Bissell and his fourteen men– of whom "seven became casualties," according to his report – set up their machine gun on the north bank of the river late in the afternoon of May 31, 1918. Youths silently fished in the sluggish green water beside the bridge just where the Seventh Machine Gun Battalion poured a hail of bullets from the other side. The dusty trees along the little boulevard there still showed bullet scars. Below the ruins on the river bank, where men of the Seventh slipped down to get water in the darkness during the battle, a public laundry barge was anchored. Sunburned women did the family wash and laughed and gossiped about their petty affairs.

Along the street facing the Marne I found bullet holes in the shutters, some filled with putty, others remaining as they were. A graceful stone span had replaced the old stone bridge that the French Colonials blew up as they retired. Practically all of the buildings in town had been repaired, with bright, new patches of tile where the shells plunged through. Most of the people had plastered up the shrapnel scars on the walls. Indeed, in most of the town it was difficult to identify traces of what happened during May and June, 1918. The population of 8,000 was about the same as before the war. The town had one movie theatre which opened twice a week. By nine-thirty at night everything was closed and most of the inhabitants had gone to bed; even the principal hotel, Jean de la Fontaine, locked up before ten at night. I went to see M. Bethincourt, the acting mayor. He was seventy-three, and wore a rough jacket buttoned to his throat and a greasy, heavy cap. He had stayed in Chateau-Thierry throughout the war. Tugging at his long white beard, he said, "Yes, things are pretty much as they were before the war." Wandering around the somnolent town, watching the snail-like canal boats slipping down the mirrorlike stream, I found it hard to realize that here along the Marne occurred a battle which will bulk large in American history. But the bottom of the tranquil Marne, dyed with American blood only a hundred months before, contained some grim relics which would belie its pleasant guise.

I visited Quentin Roosevelt's grave. The last time I was there, during the war, it was marked only by his half-buried airplane propeller, erected by the Germans to mark the spot where he was shot down from the air. Now the Roosevelt family had erected a memorial bearing Theodore Roosevelt's words: "Only those are fit to live who are not afraid to die."

The historic forest at Belleau Wood where 1,000 American boys had been killed and 7,321 wounded was being restored so that present and future generations of Americans might see the battlefield as it was the day the fighting ceased. I walked on broad paths into the centre of the wood and along the trench lines. The trenches and "fox holes" and machine-gun emplacements remained as the troops had left them. Nature had undertaken her own work of restoration. Tree tops literally mowed off by shell fire had grown out, though many of the big trees were so mangled they had died. These gaunt skeletons stood, with unexploded shells or shell fragments as big as a fist still sticking out of their trunks. Off the paths lay the horrid debris of war: torn German and American shoes, pieces of uniforms, steel helmets pierced by bullets, torn bandoleers, bits of underwear, beef cans pierced by shrapnel, twisted barbed wire, rusty bayonets, and broken rifles.

The bodies of at least fifty Americans and one thousand Germans still lay in the depths of the woods. Every few days several bodies were found and buried. Adolph Kess, in charge of the near-by American cemetery, said: "We are still identifying many American bodies by charts of their teeth. By careful checking with the army records we can usually, by a process of elimination, reduce the probabilities down to a few names. Then we consult the relatives and dentists who treated these men in their home towns, and frequently make absolute identifications by the teeth charts. No two men ever have the same teeth chart." The fact that at least 3,000 Americans and Germans were killed in this wood of only 150 acres indicates better than any words the terrible struggle which occurred here. A walk through beautiful Belleau Wood cemetery, in which there were then 2,262 graves, teaches a lesson in Americanism. One row of crosses taken at random showed the names Miconi, Patrick, Russell, Noel, Manning, Debacker, Redovanovich, Derusha, and Torlep. I brought with me statistics of the remarkable restoration work the French had done, reconstructing half a million buildings and rebuilding 3,000 miles of damaged or destroyed railways and 34,000 miles of roads. But these statistics did nothing to lift the morbid depression I felt. I could not tear my mind away from the almost ungraspable fact that 8,538,315 men from all over the world had been killed and 21,219,452 wounded, and that 867,000 houses, 17,000 public buildings, 4,061 miles of railways, 36,394 miles of roads, and 5,000 bridges and tunnels had been destroyed or damaged. From the strained faces and tear-dimmed eyes of the visitors I encountered among the acres of black and white crosses dotting the 600 miles from Switzerland to the English Channel, I caught only a glimpse of the awful load of sorrow this meant to the whole world.

Then I remembered that there were more men under arms in the world, more militarism, more oligarchies, less freedom, more new wars looming on the horizon than before all this happened. I went back to Paris in a state of dejection and depression such as I had never before experienced and got drunk trying to take the load off my mind.

◆ ◆ ◆

During the ten years from 1925 to 1935 I remained in London much of the time in my capacity as assistant European manager and later as European news manager of United Press. Frequent trips to various parts of the world broke this period.

In 1926 I went to Spain and Portugal. In Madrid I talked with Niceto Alcala Zamora, then unknown to the world at large, who later became the first President of the Spanish Republic and was deposed just before the Spanish civil war of 1936. At the time I met Zamora, King Alfonso seemed firmly seated on the throne, but Zamora accurately predicted that Alfonso would be deposed before many years and be followed by a republic. I think he little realized that he would be the first president of it.

I had several conversations with Indalecio Prieto, the Socialist leader, who became the most powerful figure behind the scenes on the government side in the Spanish civil war in 1936. Prieto, a burly, bluff, red-faced newspaper owner of Bilbao, who commenced life as a street waif, talked with me at a cafe table. Every now and then he stopped talking and burst into loud, ribald song. He explained: "See those two fellows at the next table? They are spies for Alfonso. They're trying to hear what I say; that's why I sing."

From Lisbon I sailed to South America and spent four months visiting Brazil, Uruguay, Argentina, Chile, and Peru, accompanied by James Irwin Miller, vice president of United Press for South America. We talked with scores of newspaper editors to ascertain their news requirements in the extensive service we furnished to about one hundred South American newspapers. We had interviews with the President of Brazil, President Figueroa of Chile, and the diminutive dictator of Peru, Leguia, who told me about the various attempts that had been made to assassinate him. I returned to Europe by way of the west coast of South America, the Panama Canal, and the United States.

Early in 1931 I travelled to all the principal cities of Italy to write a series of articles on Fascism in its ninth year. Late in 1932 I went to Germany and wrote a series of articles on the rise of the Nazis. This was some time before Hitler came into power.

Adolf Hitler gave me an interview at the party headquarters, the famous Brown House, in Munich. Dr. Ernst Hanfstaengl, Hitler's friend who plays Wagner on the piano for him, arranged the meeting. It was fixed for four P.M. I sat in Hitler's outer office four hours and finally told Hanfstaengl that I should wait no longer; that I had never been treated in this manner when interviewing great figures. Hanfstaengl hastily arranged that the conference General von Epp was having with Hitler be interrupted, and I was received.

Hitler greeted me briefly, sat down at his desk, stared into space, and launched into a speech. He spoke exactly as though he were addressing a public meeting. Among other things he told me that when he came into power Germany would cease paying reparations and that he would unify Germany, cast off the remaining shackles of the Treaty of Versailles, and reconstitute Germany's military power. None of those objectives seemed possible at the time; it wasn't even certain he would come into power; but he has achieved all of them.

In 1934 I went to Doom to attempt to interview the ex-Kaiser, but failed. I went to Moscow in 1935 and wrote a series of stories about how the Russians live, dress, and amuse themselves. Early in 1935 I took charge of our staff at the Stresa Conference in Italy. That was only one of many conferences I had covered, including the 1930 Naval Conference in London, the World Economic Conference, and the Disarmament Conference in Geneva.

During the summer of 1918 I met Franklin Delano Roosevelt for the first time. He came to Paris as Assistant Secretary of the Navy in connection with the anti-submarine campaign. He received about a score of French journalists in a hotel on the Rue de Rivoli, and I was present. I recall particularly the excellent impression he made upon the French newspaper men and how he charmed them with his pleasant personality and unusual frankness. He was then about thirty-six years of age, slender, handsome, and prepossessing in appearance. He leaned against the mantelpiece and chatted with the newspaper men in fluent French; that alone won them to him, because he was the first American high official to reach France who spoke their language with facility.

He astounded the French newspaper men by telling them that American cabinet members received newspaper correspondents twice daily, something unheard of in Europe. Some time afterward, Roosevelt said that Clemenceau jokingly accused him of having almost overturned the French Cabinet. All the French newspaper men, Clemenceau told him, had rushed to the Quai d'Orsay and demanded that French cabinet ministers receive the press daily, citing Roosevelt's statement that it was done in the United States. Roosevelt's famous charm of personality is no new development; he had it at least eighteen years ago.

I met Roosevelt again briefly in 1932, but the next time I talked with him was at the White House in February, 1936, after my return from the Northern Italian Front in Ethiopia. He received me privately and asked many questions about the military and political factors of the situation in Ethiopia which revealed that he had a thorough grasp of them. I am not at liberty to go into the details of our conversation, but one of the stories he told me proved that the heavy burden of office had not affected his sense of humour. Of all the men in high places I have met, President Roosevelt possesses the warmest and most attractive personality.

14

MAGIC CARPET

The telephone in my London apartment rang early one morning in May, 1930. The United Press was telephoning an urgent cable message from our New York office.

"Go to India by first available airplane cover Gandhi salt march" the cablegram read.

Thus commenced one of the most interesting assignments any newspaper man ever received. It was to take me by air over fifteen countries, over continents, mountains, seas, and deserts. Before I returned I was to travel by air nearly 16,000 miles in fifteen days of flying.

I telephoned Imperial Airways, which had only recently commenced a weekly passenger service to India. They told me the plane left at eight the next morning, that I would require ten visas and that it was doubtful if I could get them all in one day. I had to be inoculated for cholera, plague, and typhus and vaccinated against smallpox. Imperial Airways were forbidden to accept any passenger for India without a certificate of these inoculations.

I reserved a ticket for Karachi, which cost the equivalent of $586. Baggage above the free allowance of sixty pounds cost $1.25 per pound; visas for crossing Europe, Africa, and Asia about $40.

Imperial Airways assigned a man to help get the visas. I paged hospitals in an effort to get the necessary inoculations. Hospital after hospital announced they had no cholera or plague serum. I was getting worried. In mid-afternoon I located a hospital which possessed the necessary serums.

When I informed the doctor that I wanted the whole list of inoculations in one sitting he threw up his hands. "Man, I must warn you that you are going to be very, very ill. Some of these serums should be administered in three doses a week apart. I never heard of anyone taking them all at one time. However, since you insist, I'll give you the shots. But you're going to be a sick man for days." The doctor was right. I spent a feverish night. But everything was set–visas, inoculations, baggage, including the evening clothes I had to have in India. But I didn't have time to buy tropical clothes or sun topi or dark glasses.

At seven-thirty the next morning I arrived at Croydon in a gray drizzle. My wife and little boy came to see me off on my seven-day flight of 6,000 miles.

The airdrome bustled. Outside on the cement loading platform the huge six-ton biplane loomed in the mist as big as a house. Half a ton of mail for India was being stowed away. Passengers' luggage followed. Then the passengers, the wireless operator, the mechanic and a wiry, alert pilot with a face windburned the colour of a raw beefsteak. The three motors raced, blocks were jerked from the wheels, and the plane waddled awkwardly across the soggy field and roared into the air.

Of the six passengers, only two had booked through to India. Lady Leighton, snowy-haired and sixty-three, was hurrying to Basra on the Persian Gulf to the bedside of a critically ill niece. Barry Lawther, hard-bitten chief of the Intelligence Service and deputy inspector of British police of the Northwest Frontier Province, who spoke Hindu, Pashto, and Persian, veteran of many tribal skirmishes during twenty years on the Afghan frontier, his face the colour of an old saddle, was rushing back to Peshawar because the Afridis had gone on the warpath and interrupted his two years of leave. Quin-Harkin, a blond giant who survived the terrible anti-Bolshevist campaign, in the winter of 1918, with the British forces in Northern Russia, now a chief accountant, was bound for Cairo on business. Fleming, a rosy-cheeked Glasgow shipbuilder on his first airplane flight, and nervous about it, was going to Athens to sell ships to the Greek government. Finally there was an American business man en route to Vienna and myself.

We settled in our seats and stuffed cotton wadding in our ears to deaden the thunderous roar of the engines. Lady Leighton began knitting a half-finished "jumper," picking it up where she had left off when she decided to fly to the Persian Gulf.

We came into warm sunshine with a vast sea of woolly clouds below. At times the machine barely skimmed the white floor. One was seized by a feeling of intense, buoyant exhilaration. We were alone – alone in a world of billowy clouds, empty blue sky, and sun. The black shadow of our machine speeding across the cloud floor was the only movement in our world.

The drone of the engines gradually subsided. A flat field tilted crazily, rushed upward, and met the wheels of the airplane. Jimmy Youell, star pilot for Imperial Airways, set down the 12,000-pound machine, travelling faster than an express train, as gently as a housewife sets down a basket of eggs. Since then he has completed his millionth mile of flying – 10,000 hours, or one and one-half years in the air.

Cologne airdrome, and forty-five minutes for luncheon. But I felt too sick to eat. German passport officials in gray uniforms saluted stiffly and seized our passports. While the ground crew hurriedly pumped hundreds of gallons of gasoline into the tanks – we burned a gallon a minute–the passengers lunched in pale sunshine on the terrace restaurant.

Soon we set off for Vienna via Nuremberg. After Nuremberg appeared a meandering silver strip – the majestic Danube, which we were to follow more than five hundred miles.

Shortly after sunset we landed in Vienna as the lights were flicking on along the boulevards. From the air it seemed a noble city, built as the capital of a great empire and worthy of that role. Within a few minutes we sped by automobile through the broad, tree-lined avenues, past dignified churches, great palaces, and government offices where once a ramshackle, polyglot empire was governed, to dinner at the famous Bristol Hotel. I was still feverish and ate little.

At eight-thirty on a brilliant Sunday morning, with fleecy clouds slowly marching across the sky, we left for Budapest and in two hours sighted it astride the Danube. While we breakfasted in the open air at the airdrome, Hungarian officials in short, tight blue tunics dealt with our passports.

As we prepared to re-enter the plane a small French airplane swooped down from the direction of Vienna. The lone flyer leaped out and ran to our pilot. He carried three tiny boxes three inches square. In staccato French he explained that he had been chasing our plane more than nine hundred miles. In Cairo a young Egyptian girl was dying from a rare form of paralysis. Unless she were inoculated with a serum obtainable only in Paris she would die within a few days. Cablegrams had instructed the Paris laboratory to spare no expense to get the serum aboard the India plane. For a fee of 8,000 francs the pilot had been engaged to catch the India liner. He had missed us at Cologne the day before and had chased us ever since. Pilot Youell took charge of the precious boxes.

Off to Belgrade. In about two hours the majestic sweep of the Danube appeared again, glittering in the sun thirty miles ahead and behind like a winding silver ribbon. High, steep cliffs rose from the banks with neat farms and fertile fields extending to the edge. For the first time the air became "lumpy." The wing tips swung up and down as much as fifteen feet and the six-ton plane pitched like a motor truck on rough roads. I lay down on the floor in the aisle with an overcoat under my head.

Soon the air became smoother as Belgrade, capital of the Kingdom of the Serbs, Croats, and Slovenes, came into view miles ahead, sloping toward the river. In a shack beside the airdrome we swallowed vile coffee, surrounded by a group of slouchy conscript Yugoslav soldiers in shapeless, dirty gray uniforms wolfing sausages.

From the Danube, which we had followed off and on for five hundred miles through four countries, we struck out across the Balkans to or Skoplje, over the roughest terrain yet encountered. To left and right loomed high mountain ranges while we followed a deep, narrow valley through which a wide, muddy river looped as far as the eye reached, miles ahead. At our level hung great cottony clouds. Sometimes our wing tips seemed almost to touch them and one instinctively shrank back—they looked as solid as snow peaks. The white masses whipped past our wing tips at a hundred miles per hour.

The roar of our motors in the thin upper air caused curious

aural illusions. I thought I heard cathedral bells and sometimes human voices singing. As we came over a gap in the mountains the plane shot rapidly upward, borne up like thistledown by a great rising column of air deflected skyward by the configuration of the pass. Ahead lay Skoplje, in the midst of the Yugoslav Balkans. The plane landed in a field of growing wheat, its makeshift airdrome. A rattletrap American car bounced us over atrocious roads, past rude, toiling bullock carts and Mohammedan peasants wearing red fezzes and baggy Turkish trousers.

We passed the night in the Hotel Moskva, a primitive inn with one bathtub filled by buckets carried up from the courtyard to our bare, squalid rooms.

Early next morning we set off over more mountains into Macedonia, following the fertile valley of the Vardar, covered with wheat fields flecked by scarlet opium poppies. At our feet lay Salonika, raw and new, as it was largely rebuilt after the great fire. Here we transferred into an eleven-ton three-motored flying boat for the 860-mile flight across the Mediterranean to Egypt.

The flying boat skimmed the glassy surface of the water, rose to 2,000 feet, and drifted down the coast about twenty miles off shore. The air was crystal clear and gave us a visibility of fifty or sixty miles. Silhouetted on the horizon like a gigantic relief map in pastel-blue shades was the coast line of Greece. On our right rose the bulks of Mount Olympus and Mount Ossa. Directly below, the Northern Sporades islands shone in the warm sunlight.

About noon a sudden stir ran through the cabin and there were excited gestures and exclamations. We crowded to the starboard side and peered down through the portholes. Athens! The steep rock of the Acropolis surmounted by the magnificent ruin of the Parthenon and the fragments of the Temple of Jupiter. Around stretched the gray expanse of the modern city.

Ten minutes later our flying boat gently splashed into the vivid blue of Phaleron Bay. The passengers remained aboard during a hasty refuelling from a motorboat. With three hundred gallons of gasoline aboard we were off for the next hop of 220 miles to Mirabella Bay in the eastern end of Crete, in the middle of the Mediterranean.

We soared over the Cyclades islands and skirted the famous island of Milo. Our modern magic carpet swooped straight across the islands, scattering panic among the peasant goatherds and their flocks. Goats scuttled over the stony slopes. In thousands of miles of flying in many countries I experienced no flight so delightful. I could see an expanse of hundreds of square miles of the unbelievably blue Mediterranean, studded with reddish islands. Over a smooth sea the flying boat remained steady as a becalmed ship.

About three o'clock we sighted the dark bulk of the island of Crete, some twenty miles wide and a hundred and forty miles long. The snow-covered peak of Mount Ida rose 8,000 feet from the sea about a hundred miles away.

Below, Mirabella Bay suddenly appeared, narrow, land-locked, and hemmed tightly around by gray mountains. We pointed sharply downward, planed over a tiny island, and splashed down into the bay beside Spinalonga Island, an isolated rock a few hundred yards square, covered with ancient battlements and crowned by a citadel with walls twenty feet thick, fortified by the Venetians when they were masters of the Mediterranean. For fifty years the Turks besieged the rock and finally captured it. During the last Balkan war the Greeks gained possession and ejected the few lingering civilian Turks by populating Spinalonga with lepers.

Today two hundred and sixty lepers lead hopeless lives amid the splendours of this lovely little bay, with only a lingering, horrible death as release. They have no work, no amusements. The rock is too barren to permit gardens. Once daily a heroic Greek doctor goes over from the mainland. Nobody else ever visits the island prison. Despite their dread malady, the lepers bring babies into their hopeless world. If their children show no signs of disease when they are five years old they are taken from the parents, but those revealing leprosy must live out their lives on the rock. As our flying boat zoomed down over Spinalonga and landed we distinguished listless, black-hooded figures with ravaged faces staring upward. They showed no animation, no excitement.

After studying the weather report the pilot decided it was too late to try to make Egypt that day and we therefore went aboard the old hundred-ton yacht lmperia, which constituted the air base. As there were no inns at this end of Crete the air line kept the yacht moored in the bay to accommodate pilots and passengers. Knowing that one night's delay of the boxes of serum we carried might jeopardize the life of a girl in Cairo, the pilot was worried.

We were called at four in the morning and breakfasted, unwashed, by the light of the cabin lamps. Just as dawn broke we took off for Alexandria, 370 miles away, the longest regular overseas flight in Europe. Crete soon sank below the horizon in the dim early morning light.

In the cramped lavatory I achieved a fairly satisfactory shave while we roared along 2,500 feet above the deserted Mediterranean. In the whole flight to Alexandria only two ships were sighted. About nine o'clock the low, yellowish coast of Egypt rose on the horizon and soon we swooped down into the crowded harbour of Alexandria.

A swift motorboat nosed alongside to take the tiny cargo of serum to Cairo in the race against death. They told us the girl was still alive and that a special train was waiting in Alexandria to rush the serum to her. After reaching India we heard it had arrived in time and saved the girl's life.

A quick lunch in Alexandria, purchases of dark-tinted glasses to shield our unaccustomed eyes from the blinding glare of the sun, and we set out by motor car for Abukir airdrome for the flight across the Sinai Desert. The plane carried extra water jars in case of forced landing in the desert.

The Nile delta, studded with flat-roofed, earth-colored towns, sped beneath. Then the ribbonlike Suez Canal, the ganglion and connecting link of the British Empire, where man has severed two continents. From a height of 4,000 feet we saw it from end to end, sharply defined against the yellowish brown of the desert sands. A half-dozen ships were steaming between the Red Sea and Mediterranean.

Below stretched the brownish wilderness of the Sinai Desert, where the children of Israel wandered forty years – sand ridges, sand valleys, hard sun-baked earth, scrofulous alkali or salt sinks quivering in the burning heat – with here and there a tiny oasis of dejected palms. We saw no sign of life but glimpsed the ancient caravan track from Egypt to the Holy Land. Near Gaza we sighted the railway Allenby built to fight the Turks. In the middle of the afternoon we landed outside Gaza, the ancient city of the Philistines, and spent the night in the wooden shanties used as quarters by the air line.

In Biblical times Gaza was an important city; in 322 B.C. it withstood Alexander five months; and 1,400 years ago it was a great seat of learning. But nowadays it is a dejected, squalid town of about 17,000, still partly in ruins from the British bombardment of the Turks.

The affable British policeman from Glasgow in sun helmet and khaki shorts patrolling the dusty main street amid flocks of goats, camels, donkeys, and strolling groups of grave Arabs in multicoloured silk headdresses was surprised to learn that Sampson performed his immortal gate-carrying feat here and that the round hill beyond the airdrome was where the champion weight-lifter of ancient days deposited the gates of Gaza. However, he readily confirmed that Gaza is gateless now.

At 3:20 A.M. they routed us out for breakfast. Only three passengers remained – Lawther, Lady Leighton, and I. Lady Leighton, despite her sixty-three years, was bearing the heat, fatigue, and early rising surprisingly well. During the night a party of nomad Arabs had camped near by and the noise of our motors threw their camels and goats into a panic. Lights appeared in the low, black-leather tents while the Arabs hurled guttural curses at the infidels and their ancestors, offering unprintable suggestions of what camels should do on our mothers' graves.

While we were preparing to take off, a wireless from Ramleh informed the pilot that the Indian aviator, Singh, flying alone to India for the Aga Khan Prize, had disappeared in the desert between Gaza and Bagdad during the night. We were instructed to search for him.

We climbed to 4,000 feet. Ahead lay the Holy Land, which looked to us like a corrugated olive-drab jumble of rocky hills and narrow valleys eroded by ages of weathering. The hillsides were thickly terraced with stone walls to permit cultivation of every yard of soil. Here and there bleak villages clung to the hilltops. At this hour nobody was visible. We roared over Hebron and its olive groves. As the sun rose higher we distinguished white buildings on hillsides shining in the sun many miles to the left. Jerusalem! The Judean Hills loomed on the horizon. We climbed higher to cross them.

An hour after leaving Gaza our amazed eyes suddenly looked down on a scene unequaled for weird grandeur by anything in the world except perhaps the Grand Canyon of the Colorado. In an awesome gorge between the mountains of Judea and the mountains of Moab lay the Dead Sea, 1,300 feet below sea level, at the bottom of a vast rift in the earth –forty-seven miles long and ten miles wide. In some titanic cataclysm the earth had split open, and the wound lies gaping with the Dead Sea at the bottom. We could see in one glance the entire 340-square-mile expanse of the sinister sea, which has inspired awe and curiosity down through the ages.

From the slate-green water heavy vapours rose. On either side the tawny jumble of desolate, barren mountains towered 3,000 feet. In the early morning light the shadows in the gorge and on the mountains changed colour every moment. They were now ashen, then lemon, lavender, mauve, shading into pastel blue against the dark red precipices. At the north end we saw the green valley of the Jordan.

Beyond the Dead Sea we flew over the yellowish uplands of Transjordania, the granary of the Middle East in Roman times. Nowadays it is semi-arid, like parts of the Wyoming plateau. On many hilltops we looked down into vestiges of outposts erected by the Romans nineteen centuries ago to guard their wheat supply and glimpsed the beaten path from Damascus over which millions of faithful Mohammedans have made the perilous pilgrimage to Mecca to view the sacred black stone which they believe fell from Heaven. We saw no houses, no human beings.

Beyond Transjordania began the great Syrian Desert, haunt of roving Bedouin tribes and one of the most desolate areas in the world.

Here we picked up the beginning of a plough furrow six hundred miles long which guides flyers across the sun-baked wastes to Bagdad. Over arid ridges and bare plains it stretched, plainly visible from the air. Every thirty miles a huge circle on the ground enclosed a letter of the alphabet. These aerial guide signals had been formed by running a tractor over the outlines until its marks had worn deeply into the baked earth.

I was told that the Royal Air Force ploughed this furrow, the world's longest, in 1918 and that it took two parties working from each end seven months to etch the guide line across the desert. For three hundred miles we saw no human being, animal, or habitation. The pilot and mechanic kept a sharp watch on each side for the lost Indian flyer.

In the middle of the morning we landed on the open stony desert beside the military blockhouse of Rutbah Wells, the only structure for hundreds of miles in any direction. It consisted of a rectangle of thick stone walls about two hundred yards by one hundred, guarded by sand-bag outposts, trenches, and barbed wire to ward off attacks by Bedouins. A detachment of swarthy Iraqi soldiers with red fezzes, khaki uniforms, and brightly beaded cartridge belts, carrying carbines and silver-handled daggers, garrisoned the fort. They admitted us through a small iron door. Inside we found a rest room with easy chairs, electric fans, and ice-cold beer. Provisions had been brought from Bagdad and we ate a passable lunch served by Arab servants.

From Rutbah we flew four hours over the monotonous desert. A sudden blast of heat enveloped the plane. The metal arms of the seats became too hot to touch with comfort. Since leaving Egypt I had suffered from heat, as I still wore my heavy London suit.

On the horizon loomed a mass of earth-coloured buildings and a mud-coloured river – Baghdad, "Pearl of the East," where centuries ago the world's richest literature and a great civilization had flowered. Eleven centuries ago this was a city of two million, the second city of the world. Today it is the dusty, squalid capital of Iraq astride the muddy Tigris, fringed by dusty date palms, living on memories of its past.

As we climbed out into the blinding glare of the sun the pilot warned me to hold a newspaper over the back of my neck. He said that without an insulated sun topi to shield my head I might suffer sunstroke while walking the few hundred yards to the rest room. Inside the rest room the curtains were tightly drawn and punkahs revolved to stir a breeze. Cool drinks and food and an hour's rest refreshed us. We were told a radio message had just arrived announcing that the Indian aviator was found. He had spent the night in the desert and reached Rutbah after repairing his machine.

As soon as the plane was refuelled we took off for Basra, at the head of the Persian Gulf, the hottest region in the world. We pulled the curtains over the windows, and Lawther and I removed our shoes because our feet had swollen in the heat. Soon we reached the marshes of the Euphrates, where a semiaquatic tribe of Arabs has lived for centuries in the vast, inaccessible sedgy marshes. They are still untamed and often fire at passing airplanes. A few years ago they hit Sir Alan Cobham's mechanic, who bled to death while Cobham flew on to Bagdad ignorant that his mate was wounded. The roar of our motors frightened herds of the marsh Arabs' amphibian cattle, which took to the water and swam. Turbaned Arabs rushed out of their low, leather huts and pointed at us. The lower reaches of the Euphrates are fringed with miles of date gardens, and most of the world's supply of dates comes from this region. We landed at the air field seventeen miles outside Basra on a flat desert absolutely bare of vegetation. The thermometer stood at 117 in the shade and at 156 in the sun. We heard rumours of cholera and plague in Basra and pulled our cots outside and slept under the stars. Lady Leighton had reached her destination, leaving only Lawther and me as passengers for India.

We took off at 5:30 A.M. for the flight across the Persian Gulf – 130 miles over the water in a land machine – to Bushire in Persia. As soon as we were in the air we undressed and sat in our B.V.D.'s. It was unbelievably hot. The Gulf looked like curdled milk and we could not distinguish where the sky left off and the water began. The Gulf is full of sharks, and as we planed down near the Persian coast we could see scores of them in the water.

After refuelling at Bushire we hopped off for Lingeh, a pearl-and shark-fishing village. Since the air field had no building, we sheltered ourselves under the wings and hastily ate the box lunch we had brought from Bushire. The sandwiches had dried so in a few hours that the bread was toastlike. Just beyond Lingeh we flew over a great lake of solid salt, so blindingly white that we could not look at it even through dark glasses. Furnacelike heat rose from the salt. The Persian coast during the last three hundred miles was appallingly desolate and resembled a vast mountainous ash and slag heap. There were only a few squalid villages, which existed on shark fishing.

After leaving Lingeh the pilot departed from the usual route; a wireless message had informed him that a tribal war was in progress on the tip of Arabia and that the natives might fire upon a passing airplane. The plane climbed to 8,000 feet; below lay a confused mass of brownish mountains rising sheer from the poisonous-looking green sea. This was my first glimpse of Arabia, perhaps the least westernized and least known of any large body of inhabited land in the world.

The atmosphere was so dry that I could not moisten my dark glasses with my breath, even when I put the lens inside my mouth. When we drank from the thermos flask any water we spilled evaporated in a few seconds before our eyes. I was suffering from the heat so much in my London clothes that Lawther insisted upon loaning me one of his thin suits.

In the evening we landed at Jask in Persia for the night. Only one European lived in this tiny native village of shark fishers and we spent the night in his house. His name was W. C. Janes, superintendent of the relay station of the Indo-European Telegraph Company, and he had spent more than twenty years in this God-forsaken spot. Until a few weeks previously, when the regular passenger service by airplane to India had started, Janes often had not seen a European for months on end. He had developed two hobbies to while away the tedious days. He collected volume after volume of "art pictures" of lightly clothed or unclothed women of various nationalities. He had one volume devoted to France, one to Austria, another to Germany . . . "When I long for Europe, as I often do, I open these books and take a mental trip to Paris or Vienna," he grinned. His other hobby was fret-saw work. He exhibited numerous intricate designs which he had spent days sawing, and I noticed that the feminine form predominated in the designs and could imagine the loving care with which he sawed around the curves.

The stench of rotting carcasses of sharks on the beach was almost intolerable, but we had a bath, whiskey-and-sodas, and an excellent dinner in Janes's house, and slept on his flat roof under a huge bright moon, lulled to sleep by the surf pounding on the beach near by. We were awakened at 3:30 A.M. with tea and toast and started for the air field in the darkness mounted on donkeys and guided by the flashlight of Atwood, the pilot, who told me that on a previous trip the heat was so intense it had burst a tire in the air, forcing him to land on one wheel. We took off for the last day of our flight to India while it was still dark and at about 1,000 feet we suddenly entered a layer of air so intensely hot that for a moment I thought the plane had caught fire.

Our next stop was Gwadar, a tiny village in Baluchistan without motor cars or anything else modern. A group of wild-looking Baluchi with long tangled black hair, dressed in baggy homespun trousers and rough turbans, rode out from the village on camels to stare at the plane and the strange beings it brought. We breakfasted on boiled eggs, sardines, and the inevitable hot tea, sheltered from the searing sun under the wing of the plane, and then took off on the last hop to India. We flew 130 miles over the sea, at times as much as fifty miles from land. Halfway to Karachi the pilot received a wireless asking him to search for a sailboat which was carrying Royal Air Force stores to Pasni and which had been missing ten days. The pilot came down low over the water and made several circles over fishing vessels, but we found no trace of the missing boat.

In the afternoon we landed on the hard-baked Sind Desert, about twenty miles outside Karachi, beside a vast empty hangar, the largest structure of any kind in Asia. It had been erected as the Indian terminus of the projected British airship line from England to India. When the R-101 crashed in France the entire project was abandoned.

Seven days of continuous flying had reduced me to a state of exhaustion. The roaring of the motors hour after hour and day after day had a curious mental effect, after the first few days. Sometimes I could not remember which country we had been in a day or two before, and my memory was affected so that I often forgot my passports, notebooks, and articles of clothing until reminded of them. I stayed in bed in Karachi the greater part of two days recovering from the physical strain of the trip.

15

THEY THAT TURN
THE CHEEK

In India I plunged into the strangest experiment in mass political rebellion in history, a rebellion based upon a strange philosophy of nonviolence and nonbloodshed. This was diametrically opposed to previous conceptions of rebellion, which were always based upon the use of violence and bloodshed. This rebellion arose from the remarkable concept of imposing the will without resort to instruments of injury or slaughter. It took the form of nonviolent action and confined its weapons to the boycott and mass disobedience of certain laws imposed by the dominant power – the British Empire. The fundamental idea aimed at rendering the mechanics of government so difficult that the government would throw up its hands and submit to the will of the rebellious mass, as people give in to a nagging wife or crying child.

Subsidiary factors also entered into the workings of nonviolent political rebellion. These included nonpayment of taxes that provided the income used to maintain the government, boycotts of goods made in England, and humiliation of the government before world and home opinion when, as was foreseen, it had to use violence against a supinely non-resisting people.

With the strange appeal of this idea and his own personal influence, M. K. Gandhi, a wizened, 104-pound Hindu lawyer, inspired millions of underfed, illiterate, unarmed people to defy the power of the greatest empire in the world. He was largely instrumental, through their action, in forcing the British Empire to give the great subcontinent of India a measure of self-government. Gandhi imposed his will upon his followers and the government by the grotesque practice of frequently attempting to starve himself to death. The idea worked successfully because the British government did not desire to inflame the rage of the masses by permitting Gandhi to die in a British prison. In likemanner, Gandhi's subleaders refrained from opposing his ideas because they feared being held indirectly responsible for his voluntary death.

Gandhi, who had often been in jail before, was arrested again during his famous "salt march" to the sea, while I was flying to India. He cleverly made the salt tax the spearhead of his attack because it affected every one of India's 350,000,000 people. He claimed this tax was unfair and iniquitous and should be abolished because hundreds of millions of wretchedly poor Indians each required as much salt to live as the prosperous few. Thus the incidence of the tax weighed much more heavily on the poor than on the others. The salt tax was an important source of government revenue, and unauthorized persons were forbidden to make salt from sea water. As a gesture Gandhi therefore led a party in a march to the coast to make salt from sea water in defiance of the law. As Gandhi foresaw, his arrest infuriated his followers, and when I reached Bombay after a two-day boat trip from Karachi the situation had become explosively dangerous.

After witnessing two serious riots at the Wadala salt pans in the suburbs of Bombay, I received on the evening of May 20, 1930, an important tip from a friendly Gandhi sympathizer. He told me they were planning the biggest demonstration yet at Dharasana, about a hundred and fifty miles north of Bombay.

"Sarojini Naidu, the famous Indian poetess, is leading a non-violent demonstration against the big salt pans near Dharasana. The nearest railway station is Dungri. It is an isolated spot and you will have to take your own food and water. You'd better telegraph Mme. Naidu to provide transportation from Dungri, otherwise you will have to walk many miles. Be sure to take an adequate supply of bottled water, because the water from native sources is unhealthy for white men."

I telegraphed Mme. Naidu, asking her to provide transportation.

That was a mistake because the British government authorities learned from my message that I was going, confiscated the message, and took measures to prevent me from reaching Dungri.

I went by night train, carrying a packet of a dozen sandwiches and three bottles of water. Even at night the heat was terrific, and I tossed around in the dusty compartment, unable to sleep. On that railway line the passenger was supposed to provide his own bedding, but I had none nor did I have the native servant which Englishmen carry on journeys.

About four o'clock in the morning the train halted; the station master informed me he had instructions from Bombay to see that I got out there. It was a small town called Bulsar. My protests that I had a ticket for Dungri and that the train was scheduled to stop at Dungri were unavailing; the authorities had decided that the train would skip Dungri that night. In the course of the argument the train pulled out, leaving me at dawn on the deserted platform with only the native station master and his servant.

When he learned that I was an American correspondent bound for the Dharasana demonstration the station master, an English-speaking Parsi dressed in a soiled Palm Beach suit, tried to help me. He spoke English well. Bulsar was a small native town apparently without European inhabitants.

"There is only one motor car in this town," the station master said, "but I'll try to hire it for you. I don't know whether you can reach Dharasana by motor car because you have to go through a river where there is no bridge. If the water is high you may not be able to make it."
He sent his servant for the owner of the motor car. When he arrived, a tall, swarthy Gujar dressed in the Gandhi or Congress costume of a dhoti of undyed homespun cotton, which looked like a loose infant's didy, he indignantly refused to have anything to do with me. He explained to the station master that he was a Swarajist and boycotted foreign cloth or anyone who wore it.

My luck seemed to be out, but the station master learned that a freight train which would stop at Dungri was due soon, and promised to put me aboard if the train crew made no objections. When it arrived he laid the proposition before them; they agreed to take me. I climbed into the tiny caboose at the end of the train. None of the crew spoke English but they were quite amiable, smoked my British cigarettes, and communicated by sign language.

Dungri consisted of a little huddle of native huts on the dusty plain. There were no means of transportation because Mme. Naidu had not received my telegram. I could find nobody who spoke English. By repeatedly pronouncing the word "Dharasana" and pointing questioningly around the horizon, I got directions and set off across country on foot through cactus hedges, millet fields, and inch-deep dust, inquiring my way by signs.

After plodding about six miles across country lugging a pack of sandwiches and two quart bottles of water under a sun which was already blazing hot, inquiring from every native I met, I reached the assembling place of the Gandhi followers. Several long, open, thatched sheds were surrounded by high cactus thickets. The sheds were literally swarming and buzzed like a beehive with some 2,500 Congress or Gandhi men dressed in the regulation uniform of rough homespun cotton dhotis and triangular Gandhi caps, somewhat like American overseas soldiers' hats. They chattered excitedly and when I arrived hundreds surrounded me, with evidences of hostility at first. After they learned my identity, I was warmly welcomed by young college-educated, English-speaking men and escorted to Mme. Naidu. The famous Indian poetess, stocky, swarthy, strong-featured, barelegged, dressed in rough, dark homespun robe and sandals, welcomed me. She explained that she was busy martialing her forces for the demonstration against the salt pans and would talk with me more at length later. She was educated in England and spoke English fluently.

Mme. Naidu called for prayer before the march started and the entire assemblage knelt. She exhorted them: "Gandhi's body is in jail but his soul is with you. India's prestige is in your hands. You must not use any violence under any circumstances. You will be beaten but you must not resist; you must not even raise a hand to ward off blows." Wild, shrill cheers terminated her speech.

Slowly and in silence the throng commenced the half-mile march to the salt deposits. A few carried ropes for lassoing the barbed-wire stockade around the salt pans. About a score who were assigned to act as stretcher-bearers wore crude, hand-painted red crosses pinned to their breasts; their stretchers consisted of blankets. Manilal Gandhi, second son of Gandhi, walked among the foremost of the marchers. As the throng drew near the salt pans they commenced chanting the revolutionary slogan, "Inquilab zindabad," intoning the two words over and over.

The salt deposits were surrounded by ditches filled with water and guarded by four hundred native Surat police in khaki shorts and brown turbans. Half a dozen British officials commanded them. The police carried lathis–five-foot clubs tipped with steel. Inside the stockade twenty-five native riflemen were drawn up.

In complete silence the Gandhi men drew up and halted a hundred yards from the stockade. A picked column advanced from the crowd, waded the ditches, and approached the barbed-wire stockade, which the Surat police surrounded, holding their clubs at the ready. Police officials ordered the marchers to disperse under a recently imposed regulation which prohibited gatherings of more than five persons in any one place. The column silently ignored the warning and slowly walked forward. I stayed with the main body about a hundred yards from the stockade.

Suddenly, at a word of command, scores of native police rushed upon the advancing marchers and rained blows on their heads with their steel-shod lathis. Not one of the marchers even raised an arm to fend off the blows. They went down like tenpins. From where I stood I heard the sickening whacks of the clubs on unprotected skulls. The waiting crowd of watchers groaned and sucked in their breaths in sympathetic pain at every blow.

Those struck down fell sprawling, unconscious or writhing in pain with fractured skulls or broken shoulders. In two or three minutes the ground was quilted with bodies. Great patches of blood widened on their white clothes. The survivors without breaking ranks silently and doggedly marched on until struck down. When every one of the first column had been knocked down stretcher-bearers rushed up unmolested by the police and carried off the injured to a thatched but which had been arranged as a temporary hospital.

Then another column formed while the leaders pleaded with them to retain their self-control. They marched slowly toward the police. Although every one knew that within a few minutes he would be beaten down, perhaps killed, I could detect no signs of wavering or fear. They marched steadily with heads up, without the encouragement of music or cheering or any possibility that they might escape serious injury or death. The police rushed out and methodically and mechanically beat down the second column. There was no fight, no struggle; the marchers simply walked forward until struck down. There were no outcries, only groans after they fell. There were not enough stretcher-bearers to carry off the wounded; I saw eighteen injured being carried off simultaneously, while forty-two still lay bleeding on the ground awaiting stretcher-bearers. The blankets used as stretchers were sodden with blood.

At times the spectacle of unresisting men being methodically bashed into a bloody pulp sickened me so much that I had to turn away. The western mind finds it difficult to grasp the idea of nonresistance. I felt an indefinable sense of helpless rage and loathing, almost as much against the men who were submitting unresistingly to being beaten as against the police wielding the clubs, and this despite the fact that when I came to India I sympathized with the Gandhi cause.

Several times the leaders nearly lost control of the waiting crowd. They rushed up and down, frantically pleading with and exhorting the intensely excited men to remember Gandhi's instructions. It seemed that the unarmed throng was on the verge of launching a mass attack upon the police. The British official in charge, Superintendent Robinson of Surat, sensed the imminence of an outbreak and posted his twenty-five riflemen on a little knoll ready to fire. He came to me, inquired my identity, and said: "You'd better move aside out of the line of shooting. We may be forced to open fire into the crowd." While we were talking one of the Gandhiites, a young university student, ran up to Robinson, his face contorted by rage, tore open his cotton smock, exposing his bare breast, and shrieked: "Shoot me, shoot me! Kill me, it's for my country!"

The leaders managed to calm the crowd.

The Gandhi men altered their tactics, marched up in groups of twenty-five and sat on the ground near the salt pans, making no effort to draw nearer. Led by a coffee-colored Parsi sergeant of police named Antia, a hulking, ugly-looking fellow, detachments of police approached one seated group and called upon them to disperse under the nonassemblage ordinance. The Gandhi followers ignored them and refused even to glance up at the lathis brandished threateningly above their heads. Upon a word from Antia the beating recommenced coldly, without anger. Bodies toppled over in threes and fours, bleeding from great gashes on their scalps. Group after group walked forward, sat down, and submitted to being beaten into insensibility without raising an arm to fend off the blows.

Finally the police became enraged by the nonresistance, sharing, I suppose, the helpless rage I had already felt at the demonstrators for not fighting back. They commenced savagely kicking the seated men in the abdomen and testicles. The injured men writhed and squealed in agony, which seemed to inflame the fury of the police, and the crowd again almost broke away from their leaders. The police then began dragging the sitting men by the arms or feet, sometimes for a hundred yards, and throwing them into ditches. One was dragged to the ditch where I stood; the splash of his body doused me with muddy water. Another policeman dragged a Gandhi man to the ditch, threw him in, then belaboured him over the head with his lathi. Hour after hour stretcher-bearers carried back a stream of inert, bleeding bodies.

I went to see Mme. Naidu, who was directing the subleaders in keeping the crowds from charging the police. While we were talking one of the British officials approached her, touched her on the arm, and said: "Sarojini Naidu, you are under arrest." She haughtily shook off his hand and said: "I'll come, but don't touch me." The crowd cheered frantically as she strode with the British officer across the open space to the barbed-wire stockade, where she was interned. Later she was sentenced to prison. Mariilal Gandhi was also arrested.

In the middle of the morning V. J. Patel arrived. He had been leading the Swaraj movement since Gandhi's arrest, and had just resigned as President of the Indian Legislative Assembly in protest against the British. Scores surrounded him, knelt, and kissed his feet.

He was a venerable gentleman of about sixty with white flowing beard and moustache, dressed in the usual undyed, coarse homespun smock. Sitting on the ground under a mango tree, Patel said: "All hope of reconciling India with the British Empire is lost forever. I can understand any government's taking people into custody and punishing them for breaches of the law, but I cannot understand how any government that calls itself civilized could deal as savagely and brutally with nonviolent, unresisting men as the British have this morning."

By eleven the heat reached 116 in the shade and the activities of the Gandhi volunteers subsided. I went back to the temporary hospital to examine the wounded. They lay in rows on the bare ground in the shade of an open, palm-thatched shed. I counted 320 injured, many still insensible with fractured skulls, others writhing in agony from kicks in the testicles and stomach. The Gandhi men had been able to gather only a few native doctors, who were doing the best they could with the inadequate facilities. Scores of the injured had received no treatment for hours and two had died. The demonstration was finished for the day on account of the heat.

I was the only foreign correspondent who had witnessed the amazing scene – a classic example of "Satyagraha" or nonviolent civil disobedience. My problem now was to get the story out to the world. The nearest telegraph facilities were at Bulsar and I realized that although the British claimed they imposed no censorship on messages going abroad I would probably have difficulty in cabling the story. One Gandhi volunteer who possessed a ramshackle automobile promised to take me to Bulsar if we could ford the river. We stopped for food at a squalid native inn in the village of Untadi. Lunch consisted of parched rice, ground nuts, and tea I dared not drink because I saw that the water came from a muddy pond in which half a dozen water buffalo were wallowing. Obviously few white people had visited Untadi because I was greeted with intense curiosity. Hundreds of half-naked, barefooted villagers surrounded the inn and craned through the open door and windows, watching every move I made. We managed to ford the river and reached Bulsar.

From previous experiences I knew that sometimes unexpected messages from the interior of a country addressed abroad slip through the censorship at the cable head. I therefore determined to telegraph several messages from Bulsar to London covering the essentials of the story, and then take the train for Bombay to cable a more complete dispatch, hoping that the Bulsar messages would slip through. I sent five messages of about a hundred words each before catching the train to Bombay. Three of them and about a half of the fourth reached my London office, I learned later. Then the cable office telephoned my office and stated that the Government of India desired that the messages be cancelled; that they had been transmitted "by error." My London office refused to cancel them.

On the train going down to Bombay I wrote in pencil about 2,000 words, typed them out when I arrived at my hotel, and took them to the telegraph office. The Government of India had consistently maintained that it imposed no censorship upon outgoing messages. Of course, there was a drastic censorship on the newspapers in India. Within a few hours after my message was filed I received a rumpled scrap of paper upon which were pencilled the words: "Mr. Miller: The messages you deposited about Dharasana have not been telegraphed." There was no signature; when I inquired from the porter who had brought the note he said it was an Indian youth whom he did not know. I concluded that the note had been sent by some Gandhi sympathizer in the telegraph office, which was manned chiefly by natives.

I went to the telegraph office and demanded to know what time my messages had been transmitted to London. They would tell me nothing and would not admit that the messages had been stopped. I went to the government headquarters of the Bombay Presidency and was passed from official to official without obtaining any satisfaction. Eventually I was sent to a pleasant young Oxford man who held the position, as I recall, of Secretary for Ecclesiastical Affairs.

"Of course, there is no censorship," he said. "Your messages must have gone. The government is not interfering in any way with the messages of foreign correspondents."

"I have means of knowing that my messages about Dharasana have not been sent. I cannot tell you how I know but I am absolutely certain. Unless you or someone in authority releases those messages immediately I'm going to fly to Persia and send them from there. This demonstration at Dharasana is the biggest story that has happened during the Gandhi rebellion. I'm going to get it out to the world in full even if I have to go to Persia and am prevented from coming back. If the newspaper readers of the world learn that the government is censoring or killing messages they won't believe a word of British officials' statements thereafter."

The young Oxford man realized I was in earnest, pressed a button, and spoke a few words in Hindi to his servant, who promptly appeared with my messages on a tray. Not one word of the messages filed at Bombay had been transmitted. The Secretary for Ecclesiastical Affairs now admitted that he had been assigned to act as censor; he said that most messages were not interfered with but that mine concerned such a grave matter that it had been decided to hold them up for the time being.

We quarrelled for an hour over the context of my messages, which he was loath to pass in any form. Several times I reiterated the threat to fly to Persia Finally I bludgeoned him into agreeing to pass the whole story except three points concerning the actions of the police. In order to get the bulk of the story out immediately I reluctantly agreed to the deletions.

"But I'm going to get those points you have deleted to the United Press somehow or other eventually," I said.

"That's all right with me. My only job is concerning telegrams. There is no censorship whatever on air-mail letters abroad. I assure you of that."

The remaining material was air-mailed and it reached London and New York about ten days later, along with the story of my troubles with the censorship. My story of the beatings at Dharasana caused a sensation when it appeared in the 1,350 newspapers served by the United

Press throughout the world, Senator Blaine read the text of my story into the records of the United States Senate. Representatives of the Gandhi movement in the United States printed it as a leaflet and distributed more than a quarter of a million copies.

Throughout my stay in Bombay, whenever one of my messages was delayed or cancelled by the censorship, I received a pencilled scrap of paper from the same mysterious source in the telegraph office, informing me that my message filed at such-and-such a time had not been transmitted. I never learned where these messages came from. They were not all in the same handwriting, but they were always left in my box at the Taj Mahal Hotel. The porter said a different man brought the slip of paper every time.

By accident I discovered a hole in the censorship. Through talking with a British business man I learned that full-rate or deferred-rate messages not addressed to a newspaper or press association did not pass through the hands of the censor. Apparently it was presumed that all news messages were sent at the press rate and addressed to newspapers or press agencies and that all others were personal or commercial messages. After making that important discovery I occasionally transmitted brief important news out of Bombay under the nose of the censorship by telegraphing it at the deferred rate to Ed L. Keen, the European manager of United Press, at his private address in London. It was expensive; it cost six times as much per word as at the press rate; but it was worth the money on important bulletins.

16

THEY THAT
TAKE THE SWORD

Six days after the beatings at Dharasana I heard that mobs had attacked police stations in the Bhendi Bazaar quarter in the central part of Bombay during the night and that a critical situation had arisen. I did not want to go alone into the native quarter; Europeans were being attacked daily even in the European section of the city and I'd made it a rule never to carry a revolver no matter how dangerous conditions were.

Carl J. Ketchum, of the London Daily Express, was willing to accompany me unarmed. Early in the morning we took a taxi with a native driver from the Taj Mahal Hotel and went into the teeming native quarter. The streets were crowded and frequently natives jeered at us or spat contemptuously at our car. About nine o'clock we reached the Sandhurst Road police barracks and found a crowd of several thousand natives surrounding the station. The throng was highly excited and buzzing like a hornet's nest but it opened up to let our car through. At the entrance to the police station we halted a moment to talk with Sergeant A. J. Brown, who had been brought in with injuries to his head. Something in our action suddenly infuriated the crowd; perhaps they thought we were plain-clothes police. In an instant a shower of rocks the size of a fist began bouncing around us and smashing through the windows of the police station. We ran hastily upstairs, dodging the bayonet points of the soldiers who were clattering down to deploy in front of the station. Ketchum and I reached a window on the second floor which had been smashed by stones and from there watched the terrifying rage of the mob. Half a dozen police rushed out and opened fire with revolvers point-blank into the screaming mob. Deputy Inspector Beart standing in the street just below us was hit by a bullet and his white uniform splashed with blood. Big splotches of blood also showed on the white uniforms of several other British sergeants, but they stood and fired methodically into the mass of human beings. With shrieks of rage and yells of agony the mob quickly broke and scattered in all directions. We could see people falling as they ran and the street for a couple of blocks was splattered with blood.

After scattering into side streets the mob made several attempts to approach the police station again but revolver shots drove them back. Some reached the tops of buildings adjoining the police station and hurled down rocks. This situation continued for an hour. Ketchum and I wanted to escape back to the European quarter to cable our stories, for the telephone wires at the police station had been cut. We made three attempts to leave the police station but each time showers of rocks from adjoining buildings drove us back. Finally the Inspector of Police decided we should have to wait until he could spare a detachment of soldiers to escort us through the native quarter. Twelve British police sergeants were more or less badly wounded during the fracas; we learned afterward that about eight natives had been killed and eighty wounded in the firing. Two attempts were made to set fire to the wooden parts of the barracks, once with kerosene and once with tar, but both were quickly extinguished.

The affray at the Bhendi Bazaar differed entirely from Dharasana. It had nothing to do with the Gandhi movement but began with a trifling incident when a Pathan kicked a dog belonging to a British police sergeant, who then tried to catch the Pathan. A crowd quickly gathered and attempted to beat the sergeant, who opened fire to save himself. News of the incident spread and mobs rushed to attack the police station. They were Mohammedans, whereas Gandhi's followers were Hindus, normally enemies of the Mohammedans. The British regarded the incident as serious because it revealed the dangerous state of tension among the Mohammedan population, which had hitherto largely ignored the Gandhi campaign.

About eleven o'clock, after having been besieged two hours, the Inspector of Police considered that things had quieted sufficiently to spare a truckload of troops to take Ketchum and me back into downtown Bombay. About twenty East Lancashire soldiers armed with bayonetted rifles preceded our car in a motor truck. Street cars had resumed operation and the passengers frequently spat at us and the soldiers, but no further attack occurred. Ketchum and I were the only correspondents who witnessed the Bhendi Bazaar rioting. Owing to the severed telephone wires, even Commissioner Healy had not learned of the riot when we went to his office after escaping from the native quarter.

Within a few days I witnessed one of the largest and most exciting mob scenes I encountered anywhere in years of covering riots and civil disturbances. Gandhi's leaders organized a great demonstration of more than 100,000 people as a protest against his arrest. With other correspondents I gained a point of vantage on a balcony in the Victoria Terminus Station. The procession flowed slowly along for miles like a white river, shouting "Gandhi kai jai" and intoning "Inquilab zindabad," the slogans of the movement. Opposite the Victoria Station the police blocked the street with a cordon of about two hundred swarthy, bare-legged native police from the Deccan uniformed in khaki shorts and little yellow caps like pin-cushions and armed with lathis. There were also fifty Bombay police armed with rifles and a score of British police sergeants with revolvers. The procession carried dozens of Nationalist flags and banners attacking England and urging boycotts of British goods.

This was the first time that Bombay police had attempted to halt a peaceable procession. The Gandhi leaders tried to prevent the crowd from advancing upon the police by linking arms but had the utmost difficulty in holding back the milling thousands. Often the situation was extremely dangerous and we thought a bloody clash could not be avoided. But the Gandhi leaders succeeded in inducing the vast procession to sit down in the street facing the police while British sergeants paced up and down in the narrow space between the opposing forces. There were continual roars of shouting and cheering. All street cars in the centre of the city had halted and hundreds of people covered the tops of surrounding buildings.

This tense situation continued for four hours. Time after time petty incidents nearly precipitated a furious charge upon the police, which would have resulted in many hundreds of casualties. One Gandhi man circulated among the demonstrators shouting, "If you are prepared to die, stay; if not, go home," but none left. One youth laboriously climbed the tall statue in front of the Municipal Building to display the Nationalist flag; this caused a great demonstration and a wave of excitement through the masses of white-clad human beings. Tearing open his shirt, one frenzied Gandhiite rushed in front of the police, shouting repeatedly, "Shoot me in the breast." Others exhibited samples of the vile bread given to the Gandhi prisoners in Worli prison. Each of these incidents provoked a flutter of excitement that ran through the multitude like an electric current. Volunteers passed through the seated throng carrying jars, pails, and canvas sacks of water. Sometimes as a gesture they even gave the native police a drink, for Gandhi's followers frequently used these demonstrations to try to win over the native police.

Throughout the afternoon the remarkable spectacle of 100,000 unarmed followers of Gandhi facing less than 300 armed police went on. The entire centre of Bombay, a city of a million and a quarter people, was paralyzed. Gandhi leaders began discussing maintaining the impasse all night and for as many days as necessary to break the will of the British authorities. Additional cordons of khaki-shorted Gandhi volunteers arrived to make certain that their demonstrators did not attack the police. Arrangements were discussed for bringing food so that the multitude could remain indefinitely. One of the strangest characters I saw that afternoon was a holy man wearing a dhoti smeared with sacred cow dung sitting all afternoon absolutely immobile, not moving a muscle so far as I could see, looking straight ahead without a flicker of an eyelash in the midst of the tension and confusion.

About eight o'clock at night the British authorities decided to withdraw the police and permit the procession to proceed into the heart of the European quarter in order to prevent what seemed like inevitable bloodshed. The Gandhi leaders shouted the news through megaphones to the squatting masses. When the police drew aside the procession instantly surged ahead like a tidal wave in a pandemonium of cheers, waving flags and banners. Like a river bursting a dam, the torrent of white-robed humanity raced through the main streets toward the seafront and the Taj Mahal Hotel, yelling in a frenzy of excitement. It took them more than an hour to pass the hotel. This triumph of nonviolence over armed force gave Gandhi's idea of nonresistance its first spectacular victory. The racing, shrieking mob shouted curses and jeers at every European in sight; they were particularly hostile in front of the Taj Mahal Hotel, which was regarded as the citadel of the "sahibs," but the night passed peacefully.

Another demonstration which I witnessed emphasized the high pitch of nationalistic feeling which the Congress, or Gandhi, movement had aroused. It was the funeral of Vithaldas Chandran, a young captain of the Congress Volunteers. When I reached the swarming native quarter, where no white people could be seen, a chattering crowd of natives surrounded my car, shouting and jeering at me. An English-speaking Congress Volunteer extricated me with considerable difficulty. He explained to the crowd who I was and found me a place on the balcony of a native home. Inadvertently I offered my hosts some cigarettes which happened to be British. They indignantly rejected them and proffered American cigarettes. As the only white man in sight I was the object of highly uncomfortable attention and greeted with shouts: "Come down and join the procession." There was not a single policeman in sight, and Congress Volunteers acted as unofficial police.

The volunteers cleared the swarming streets of the lumbering, high-wheeled buffalo carts, wandering goats and cows, and the majestic fawn-colored sacred bulls which wander at will through Bombay. The sacred bulls impede traffic, lie down on the street-car tracks and have to be coaxed to get up. Sometimes they enter shops to eat vegetables or grain. It is sacrilege to strike them. If a European automobile happens to hit one a riot invariably ensues.

The khaki-shorted volunteers linked arms and formed cordons, opening an avenue for the funeral. The procession was headed by Congress officials bearing large white, green, and red Nationalist flags and followed by a vast procession of white-clad people who walked slowly, chanting Hindu prayers for the dead and burning incense sticks. The white smocks of all the marchers were splotched with the scarlet powder of perfumed sandalwood, signifying joy and happiness, which they continually threw over the procession in handfuls and smeared upon their faces. Fifty women in flowing, cherry-colored saris, with small Nationalist flags sewed to their breasts, marched ahead of the rest. Twelve men literally drenched with scarlet powder carried on their shoulders bamboo poles to which Chandran's body was tied. The face of the corpse was uncovered and splashed with scarlet sandalwood powder. The body was half buried under white, green, and red flowers representing the Nationalist colours, and crowds in the streets and balconies showered it with more red flowers. The din and excitement as the body passed was awe-inspiring. The procession took several hours, marching many miles to the grounds where the body was to be cremated.

At Wadala in the suburbs of Bombay about one hundred Congress Volunteers leading a mob of about 40,000 made a mass attack on the salt works, giving rise to a series of sporadic mêlées lasting three hours. In this instance Gandhi's injunctions of nonviolence were ignored. Time after time the mob broke through the police cordons, invaded the salt pans, and carried away hatfuls and sackfuls of salt. The police belaboured the mob with clubs and I counted fifty-six hit at various times. The mob showered the British police with large stones and at one time I estimated about fifty stones were in the air simultaneously. Since the salt-pan area was two and a half miles in length, the police could not cope with the situation when the mob rushed from place to place, tearing down the barbed-wire fence. Mounted Punjabi police charged into the crowd with rearing horses, striking heads with clubs. At least one hundred were injured in the mêlée.

I saw a British sergeant grab a turbaned Sikh just as he was squirming through a barbed-wire fence with a bag of salt. The mob on the other side grabbed the Sikh and a tug of war ensued in which the Sikh's body was lacerated by the barbed wire at every tug. The crowd won, but the sergeant courageously climbed through the fence, smashed his way into the crowd with his club, and re-seized the Sikh, whom he finally arrested with the aid of several native police.

Once I became isolated in the confusion and a yelling group surrounded me twenty deep. They demanded that I take off my sun helmet, wear a Gandhi cap, and shout, "Gandhi kai jai." I was in a tight spot and probably would have been beaten had not a college-educated, English-speaking volunteer seen me. He quieted the crowd by explaining that I was not British, had not been in India long, and would suffer sunstroke without the protection of the sun helmet.

The demonstration at Wadala was regarded as critically significant because the mobs were getting out of hand and disobeying Gandhi's nonviolence orders. In the course of two such demonstrations which I witnessed nearly a thousand arrests were made and several hundred people suffered more or less serious injuries. It was always difficult to get casualty figures because the Congress followers carried off their wounded, for obvious reasons, and did not report them to the authorities.

After the situation quieted in Bombay I decided to cross the country to Calcutta. Experienced travellers warned me that it would be necessary to have a native servant who spoke several of India's 242 languages, so I acquired an ebony-black Madrasi whose name I couldn't pronounce and whom I therefore called George. He spoke a smattering of English, Hindi, Tamil, Gujarati, and Pashto. I agreed to pay him what he asked, which was the equivalent of $3.50 a week, for which he was to board and room himself, while I was to pay his railway fares. British friends told me I was paying him too much; that I could have had him for $2.75.

George was well trained in the traditional way of taking care of British sahibs, but since I was not accustomed to body servants his incessant attentions made me uncomfortable. Whenever I changed my clothes, which was necessary several times a day because they became soaked with perspiration every few hours, George insisted upon helping me put on my pants. When I bathed, George drew the water and tried to scrub my back and dry me with a towel. Even when I reached for a match George would grab it and light my cigarette; if I wanted to write George would hand me the pencil. My evening clothes were laid out punctiliously every evening at the proper time with the studs inserted. He cleaned my shoes, took care of my laundry – knocking down his commission thereon – brought iced tea whenever he thought I should have it, kept my books and papers arranged, and when doing nothing else squatted on a mat just outside the door of my hotel room. Where and when he slept and ate I never knew.

The railway trip to Calcutta, as I recall, took about a day and a half, but the unbelievable midsummer heat made it seem much longer. British friends told me I must have a portable ice box, such as all British travellers in India carry in summer, to put in my compartment, but I could not bring myself to burdening my equipment with it. The servant travels in a tiny compartment adjoining the sahib's. His fare is a mere fraction of the fare the European pays. At each ice station he brings ice to replenish the ice box, which, if you have one, you keep open with the electric fans in the compartment aimed at the ice.

I had not been travelling many hours before I wished I had brought an ice box. Even with the fine screen and the two windows of dark blue and of white glass, which kept the compartment in semi-darkness, the heat was almost unbearable. All the way across the subcontinent I lay naked in my compartment while three electric fans played on my body. About every quarter of an hour I took a shower bath in the little private shower adjoining the compartment and lay down wet. The evaporation from the current of the fans helped a little. At every stop George brought me iced soda water and at mealtimes brought me food. I arrived in Calcutta in a state of exhaustion.

Here some Indian friends put me in touch with leaders of the Bengal Terrorists, a comparatively small but active Hindu secret organization. A young Bengali who spoke perfect English picked me up at the Great Eastern Hotel. He told me that he would prefer not to give his name but would take me to an appointed place where another emissary would take me by a circuitous route to meet one of the leaders of the Terrorists. He explained smilingly that the police wanted the man I was to see and if they found him he would probably be sent to prison for the rest of his life.

We rode in an automobile through interminable streets in the swarming native quarters and after half an hour got out and walked about five minutes to another automobile. More turning and back-tracking until we entered a native compound and went into a low, darkened room. I do not know the name of the Terrorist leader I met; he said he could not tell me and asked me not to describe him physically in my dispatches or in conversation. He outlined what he said was the program which the Terrorists were already attempting to carry out. It was the extreme opposite of Gandhi's nonviolence philosophy. He said:

"Our organization believes that India can never achieve self-rule without using carefully directed violence. Of course, our people, unarmed as they are, cannot hope to fight the British on any sort of equal terms. You know that the British take the most drastic precautions to prevent the importation in any way of any kind of arms or ammunition. It is a serious matter here to be found with a revolver or to be caught bringing any arms into the country. But we are succeeding in getting a few dozen revolvers per month and a little ammunition by buying them from sailors aboard incoming ships; our men among the porters have means of getting the arms ashore.

"Our object is to use carefully chosen men to assassinate British officials whenever possible. You know what has already been done in that way. We believe that if we continue assassinations they will have more effect than Gandhi's whole movement. Also, we are cutting telephone and telegraph wires and damaging the railway lines surreptitiously and systematically at widely separated points. What we want is carefully aimed, unceasing violence applied at the right points, that is, toward British officials, and toward the telephonic, telegraphic, and railway communications by which the British carry on the machinery of government. There are only about 60,000 British troops, and we are 350,000,000. If we fight bitterly enough and long enough we shall win."

Naturally I did not make any attempt to transmit in any way the Terrorist leader's story while I was in India.

17

MEN OF INDIA

From Calcutta, accompanied by the pertinacious George, I went up the great valley of the Ganges, seat of one of the world's oldest civilizations, to Delhi. The scorching sun hurt my eyes even when I wore dark glasses; the dust stirred up by the train was smothering; again I lay most of the trip naked in my dark compartment, drinking quarts of iced soda water. A blinding dust storm kept me in my room at Maiden's Hotel throughout my first day in Delhi.

Much later, after my return to England I received a letter from an unnamable friend in Delhi who had close contacts with the government authorities. He wrote: "You may not believe it, but the British secret service examined your baggage in Maiden's Hotel. I can prove it to you by telling you that among your letters was one from your wife which inclosed some clippings from the Paris Herald." Fortunately I had no notes of my interview with the Bengal Terrorist or any other compromising material.

With the aid of Brij Krishna, son of a wealthy banker who had abandoned business to devote himself to the Congress movement, I visited the Delhi headquarters of the civil disobedience movement, which was typical of the organizations established in the principal cities throughout India. The headquarters were housed in a bare, unfurnished house, former home of a nawab, or Indian nobleman. About two hundred volunteers lived there and were being educated in the principles of Nationalism and Gandhi's nonviolent creed. They devoted themselves to enforcing the boycott on foreign cloth by picketing over a hundred cloth shops. The leader, Pandit S. N. Haksar, formerly a mechanical engineer, had abandoned his career ten years before to preach

Nationalism. In 1920 he had spent a year in prison. He conducted me through the bare rooms, in which forty of the night-shift picketers were sleeping on mats on the floor, naked except for loin cloths. In other rooms volunteers operated crude handmade spinning wheels, making yarn for Swaraj homespun.

"Our volunteers live at an average cost of sixteen cents a day," Haksar said. "Their food consists of parched grain, vegetables, and fried rice. Of course, no meat is eaten because of the religious ban of the Hindus against the killing of animals or eating flesh. We have succeeded in breaking down caste prejudices here to such an extent that the higher and lower castes eat and sleep together and actually use the same utensils and touch their lips to the same drinking vessels.

"In India that is amazing because you know how rigid the caste distinctions are. The upper castes normally would not approach within five yards of an Untouchable and none of the different castes would eat together, especially use the same drinking vessels. The Congress movement is doing all it can toward breaking down these prejudices and distinctions, but it is a stupendous work because they have been ingrained through tens of centuries." He proudly showed me a sleeping man whom he said was an Untouchable surrounded by Brahmans, men of the highest caste.

Through my Indian friends I met a Hindu high in the native government of Delhi. He took me on an automobile ride into the country with two of his friends. As we reached the open country I sensed that, they had not come to show me the scenery and when we reached a place where no one could be seen they stopped the automobile and drew a bottle of whiskey and some paper cups from under the seat. At first I regarded this as a remarkable concession to my Western appetite because I knew that under their religion Hindus could not drink alcoholic liquor. But each of the three Hindus seized a paper cup and drank avidly. "I thought Hindus were not supposed to drink," I said. "We're not," my friend grinned, "but some of us do not observe all the tenets of our religion and customs. That's why we have to come out here where no one can see us drink. Do all Americans observe every rule of their religion?"

I had to admit that they did not. The Hindus soon emptied the bottle of whiskey and on the way back to town sang what I supposed was the Hindu equivalent of "Sweet Adeline." It's the same the whole world over.

With my friend Sri Krishna, an affable, well-educated Hindu newspaper man who owned an automobile, I visited the seven cities of Delhi. Here the ruins of seven successive civilizations which flourished and vanished many centuries before lie strewn around the plain surrounding the present city of Delhi. We went to see the eighth city of Delhi, that vast new imperial city constructed by the British to house the Government of India. It is occupied only half the year; during the terrific summer heat the government moves in a body to the cool mountain tops of the Himalayas at Simla. When we visited it the entire city was empty; it gave me an uncanny feeling to ride around the broad boulevards between huge, impressive buildings, palatial homes and gardens built for the officials, with nobody in sight.

On the way to Simla I halted briefly at Lahore and encountered one of the few humorous phases of the struggle between the British and the Congress movement. Upper-caste Hindu women of Lahore had been picketing the local cloth and liquor shops until an ingenious British official devised a method of driving them away. Since he obviously could not use British police to lay hands on high-caste women, he hired Hindu prostitutes of the lowest caste to picket the same shops for a few rupees a day. When the prostitutes appeared the high-born Hindu ladies fled in indignation; their religion did not permit them to associate with the degraded classes. The British official then withdrew the prostitutes, having achieved his object.

Simla is one of the strangest cities of the thousands I have seen all over the world. It is perched 7,000 feet high on the tops of mountains in the foothills of the Himalayas, surrounded by a vast panorama of snowy peaks.

Only rickshas pushed by coolies or men on horseback can manoeuvre through its steep, unpaved streets. This cool, tranquil "hill station" is the summer capital of the Government of India.

I arrived in Simla late in the evening and after freshening up went to the Cecil Hotel for dinner. The maitre d'hotel refused at first to permit me to enter the dining room because I did not wear evening dress, but finally permitted me to sneak into an obscure corner. The scene might have been the Savoy Hotel in London, men wearing full evening dress or dress uniforms, women in rich, colourful evening gowns. An individual close by interested me greatly. Middle-aged, enormously fat, he wore a tall, peaked sheepskin cap, a black knee-length braided coat with large gold buttons, and tight black trousers. In fact, he was so fat that he could not get within two feet of the table. His paunch was bespattered with soup spilled on its way from the plate to his distant mouth.

I learned this was His Highness All Nawaz Khan, the Mir of Khairpur, ruler of the native state of Khairpur in Sind. He was the leader of the Shiite sect of Mohammedans, comprising about 2,000,000 adherents; his state covered about 6,000 square miles in which he maintrained his own army of 342 men. A minister in waiting with a retinue of forty attended him in Simla. It was rumoured he had forty wives.

Later, from his Minister in Waiting, Malik Habib Ahmed Khan, I obtained a statement of His Highness's attitude toward the political situation and the position of the native princes whose ideas he embodied. This is, in brief, what I was told:

"The interests of the Indian native rulers are identical with those of the British government. The native princes are entirely loyal to the British Crown and they are at present the chief support of the British government. They are satisfied with the present status and want to safeguard their interests if Dominion Status is given to India. They believe if the present status is altered it will injure their interests. His Highness has just issued an appeal to the Shiite sect to refrain from participation in the Swaraj or Gandhi movement. His Highness emphasizes that the Moslem community is in a minority in India and needs a strong, disinterested government like the British to protect it against the tyranny of the Hindu majority."

During my time in India I had learned that this statement fairly accurately represented the attitude of the rulers of the hundreds of native states which, although within the boundaries of India, are not a part of British India. These states range from Hyderabad, as extensive as Italy and with a population of 13,000,000, ruled by the fabulous Nizam of Hyderabad, who is perhaps the wealthiest man in the world and owns a stupendous horde of gold, rubies, and diamonds and fifty-seven wives, down to tiny states like Lawa, with only nineteen square miles and a total revenue of a few thousand rupees per year. The Presidency of Bombay alone contains 151 native states. The rulers of these native states are usually absolute monarchs in every sense of the word, some with their own currency and postal systems and armies, but owing allegiance to the British Crown, which supervises their relations with foreign countries and other native states. The British government has the right, which it occasionally exercises, to intervene in cases of gross mis-government.

Simla seemed an appropriate place to review and try to crystallize the thousands of impressions I had received in conversation with hundreds of Indians of every shade of opinion. It was a baffling problem if you tried to be fair, because the Indian question is undoubtedly the most complex political conundrum in the world. Men have spent a lifetime and learned comparatively little in this immense subcontinent where 242 languages and innumerable dialects are spoken, where religious and racial hatreds are more bitter than anywhere else on the globe, where there are 500,000 towns and villages, where the merest film of the upper classes is educated, where only fourteen per cent of the male population can read and write and 982 of every 1,000 women are illiterate and only five per cent of the 60,000,000 Untouchables have been to school, where hundreds of thousands are married between the ages of ten and fourteen, where if a Mohammedan interferes with a Hindu sacred bull it causes a bloody riot, where in one province – Assam – a hundred different languages were spoken, where thousands of cotton operatives work for the equivalent of twelve cents per day, where hundreds of thousands of families exist upon 10 rupees– about $3.50-a month. . .

Besides the political questions, all sorts of economic factors made the situation complicated and confusing: There was wide-spread dissatisfaction with the incidence of the land tax, which yielded sixteen per cent of the entire governmental revenue and affected seventy-four per cent of the population. By a colossal accounting system every cultivated field in British India was registered and taxed in accordance with an estimate of its fertility and productiveness. Revisions of the estimates occurred periodically but there was intense dissatisfaction with the amount of revision or the absence of revision. A few years' bad crops made the poor farmers' burdens intolerable.

Many Indians bitterly objected to the government's payment of thirty or forty millions of rupees a year in comparatively high pensions to retired Indian Civil Service officials. The comparatively large proportion of revenue spent on the upkeep of the military machine and the comparatively small amount spent on education also caused dissatisfaction. Others objected to the high rate of the rupee in relation to British sterling and the British practice of shipping India's raw materials to England, manufacturing goods there, and shipping the manufactured products back to India. This meant that the Indian consumer paid the freight for two trips across the world in addition to several middlemen's profits. India therefore insisted it should have its own home industries. Tens of thousands of educated Indians graduated annually from the sixteen modern universities in India imbued with Western ideas of culture and standards of living, but they could not find suitable jobs because the British filled the best positions in the army and civil service.

I had talked with such men as Sir Chimanlal Setalvad, one of the liberal leaders; Sir Tej Sapru, leader of the All-India liberals federation; Mohammed Ali Jinnah, leader of the Moslem League, Mohammed All of the Mohammedan Khalifate organization; and Sir Rao Bahadur Patro of Madras – all hitherto staunch supporters of India's connection with the British Empire. Also Congress – or Gandhi – leaders such as Manilal Gandhi; V. J. Patel, former President of the Indian Legislative Assembly; Satish Chandra Das Gupta, president of the Bengal Committee for Civil Disobedience in Calcutta; Jamshed Choksy, Congress leader in Bombay; R. K. Sidhva, Congress leader in Karachi; and many others. The two last named had been arrested since I talked with them.

The Congress, Swaraj, or Gandhi movement – the terms are practically synonymous for general purposes – had resulted in the deaths of hundreds, the injury of perhaps ten thousand, and the imprisonment

of nearly a hundred thousand. No one will ever know the exact figures.
I find from my notes of that time that I attempted in Simla to summarize
in a few words my impressions of the trend. I wrote:

"The consensus of opinion of men of widely varying schools of
political thought is that the British government is confronted with the
most serious situation in India since the Great Mutiny of 1857; that
political agitation is more widespread and has reached a comparatively
greater depth than in the outbreaks of 1920 and 1921; that the present
movement is based upon definite nationalistic and racial aspirations
toward self-government which cannot be suppressed by force indefinitely.
The British government must sooner or later implement its frequent
promises and give India a considerable share of self-government.

"The majority of the leaders with whom I talked are proponents
of peaceful negotiations with the British regarding India's future status.
All agree on one point: that unless India is granted a large measure
of self-government the situation will progressively worsen and enter
a widespread phase of violence. The extremist wing of the Congress
movement will break away from Gandhi's civil disobedience campaign
– they are already impatient – and commence a definite campaign of
violence. Already there are indications of preparations for violence, such
as the discovery of a bomb manufactory at Lahore and the discovery
of an arms depot at Chittagong. Coming up the Ganges I saw notices
at railway stations offering rewards of 5,000 rupees for information
about anyone tampering with rails or switches. Also, the Extremists
distributed circulars charging that the fat of pigs and cows was used in
the manufacture of coloured cloth in England, which was exported to
India. This was calculated to infuriate the Indians, to whom the fat of
pigs and cows is anathema. It was the rumour that such fats were used
on cartridges issued to native troops which precipitated the bloody Great
Mutiny of 1857. Both Hindus and Mohammedans regard contact with
these fats as hideously unclean."

I encountered such a myriad of hatreds, animosities, resentments,
irritations, dissatisfactions, frictions, and cross-currents of self-interest in
India that my head spun. I had come to India idealistically sympathetic

to the Congress or Gandhi cause; I had felt similarly in Ireland, Egypt, Palestine, and wherever a homogeneous people were caught in the toils of imperialism. I liked the Indian people after such contacts as I had with them individually and in the mass; so far as I could see they were kindly, tolerant,–except in their religion and certain of their customs,–likable folk much the same in the fundamentals of human life and relations as the dozens of races I had become acquainted with in other parts of the world. Almost invariably they treated me with courtesy and consideration; I made many warm friends among them and visited homes ranging from palatial establishments with richly tiled floors and cool fountains to squalid huts in which an American would hesitate to keep his cattle.

Although I had necessarily to keep my dispatches absolutely objective and free from bias or partiality, I tried to sort out my own emotions in the matter. Frequently I argued with Indians against their cause: "But granting everything you say about the British is correct, you are not yet ready in India for self-government, are you? The percentage of illiteracy is so high that you could not operate a modern democratic government." Usually the answer would be: "Look at China, look at Brazil, where the percentage of illiteracy is somewhat similar to ours. No one gainsays their right to govern themselves."

"You would have civil war or a series of internal wars owing to the inextricable mixture of antagonistic races and religions, wouldn't you?" "Yes, we should probably have civil wars, but didn't the United States have the greatest civil war in history?" "Don't the British give you better and fairer government than you could give yourselves?" "Yes, probably the British can and do, but we should rather be governed badly by ourselves than well by an alien government."

Finally I reached the personal conclusion that if the British gave India a far larger share of self-government–as they are now preparing to do–the mass of people in the long run would be better off. There would always be the risk that if the British were driven out of India or forced to relax their supervision too much, some other power would enter India in the chaos that would inevitably ensue. Certainly the British, it seemed to me, were better equipped and better disposed to do the job of governing

India and maintaining the peace in that subcontinent than any other power that might conceivably attempt it.

I was still theoretically in sympathy with the Indians, and hoped that their agitation would force more concessions from the British, but I could not hold with the Indians who wanted complete independence. Under the circumstances it didn't seem practical or for the eventual good of ninety-nine per cent of the Indians.

I sent word to Lord Irwin, Viceroy and Governor General of India, that I should like to talk with him; but I hardly expected that he would accede. As the personal representative of the King-Emperor he occupied a delicate and unenviable position. Talking with American correspondents was about the last thing I thought he would do. But within half an hour I received a summons to the Viceregal Lodge.

After I returned to London I learned the probable reason that Lord Irwin saw me so promptly. My messages about the censorship in Bombay had caused some heartburnings in the India Office in London. There had been telegrams to the Viceroy telling him about the adverse effect of a rigid censorship upon world opinion. Thus Lord Irwin already knew something about me.

Four panting barefoot coolies pushed my ricksha up the steep trail to the big stone government building, which was perched on the crest of a mountain overlooking the vast panorama of the Himalayas. At the gateway the squad of smart Gurkhas, those famous little Mongolian-featured fighters, saluted briskly. I was ushered into the lodge by a huge, barefooted, bearded Sikh in a gorgeous scarlet, gold-trimmed uniform. The Viceroy's aid-de-camp offered me cigarettes and a drink.

Lord Irwin, tall, with Lincolnesque face and figure, and wearing gray morning clothes, received me pleasantly and questioned me lengthily about the scenes I had witnessed at Dharasana, Wadala, and Bhendi Bazaar. He gave me a statement, not to be used as emanating from him, concerning the government's attitude toward the forthcoming Round Table Conference, which he defined "as a stage in India's advance toward self-government." He said: "While the government recognizes that the agitation is inspired by real nationalistic aspirations, the methods

are lawless and the government's first duty is to reassert law and order."
Lord Irwin's tolerance impressed me greatly, and I knew that he had the
respect of Gandhi and other Congress leaders.

18

TO THE ROOF OF THE WORLD

From Simla I went up to Peshawar in the northwestern tip of India, within sight of the famous Khyber Pass and the towering Hindu Kush ranges between India and Afghanistan, through which many of the great invasions of history poured down into the fertile plains of India. George and I went by train across the scorching plains from Lahore over the rushing Indus River into the Northwest Frontier Province, where the British have fought wild, fierce tribes since 1839.

In Peshawar my friend Barry Lawther, chief of the intelligence service in the Northwest Frontier, invited me to stay at his bungalow. Lawther had his hands full; the wild Afridis had attacked Peshawar the night before and were expected to renew the assault that night. Nevertheless, he took time out to tell me something about the Afridis.

"These chaps are probably the world's fiercest fighting tribe. Throughout history they have never been completely dominated. Their creed is fighting, killing, and looting. It is the principal occupation of every able-bodied man. Their strongholds are in the narrow, arid, inaccessible valleys high up in the Himalayas. This tribe has about 25,000 fighting men armed with more or less modern rifles. Every year or so they come down into the plains and attack the tribes loyal to the British. Sometimes they even come down and have a go at us in Peshawar. They are fanatically brave fighters and we have great respect for them and they for us. We could, of course, conquer and hold their country, but it would be far too expensive for the results achieved."

This situation had existed for nearly one hundred years, although the Afridis' country lay almost within eyeshot of Peshawar. To the left and right of the Afridis' country the unruly tribes in Swat and Waziristan maintained their strong-holds. This meant a total of about 200,000 tough fighting men who stood ready to commence hostilities whenever they saw the slightest chance of successful incursions into the rich plains below. British officers told me an Afridi valued a modern rifle as worth a one-in-two chance with his life. They often took amazing risks in hand-to-hand fighting to kill a British soldier to get his rifle.

A great stone fort manned by strong forces of British troops dominated the walled native city of Peshawar and its 120,000 inhabitants as well as the cantonment – or European section – with its ten or fifteen thousand residents. Although the cantonment was surrounded by electrified barbed wire and defended by machine guns, armoured cars, and airplanes, about three thousand Afridis armed only with rifles had actually dared launch an attack the night before. A few of the vanguard reached the southern part of the city and burned a few buildings, but the main body was attacked by British Gurkha troops and airplanes and driven back with about a hundred casualties. The Afridis had felled trees and destroyed culverts, cut telephone wires and strung them across the road in an effort to interrupt the pursuit. It had been an astonishingly courageous effort in view of the disproportionate strength of the British.

When I reached Lawther's bungalow in the late afternoon the cantonment was in a state of tension. A large lashkar of Afridis still lurked in the vicinity of Peshawar and expected to attack again that night. Officials and officers held frequent conferences. Toward dinnertime I saw Lawther's servant laying out his evening clothes. "You're not going to dress for dinner?" I asked in surprise. "Yes, we'll dress for dinner. I've invited in several officials you might like to meet. We're having a dinner party," Lawther said quietly. I had often read of the British dressing for dinner in the depths of Africa or come what may but that was the first time I had encountered it. Half a dozen of Lawther's friends arrived dressed in white dinner jackets and I had to wear my heavy London dinner jacket and starched shirt. We had a jolly dinner and drank amounts of whiskey that anywhere else would have put me under the table, but up there it sweated out through the pores so fast that one got little effect. From time to time they held telephonic conferences about the expected attack. "Jolly good fighters, these Afridi blighters," was the consensus of opinion.

Since the attack had not materialized we went to bed about two in the morning. Whenever the Afridis take to the warpath near Peshawar the principal British officials sleep with a guard, for the Afridis have an unpleasant habit of squirming through the barbed wire and assassinating officials in their beds. Lawther and I slept out on his veranda, while just outside the screen a big, bearded Sikh with a rifle paced up and down in the gravel all night – ten paces one way and ten paces back. I slept little, but Lawther snoozed peacefully. While I remained in Peshawar Lawther maintained a guard upon his bed every night. About seven o'clock daily several British airplanes flew out about twenty miles where a lashkar of Afridis had taken refuge in some caves, dropped dozens of bombs, and returned. I plainly heard the explosions of the bombs in Peshawar. I tried to persuade the air-force officers to take me in an airplane, but they refused. "These chaps are hidden in some caves and I don't think we have hit one of them," an officer told me. "But the news of the explosion of bombs travels up into the mountains and we consider the bombing useful for moral reasons."

Naturally I wanted to see the Khyber Pass, which lay so near, but Lawther said it would take a regiment of troops to go out in safety. He took me in his car out toward Jamrud Fort, a huge stone stronghold lying at the foot of Khyber. Even to go that far he took an armed rifleman, a rifle, and a revolver for himself and one for me. "You never can tell when one of these blighters will pop up and kill you. Sometimes individuals work themselves into a berserk rage of fanaticism and go out to kill the first white man they see, glorying in losing their lives while killing an infidel."

On the eighth of June the Shiite sect of Mohammedans in Peshawar held their annual religious festival of the Muharram. This festival always creates a period of tension for the British throughout the Mohammedan areas of India, and that year it did so more than ever. The holiday commemorates the death of Husain, one of the grandsons of Mohammed, and perpetuates the bitterness of the dispute between the Sunnite and Shiite sects over the divinity of the descendants of

Mohammed which began six centuries ago when Husain was killed in battle in Arabia. The Sunnites and Shiites hate one another almost as much as they both hate the Hindus. Almost invariably during the Muharram festival fighting breaks out between the rival sects and it is the duty of the British to intervene to prevent bloodshed.

Orthodox Shiites fast during forty days and eat frugally only after sundown; laughing or demonstration of pleasure is forbidden during this time and for ten days they cannot change their clothing. The fasting and repression put the nerves of the Shiites on edge and render them subject to sudden, unpredictable outbreaks.

Lawther arranged to have me witness the procession of lamentation for Husain. It was ticklish business because even the sight of an infidel on that day risks precipitating an attack in the native city. The British concealed detachments of troops in compounds ready to sally out in the event of fighting between the Shiites and Sunnites. I was taken into one of the compounds, from which we peeked at the procession–the most awe-inspiring demonstration of religious frenzy and ecstasy I had ever witnessed. Men carrying ornate, gaudily coloured religious banners led the procession, followed by groups of bare-headed men naked to the waist chanting dirges for Husain, rhythmically beating their breasts so hard that they boomed like muted drums. Peeping through cracks in the compound gate, we watched groups dance around in a circle, leaping into the air, working themselves into a literal frenzy, and beating their breasts until they were bruised the colour of raw beefsteak. Other groups followed, naked to the waist, whipping themselves across their backs with small chains. Every swish of the chain cut a deep crimson gash across the back. Blood spurted from the wounds in streams; their loin cloths were dripping with it. I saw two dozen men dance around whipping themselves until their backs were gashed with from ten to twenty long cuts. Three or four collapsed on the ground from exhaustion and loss of blood; onlookers carried them away. Reverently silent spectators jammed the narrow streets of the swarming native city and many of the marchers bore on their backs the wounds inflicted during a procession the night before. Dry blood still caked loin cloths. Toward the centre of the procession several fanatics with small knives repeatedly stabbed themselves in the chest; blood spurted after each jab. British officers told me Shiites frequently died from loss of blood or infection in their wounds as a result of the Muharram. Less fanatic marchers wore black shirts and beat their breasts in time without lacerating themselves. In the centre of the procession walked a gaudily caparisoned horse, saddled but without rider, representing Husain's horse after he was stricken down in battle. The procession kept up a weird, monotonous chant, repeating Husain's name occasionally interrupted by curses of Yazid, who cut Husain's head off during the battle six hundred years before. Seven similar processions wound through the crooked, narrow streets during the day, but fortunately no outbreaks occurred. The British had informed leaders of the Shiites that numerous detachments of troops were secreted throughout the city ready to intervene.

To add to the complexity of the situation in the Northwest Frontier Province there was a revolutionary organization called the "Red Shirts" with headquarters at Charsadda, about twenty miles northeast of Peshawar. They used the Bolshevistic emblem of the hammer and sickle and wore red shirts as uniforms. The avowed object of the organization was to fight the British government and attain independence.

Its connection with the Gandhi movement was uncertain as it was a Mohammedan organization. The leaders asserted there was no inspiration from Soviet Russia but the British claimed that two of the leaders had studied Bolshevistic revolutionary methods in Persia, where they fled during the Caliphate agitation in 1919. One of the leaders, Mir Shah, had been arrested by the British. They claimed that the use of red shirts as an emblem arose from the fact Mohammed once wore a red shirt, which justified their use for religious motives. The principal organizer of the "Red Shirts," Abdul Ghaffar Khan, was related by marriage to the famous unruly Haji of Turangzai, a perpetual thorn in the sides of the British on the Frontier. It was the arrest of Ghaffar Khan with about fifty other leaders which precipitated the bloody outbreak in Peshawar in April and caused the Haji of Turangzai and his blood-thirsty tribesmen to march down from their mountain fastnesses into British territory with the mad intention of releasing the prisoners and attacking Peshawar. The "Red Shirts" claimed about 20,000 adherents to their movement among the population of several hundred thousand in the Peshawar region.

Lawther had to make an inspection trip to Charsadda and offered to take me with him. We were accompanied in the automobile by a native bearer armed with a rifle, and Lawther threw two revolvers on the floor of the car within convenient reaching distance. Charsadda was a cluster of five villages lying beside a clear stream, a branch of the Kabul River, in a broad, lush, green valley covered with rice and sugar-cane fields, a veritable oasis in this sun-scorched land. The villages consisted mostly of baked-mud buildings shaded by tall eucalyptus trees. In an effort to stamp out the "Red Shirts" British troops had imposed a blockade upon the town, permitting no going or coming. As a punishment they had confiscated the cattle of the men known to be supporters of the movement.

While drinking tea with Lawther and several British officers in a low mud but under a punkah (a long flap of canvas suspended across the ceiling which a punkah-wallah kept flapping monotonously back and forth by means of a cord attached to his big toe – the Indian version of an electric fan) we heard the boom of artillery only a few miles away. The British were shelling caves in which some of the Haji's men had taken refuge. Airplanes had dropped ultimatums calling upon them to leave British territory. Whenever a British airplane appeared they sallied out of the caves and fired upon the plane.

British officials told me they considered the situation menacing because the Haji of Turangzai was making an effort to obtain the aid of the powerful tribes in the Mohmand country for the declaration of a jehad or holy religious war against the British. Declaration of a jehad would be serious because the fanatical Mohammedan tribes believed they were assured of eternal bliss in the Moslem heaven if they killed an infidel during a jehad. The Haji had sent letters to tribal leaders all along the Frontier proposing a holy war, promising to raise 100,000 fighting men to attack Peshawar. In an effort to stir religious passions the leaders were circulating erroneous reports that under the Sarda Act – or law against child marriages, forbidding marriages under eighteen for boys and fourteen for girls–the government would make medical examinations of girls. This was calculated to infuriate the ignorant tribesmen. Some villages held meetings and hastily married groups of children from ten to twelve years old.

The old Haji had fled to the hills years before after a disagreement with the British authorities over the policy of religious education and ever since had done his utmost to stir hatred against the British. With the Government of India fully occupied by the Gandhi movement, the Haji considered the time ripe to pay off old debts.

In our trip to Charsadda and back we had an opportunity to see some of the effects of the agitation. Usually villagers and peasants manifested respect for Europeans by bowing and saying "Salaam," but during our fifty-mile ride every native we met scowled, turned his back, or silently exhibited hostility.

British officers at Charsadda warned us against taking any road back to Peshawar except the one we had followed coming out; they said we would almost certainly be fired upon otherwise.

On the morning I left Peshawar while waiting on the station platform I heard the reverberating crashes of an airplane bombardment of the Haji's tribesmen about twenty miles from Peshawar. This situation on the Northwest Frontier had practically no connection with the Gandhi movement down on the hot, dusty plains of India; it was another phase of the century-old struggle between the British and the wild tribesmen of the "roof of the world."

19

JERUSALEM THE GOLDEN

From Peshawar I went down to the vast scorching plain to Delhi to catch the Imperial Airways plane back toward Europe. Before they would sell me a ticket I had to produce a certificate of vaccination for smallpox; having lost the previous certificate, I had to submit with ill grace to another vaccination.

We set out at dawn from Delhi on the thousand-mile trip to Karachi across the great Sind Desert. It was midsummer in one of the hottest regions on the globe. On this trip I encountered the most remarkable flying conditions anywhere in the world – and I have flown at least 150,000 miles in twenty countries. Great patches of outcropping rock became heated in the furnacelike sun much faster than the surrounding sand and set up great columns of ascending air like a stupendous chimney. Air flowed down around the edges of the rising currents to fill the vacuum. When our plane struck these vertically rising and descending currents of air, they carried our nine-ton machine hundreds of feet upwards or downwards like thistledown. At times we fell five hundred feet within a few seconds, so fast that I was raised to a standing position by the plane falling away from me. Just outside Jodhpur we dropped a thousand feet in a few seconds.

Crossing the Persian Gulf I had an opportunity for about two minutes to analyze how I felt when I thought I was facing imminent death. About twenty miles off the Persian coast the crankshaft of the centre engine snapped and the motor stopped with the propeller frozen. To carry the load it was necessary to speed up the two wing engines, whereupon the motor on the right wing started to fail. Normally the motors ran at about 1,800 revolutions per minute, but the gauge now showed only 300 or 400. We were settling rapidly toward the water; it was full of sharks; you could see them all the time in the Gulf. I knew that our chances of not capsizing if we landed on the water were small. The mechanic rushed to the window and stared intently at the gauge. He could do nothing. I saw the fear in his face. At Karachi we had picked up another passenger, Singh, a big, turbaned Sikh with silky black beard, the man who got lost in his plane on the desert when we were going to India. Singh had a dog in the cabin with him. Sensing our fright, the animal whined and crawled under a seat.

The ailing motor sputtered for about two minutes as we settled second by second closer to the milky-green water. It was no use trying to turn back to the Persian coast because that was a tumbled mass of arid, uninhabited mountains rising abruptly out of the sea with no possible landing place. After what seemed an interminable time the right motor picked up and carried us into Basra in Iraq, about 120 miles over the Gulf.

During those two minutes I learned what it was to face death. I felt a plainly perceptible crinkling of the scalp – I suppose my hair must have risen – a curious stiff, cold feeling of the spinal column, and a sensation of shaking in the stomach. When we climbed out of the plane at Basra my knees were wobbly. Atwood, the little wiry pilot who had taken over at Karachi, walked up and down beside the plane and relieved himself by cursing fluently. The plane was covered with oil, which shot out when the crank case cracked. We stayed at Basra a day and a half replacing the motor and waiting for a dense dust storm to subside. Then we flew on to Bagdad and Gaza.

Over Transjordania toward evening we ran short of gasoline because of a head wind. As the pilot feared there was not enough to reach Gaza, we descended on the open desert beside one of the emergency tanks buried deep in the sand. After scraping around in the sand in the centre of one of the aerial guide signals we found the brass plate indicating the cache of gasoline, screwed off the plate, and inserted a hand pump, which worked so stiffly that two men became quickly exhausted. The pilot called upon Singh and me to help pump. "It's a matter of minutes," he said. "We cannot land on the rough field at Gaza after sunset. Unless we can get this gasoline pumped within ten minutes we shall have to spend the night here on the desert. It gets dark the moment the sun sets and I should never risk landing at Gaza after sunset." We pumped frantically in relays and when exhausted lay down in the sand while the pilot and the mechanic pumped. The rest of that flight had its thrills since it was still not certain because of unpredictable head winds whether we could reach Gaza before sunset. We were lucky and got there five minutes before official sunset time.

I was met by Jacob Simon, an intelligent young journalist who was our correspondent in Palestine, a descendant of the Sephardic Jews who were driven out of Spain the year Columbus discovered America and dispersed throughout the Mediterranean Basin. He spoke English, Hebrew, Arabic, Spanish, German, and French fluently. Gershon Agronsky, a Jewish-American newspaper man drawn to Palestine by the Zionist cause, accompanied him. We motored over atrocious roads, lost our way several times, and reached Jerusalem about midnight. The Palace Hotel was dark and repeated kicking on the door and shouting failed to bring anyone to open it. Finally I had to sleep on a sofa in Agronsky's house.

Jerusalem, holy city of two of the greatest religious faiths of mankind! Although I was not an adherent of any religious faith I experienced a deep emotion in treading the ground hallowed by so many billions of human beings down through the centuries. All that Jerusalem connoted stirred me profoundly.

Only ten months before Jerusalem and Palestine had added another paragraph to the long history of bloodshed, not yet near its end, in this cockpit of strife. It originated indirectly from the phrase in the famous Balfour Declaration in which Arthur James Balfour promised, shortly after the war, that His Majesty's Government would "view with favour the establishment in Palestine of a National Home for the Jewish people." After obtaining from the League of Nations a mandate to govern Palestine, the British government encouraged Jews from all over the world to settle in a country which the Arabs claimed they had owned for thirteen hundred years. Petty incidents at the Wailing Wall, which Jews venerated as a fragment of their ancient Temple, led to a series of massacres followed by interminable controversy as to how the trouble started. The Arabs rose up, and when the slaughter and looting died down 207 Jews and Arabs were dead and 379 wounded. When I arrived Jerusalem still reverberated with horror.

During the week I spent in Palestine I could do no more than scratch the surface of a bitterly controversial situation. Furthermore, in my role of unbiased, impartial American-press association correspondent it was not for me to form a personal opinion or discuss the rights and wrongs of the Arabic-Jewish imbroglio. It seemed best to obtain statements from the highest possible authorities.

Through my friend Jamaal Husseini, Secretary of the Supreme Moslem Council, with whom I had previously been in correspondence during the 1929 disturbances, I met His Eminence Haj Mohammed Amin el Husseini, the Grand Mufti of Jerusalem and President of the Supreme Moslem Council. He was the foremost religious and temporal leader of the Palestine Arabs. His family, which was descended from Mohammed, had held the office a hundred and fifty years.

The Grand Mufti, a blond, sandy-haired, pleasant-mannered man of under forty, wore a shiny black robe and a tall red fez swathed in white silk. He greeted me smilingly in halting English, which he had just started to learn. He offered me tiny cups of syrupy black coffee and Turkish cigarettes. His office overlooked the site of Solomon's Temple, now occupied by the famed Mosque of Omar, built in 691 A.D., the second most sacred place in Islam, covering a great bare outcropping of rock. Here, according to tradition, Abraham prepared the sacrifice of Isaac, and Mohammed ascended to heaven.

Gravely stroking his short, sandy beard, the Grand Mufti outlined the Arab attitude toward the political and religious situation. Through an interpreter he said: "We affirm that we are merely seeking our just rights and safeguarding our national existence. We demand the fulfilment of the clear promises which the British gave the Arabs in 1915 regarding the independence of Arab territories, including Palestine. Our principal grievances at present are: First, agricultural land is being increasingly acquired by Jews, leaving the Arabs homeless or on restricted land insufficient for them. Second, abnormal Jewish immigration has caused widespread unemployment of Arabs and introduced Bolshevik elements into the Holy Land. Third, the system adopted by the British government gives the Arab no representation. Fourth, heavy taxes are levied to secure the establishment of a Jewish National Home. Fifth, the general lines of policy adopted by the British are deeply affected by Jewish influence and aim gradually to annihilate the Arab people in Palestine. Sixth, Palestine has been Arab for more than thirteen centuries and there is no way of reconciling the divergencies between the Arabs and the Zionists; the latter will have to accept a parliamentary government in which they will be represented according to their numerical proportion. Seventh, the aspiration of the Arabs is to have a national government responsible to a parliament, under a constitution passed by a national assembly. Eighth, Palestine is sacred to all Moslems and particularly to the Arabs. We demand nothing more than the liberty to be independent in our own homeland. The policy of establishing a National Home for the Jews in Palestine will be fruitless because the Arabs and other Moslem countries will cooperate to oppose this policy."

As I left the Grand Mufti's office, a dozen immobile, silent sheiks from Transjordania in colourful Arab robes crowded the anteroom. On the way back to my hotel we passed some of the most hallowed spots of Christendom – the Valley of Jehoshaphat, Absalom's Tomb, the Garden of Gethsemane, the Mount of Olives, and the Via Dolorosa where Christ carried the Cross to Calvary.

From Morris Margulies, Secretary of the Zionist Organization of America, I recently obtained an up-to-date statement of the present Zionist viewpoint: "Ever since their second dispersion from Palestine in the year 70, the Jewish people have made their return to Palestine an integral part of their national aspirations. During the centuries following the destruction of Jerusalem, Jews returned at various periods to their ancient homeland. The majority of these came back to Palestine with the wish to die on its sacred soil. Jewish colonization on a large and practical scale started in the 1880's.

"With the end of the World War, Jewish colonization began in earnest. As persecution and economic misery pressed ever greater burdens upon the Jews in European lands, the flow of Jewish immigration increased year by year until, in 1935, 61,541 Jews entered Palestine. By the end of 1935 the Jewish population of the country was approximately 400,000, having been 12,000 in 1868, 59,000 in 1919, and 163,000 in 1928.

"With the return of this great mass of Jews into Palestine a new economic and cultural life has been created. The Jews returning to the soil have proved their ability at farming. They have rehabilitated the ancient Hebrew language and made it an instrument for daily usage. In recent years, particularly as a result of the large number of German refugees, the Jews have expanded the economic and industrial life of the country so that Palestine today manufactures and produces virtually all the products of a modern country.

"In returning to Palestine, Jews aim at a free life in which economic opportunity and political security are theirs without restriction or reservation. In so far as the official policy of the World Zionist Organization is concerned, its purpose is to establish a homeland in which the Jew is assured of full rights of citizenship and participation in the life of the country commensurate with his gifts and numbers, and this refers not merely to Jews in Palestine, but to Jews outside Palestine to whom the Balfour Declaration was issued.

"The Jews base their claim upon Palestine on three factors: (1) their historic connection with the land; (2) recognition of that historic connection in international law, i.e., in the Balfour Declaration and the Mandate for Palestine issued by the League of Nations; and (3) the claim of the Jewish people upon civilized mankind for redress against the persecution and discrimination which have made life intolerable for great masses of Jews in numerous lands. Jews believe that a progressive modern civilization has an obligation to make a place in their historic homeland for the Jews whom peoples elsewhere reject.

"Responsible Jewish leadership has repeatedly affirmed its desire to co-operate whole-heartedly with the Arabs of Palestine, convinced that out of the joint co-operation of these two peoples there will be assured peace and prosperity for the Holy Land. During the past decade and a half, Arabs have benefited measurably from Jewish immigration. Their rate of wages and their standards of living have been improved as a result of the example set by their Jewish neighbours. Some 275,000 Arabs have entered Palestine since 1922, as against 250,000 Jews who entered during the same period. Arab employment in agriculture and industry, acreage of Arab farms, and the number of Arab industrial plants have increased because of the economic prosperity and the example of initiative introduced by Jewish immigrants.

"It is the contention of Jewish experts that Palestine has room for at least several more millions of people. Arab leaders contend today that additional Jewish immigration will undermine the country's economic structure; but ten years ago, sceptics of Palestine's absorptive capacity would have scoffed at the prediction that Palestine would hold 400,000 Jews today. The Arabs had centuries of time in which to develop Palestine; they neglected the opportunity because they had neither the will nor the initiative. The Jews who live on the land in Palestine today have not dispossessed Arabs. They have merely salvaged great areas of swampy, malarial land and made it habitable. There are still great areas of land in Palestine to be rescued from their desolation of centuries.

"The Jewish people recognize that consideration must be given to the Arab population if Palestine is to have a sound and steady growth, but the Jews are equally determined that no amount of violence and intimidation shall restrain their up-building activities, for Jews feel that Palestine represents the last stand of an oppressed people saving itself from destructive forces."

From Jerusalem I went to Cairo, where the Egyptian government was in the throes of a political crisis. There I had interviews with Ismail Sidky Pasha, the new Premier, and with Nahas Pasha, the leader of the opposition. What they said does not matter now; they were immersed in petty domestic ward-heeling politics and were apparently too close to the trees to see the forest. Or if they did see the forest, they didn't tell me. The forest was the inescapable fact that Egypt unfortunately occupies such a geographical position at the crossroads of the world between East and West that some strong European power will always exercise lordship over it, and so long as the British Empire remains powerful the Egyptians can never hope to attain complete independence. Some intelligent Egyptians told me they realized these facts and would rather have England rule them than any other European power they knew, but that they hoped by riots and disturbances to force the maximum concessions from the British. Nevertheless, they always wanted the British imperial connection for their protection.

I flew across the Mediterranean to Athens and from there took an Italian seaplane to Constantinople, now Istanbul. This flight up the Dardanelles and over the Sea of Marmora to the Golden Horn, where Asia meets Europe, is one of the most beautiful in the world. As soon as I stepped ashore there were evidences of the revolutionary changes Mustapha Kemal (who now calls himself Ataturk) had wrought in the lives of his countrymen. He had just imposed the obligatory use of the Latinized alphabet instead of the Turkish curlicues, and the passport officials struggled twenty minutes over my passport, trying to cope with writing in the new alphabet. They were wearing derby hats instead of the traditional red fezzes, another of Kemal's revolutionary impositions. Somehow a Turk in a derby looked ridiculous, but no more ridiculous than the Persians I saw in stiff visored caps like American railway conductors' hats, for Riza Khan had imitated Kemal and imposed upon all his countrymen a headgear utterly unfitted for a torrid climate like Persia. I could not see Kemal; newspaper friends told me he was away on a binge. Another of his revolutionary actions was to indulge heavily in alcohol, which is traditionally forbidden to Moslems.

From Constantinople I flew to Bucharest as the only passenger in a tiny cabin plane, which took off from the rough, unlighted air field at three A.M. in darkness. The pilot smoked cigarettes constantly, throwing the butts on the floor. This surprised me as smoking was strictly forbidden in that type of airplane. We encountered a severe rainstorm that buffeted us around for an hour, making us lose our course, but the pilot did not dare to fly low to try to pick up a landmark. When we came out of the storm into clear weather we were twenty miles from land, heading out across the Black Sea off Varna, Bulgaria. The pilot grinned joyfully, wheeled the nose of the plane around, and we reached Bucharest safely.

While spending a few days at the beautiful country place of Prince George Bibesco in the wooded Carparthians I happened to mention the incident of the pilot smoking. Bibesco, one of the earliest amateur fliers, who had trained under the Wright brothers in France, strongly urged me to report the incident to the offices of the air line when I returned to Bucharest. I neglected to do so, and a few months later an airplane on the same line mysteriously exploded in mid-air, killing everyone aboard. I often wondered whether it was the same pilot and whether I might have saved seven lives by reporting him for smoking.

From Bucharest I flew to London, where I resumed my regular job as European news manager of the United Press in charge of our bureaus in Europe, Africa, and Western Asia. In the airplane trip to India and back I had flown 16,000 miles, was in the air fifteen days, visited sixteen different countries in Europe, Africa, and Asia, and lost twelve pounds.

But I had gained an idea of the seething currents of unrest in the world of brown people east of Suez, where Woodrow Wilson's ringing phrase, "self-determination of peoples," still reverberated; where a current of nationalism among the brown races under white domination ran like a rip-tide and would give the guardians of empire in Whitehall many anxious moments in the years to come.

20

HOMAGE TO GANDHI

I had left India without seeing the little brown man who had inspired the most remarkable mass political movement in history. Mahatma Gandhi remained in prison throughout my sojourn in India. Despite my efforts to reach him the authorities refused to permit me to see him. I did not meet him until he came to London the following year for the Round Table Conference.

I first encountered him at a tea party at the Dorchester Hotel. He cut a bizarre figure among the smart, morning-coated Englishmen in the de luxe hotel, for he wore his usual dhoti of coarse white homespun cotton that looked like jute sacking. His skinny brown legs were quite bare, but his feet were encased in crude native sandals.

He invited me to sit with him on a silk and gilt sofa, remarking jocularly: "Why didn't you come to see me when you were in India?" "But you were in jail then, and they wouldn't let me see you," I replied. The shrivelled, little brown man grinned toothlessly and blinked through his cheap, steel-rimmed spectacles. "So I was. I spend a good deal of my time in jails." "How much of your life have you spent in jails?" I asked. Gandhi counted thoughtfully on his fingers and pondered awhile. "I don't really know. I've been in jail seven or eight, maybe ten times, but I don't remember how many years. Since about 1907 in South Africa I have spent much time in jail. I don't really mind it much because it gives me a chance to think and write better than when I am out. I am not interrupted so much in jail. They have always treated me well and I shall probably spend a great many more years in jail and may die in jail."

As a former vegetarian, I was interested in Gandhi's lifelong abstinence from meat and his extraordinarily frugal diet and frequent fasts, during which he drinks salted water. He told me he had tasted meat only once in his life.

"When I was a young man I thought much about the reasons for the superior physical strength of the British. I wondered why they were the dominant race in India and in so much of the world. Finally I thought that perhaps it was because they are heavy meat-eaters; I thought perhaps they absorbed some of the strength of the animals they ate. As you know, our religion forbids the eating of meat or the killing of any animal. But I decided to start eating meat to see whether it had any useful effect upon me. I ate it once, then my conscience hurt me so much that I never ate it again. I was afraid my mother would be horrified if she knew I had put the flesh of a dead animal in my mouth. As I grew older I began to doubt that the British are the strongest race."

I asked him about his personal habits and diet.

"I rise at four A.M., pray for twenty minutes, write letters about an hour, take about half an hour's walk, and then breakfast at six o'clock on goat-milk curds, dates, and raisins. Since the civil-disobedience campaign started I card, spin, and sew cotton between six and nine. I made a vow to spin at least two hundred yards of cotton every day. I want to influence our people to spin their own cloth and make themselves independent of importation from England. The largest single item of British importation into India is cotton cloth. At noon I lunch on bread, goat-milk curds, boiled vegetables, raw tomatoes, and almond paste, take a nap, and spend the afternoon in reading, meditation, and receiving visitors. I do not eat at night. Before my bedtime at nine-thirty I write in my diary. Until recently I always slept on the floor, but now I am old [he was then sixty-three] I sleep in an iron bed. Every Monday I have a day of silence; I speak to no person, no matter how urgent the matter may seem."

Gandhi told me that his only possessions in the world were two changes of dhotis, which he said cost the equivalent of about $2.25 each to make, a blanket, a dollar watch, a small hand spinning machine, writing materials, and a few books. When he started the civil-disobedience campaign he gave away his property and took vows of poverty and celibacy; he insisted upon the same oath for members of his ashram, the school in which he trained his disciples and the leaders of his movement. Gandhi took the vows of his disciples so seriously that once he nearly starved himself to death in penitence for the transgressions of one of his female disciples. Before being permitted to join the ashram she had taken the vows of poverty and celibacy, but it came to Gandhi's ears that she was neglecting one of them – and it was not the vow of poverty. He summoned her and she tearfully confessed to twenty-one transgressions. The Mahatma was profoundly shocked and in penitence imposed upon himself a twenty-one-day fast – one day for each transgression. The young Gandhi adherent who told me this tale added: "It's a good thing the Mahatma found out about it when he did, because if she had been in the ashram much longer Gandhi would have starved himself to death." The Mahatma subsequently ejected the girl and all the men involved from the ashram.

Later I had a long talk with Gandhi in the dingy apartment in Knightsbridge where he stayed during the Round Table Conference. He greeted me with the curious characteristic Hindu salutation, holding his hands palm to palm in a gesture of prayer and supplication. Then he led me to a little, smoky coal fireplace and sat down on the floor on a blanket. At first, I sat on a chair talking at the top of his head, but finally squatted on the floor beside him. During the whole conversation Gandhi deftly spun cotton on a homemade spinning machine.

As an admirer of Thoreau, I thought I detected similarities in Gandhi's ideas and Thoreau's philosophy. The first question I put to him was: "Did you ever read an American named Henry D. Thoreau?" His eyes brightened and he chuckled.

"Why, of course I read Thoreau. I read Walden first in Johannesburg in South Africa in 1906 and his ideas influenced me greatly. I adopted some of them and recommended the study of Thoreau to all my friends who were helping me in the cause of Indian independence. Why, I actually took the name of my movement from Thoreau's essay, 'On the Duty of Civil Disobedience,' written about eighty years ago. Until I read that essay I never found a suitable English translation for my Indian word, Satyagraha. You remember that Thoreau invented and practiced the idea of civil disobedience in Concord, Massachusetts, by refusing to pay his poll tax as a protest against the United States government. He went to jail, too. There is no doubt that Thoreau's ideas greatly influenced my movement in India."

I think I was perhaps the first to discover the curious fact that the wizened Hindu mystic adopted from the hermit philosopher of Concord the strange political concept of nonviolent civil disobedience which deeply influenced the teeming millions in India; that the example of the gentle visionary of Walden Pond inspired millions to defy without arms the power of the world's greatest empire; that the ideas of the sensitive man in Concord who detested violence and bloodshed had after eighty-one years resulted in hundreds of deaths, the injury of ten thousand, and imprisonment of perhaps a hundred thousand in India, on the other side of the world.

When Thoreau wrote the essay, "On the Duty of Civil Disobedience," in 1849 he was thinking of negro slavery and the Mexican war of 1848. He was making a one-man rebellion against the American government because he disagreed with its policies on these questions. He conceived the idea of manifesting his rebellion against the national government by refusing to pay his poll tax, and went to jail. This was the genesis of the concept which Gandhi used in his rebellion against the British government for not granting self-government in India. There can be little doubt that the inspiration of Thoreau had much to do with India's attainment of a wide measure of autonomy and self-government from Britain in the Government of India Act of 1935, which Gandhi's civil-disobedience campaign hastened. When I stood beside Thoreau's grave in the mellow sunlight of a May afternoon several years later, I wondered what Thoreau would think if he could know that his ideas and one night in jail in Concord had indirectly influenced the current of history and the lives of 350,000,000 Indians three generations later.

From long reading of Thoreau I am convinced that his philosophical conceptions emanated largely from Indian literature. In Walden he repeatedly mentions the Vedas and other Hindu literature and once says: "I . . . who loved so well the philosophy of India. . . ." It would seem that Gandhi received back from America what was fundamentally the philosophy of India after it had been distilled and crystallized in the mind of Thoreau. This perhaps explains why the Hindu mentality so readily accepted his ideas.

I asked Gandhi to sign his name in my cigarette case – a cigarette case in which at various times Clemenceau, Lloyd George, Pershing, and other world figures had written their names in pencil. Gandhi examined it closely, chuckled, and said: "Why, this is a cigarette case, isn't it? You know what I think about the use of tobacco. I would not want my name covered with tobacco. If you will promise never to put cigarettes in it, I will sign for you."

I promised and have since used it as a card case. Gandhi's signature was the clearest and most legible of any of the notables represented. The most illegible, indecisive handwriting is that of Adolf Hitler, and the most flamboyant that of Dollfuss, the tiny Austrian Chancellor. When he signed it in Vienna shortly before his tragic assassination he laughed boyishly and said, "I'm a little man but I write big."

While the emaciated little brown man talked, he twirled his spinning machine with skinny fingers. Whenever I asked a question which he wished to ponder or evade he managed to break the cotton thread and while splicing it gained time to consider his reply. Of all the notable figures I ever met I found Gandhi the most fascinating and inscrutable. He spoke slowly and deliberately, in excellent English (he was educated for the law in England), with a slight lisp because of his missing teeth. He kept his eyelids lowered constantly, and you saw his mild brown eyes only now and then when he looked up to emphasize a point. At other times he resembled a shrivelled, animated nut-colored mummy, but his eyes were full of intelligence and twinkled with humour. His nearly bald head was shaped like a pointed egg set at an angle on a scrawny neck, the withered brown skin stretched tightly over the bony skull, a wispy moustache drooped over his almost toothless mouth.

"In India we have the oldest continuous civilization in the world," he said, whirling the spinning wheel. "We had a cultured civilization when Europe was inhabited by uncouth tribesmen. We do not want or need European machine civilization. We want to be free to develop according to the genius of our own people. Our people are inherently simple folk and I want to inspire them to go back to their ancient simplicity. Modern mechanical civilization does not suit our people. We don't want its machines, its cloth, its tobacco and alcohol."

Gandhi accepted an invitation to lunch with the Association of American Correspondents in London and to make a speech. He brought Madeline Slade, the daughter of a British admiral, who had joined his movement as a disciple, lived in his ashram, and adopted Hindu customs and the dress of a Hindu woman. In deference to Gandhi's habits Negley Farson, president of the Association, chose a vegetarian luncheon prepared without animal fats. When Gandhi arose to speak he said: "I have nothing new or confidential to tell you. There is really no reason why you gentlemen should not write what I shall say. But I think the exercise of self-restraint now and then is good for newspaper correspondents. I think this should be a day of silence for you. Therefore, please do not write anything about what I am going to say to you." Although we had attended the luncheon with the idea of writing about it, we observed Gandhi's whimsical request.

This grotesque, wizened man is, I believe, despite his present comparative eclipse, destined to find a place in history as one of the great men of the century for his effect upon the course of human events. His people have given him the title of Mahatma, which means "great souled."

21

ASMARA – CITY
WITHOUT WOMEN

Early in August 1935, I received in London, my headquarters as European news manager of United Press, a cablegram from Hugh Baillie, president of United Press, suggesting that I cover the Northern Italian Army in the Italo-Ethiopian War as I was the most experienced war correspondent in our organization.

Since about May, those of us who had spent years following European affairs and the career of Mussolini were convinced that war was inevitable. During May and June we commenced our preparations to cover the forthcoming war; in June Edward Beattie was sent from our Berlin office to Addis Ababa.

But even while I was preparing to start, officials in the British Foreign Office persisted in believing that the Duce was bluffing; that he dared not fly in the face of England, of his obligations to the League of Nations, and of world opinion. They should have known better; they should have known by that time that Mussolini usually said exactly what he meant. But career diplomats can never accustom themselves to that kind of dealing.

My emotions were tangled and conflicting when the question of going to witness another war arose. I was disgusted by the hypocrisy, two-faced maneuvering, and double-dealing of the British, French, and Italian statesmen and by the prospect of watching the aggression of a nation with all the modern resources for slaughter upon an ignorant, backward, comparatively defenseless people.

Yet it promised to be the most important event in the Western World since the World War; an event which could not fail to have vital repercussions upon the course of history; an event which no foreign correspondent with the opportunity to witness it could afford to miss. I remembered that I had permitted my emotions to impel me to miss the Peace Conference, and I had always regretted it since it had left a gap in my education as an international correspondent. I told myself that my duty as an objective reporter compelled me to stifle my personal opinions and to sit in the grand stand, watching and describing the parade, not to join the procession carrying a banner. I knew that a writer who detested war made the best war correspondent because the scenes impinged more vividly upon his senses. I decided to go.

People knew so little about Ethiopia that I found difficulty ascertaining what equipment to take. I bought a khaki uniform, a tropical sun helmet, dark tight-fitting goggles edged with rubber to protect my eyes from dust and sun glare, high boots, a folding cot and blankets, woolen "cholera belts" to protect the abdomen from sudden chills, a complete kit of medical supplies, mosquito netting, a felt-padded water canteen, candles, an electric flashlight, toilet paper, a Flit gun, matches, and enough writing materials to last several months.

Experts on tropical diseases said I must be inoculated against cholera, plague, typhoid, and paratyphoid and take five grains of quinine daily. The shots made me ill for several days and delirious for one night. On August 27 I left London for Rome to get official permission to join the Italian army in Eritrea, a country of which I had never heard until a few months before.

I remained in Rome nearly a month trying to obtain official authorization to proceed to Eritrea. One evening Count di Minerbi, assistant to Minister Grazzi of the Ministry of the Press, informed me that Mussolini would give permission for fourteen foreign correspondents to go to Eritrea with the Northern Italian Army. I urged him insistently to give me my press card at once. He demurred, saying that the correspondents were to go in a body on the Vulcania about two weeks hence and that there was no other way of reaching Eritrea earlier since the airplanes were booked weeks in advance. I knew this was true because our London office had been offering vainly large sums of money to anyone who would release a seat for me aboard an Imperial airliner to Khartoum in the Sudan.

I told Di Minerbi that I wanted to catch a ship the next morning from Naples across the Mediterranean to Egypt. He pointed out that I could not buy a ticket on any passenger ship as the war scare in the Mediterranean had filled them all and that even if I did manage to reach Egypt I should have to take the Vulcania when she passed Suez.

I agreed to take my chances if he would only give me the precious card. He kept on stalling, first on the ground that I had no photograph, though it happened I had one in my pocket, and then on the ground that at that late hour the Ministry of Colonies could not visa a press card. I urged him to telephone the Ministry, and by great good luck one of the officials was still working and agreed to wait until my arrival; where-upon Di Minerbi, bless him, reluctantly filled out my card – Press Card Number 1.

I rushed breathlessly to the Ministry of Colonies for my visa and then to the hotel to fling my equipment into a duffle bag because I had just half an hour to catch the train to Naples. Only a newspaper man can appreciate the joyful thrill of getting such a head start on a story of world-wide importance.

True enough, through a special and personal dispensation from Il Duce my old-time competitor and friend, Floyd Gibbons, was already on his way, but I hoped to catch him. I knew that if I could get an airplane at Alexandria, Egypt, I should arrive in Eritrea many days before any other competitor.

After a few hours' sleep in Naples I went to the docks without a ticket – Di Minerbi was right, no steamship tickets could be had – hoping to get aboard the Italian liner Esperia, which was sailing for Alexandria that morning. If I failed, all of my schemes to reach the Italian army ahead of my colleagues would tumble.

I sent the hotel porter ahead of me up the gangplank with my baggage. When the ticket taker at the foot of the gangplank asked to see my ticket I pretended to misunderstand and argued with him in English. He spoke only Italian and, after haranguing me angrily, finally permitted me to go aboard, apparently under the impression that I was just a stupid foreigner who must have a ticket.

About half an hour before the Esperia sailed the purser found me and demanded my ticket. I explained that I had had no time to buy one but would pay him in British sterling, for I knew the Italians wanted foreign currency badly. The purser protested that the ship was loaded to capacity and that I should have to debark. After a long argument during which I told him I would sleep in a deck chair the two nights of the passage, and kept tendering two ten-pound notes, he agreed to permit me to go. Several hours after we sailed the purser told me he had taken the Third Engineer's bunk for me – a mere pallet in a tiny, hot cubicle.

We arrived in Alexandria late at night and the semi-weekly Imperial Airways plane left at three o'clock the next morning for Khartoum, where I hoped to catch the connecting Italian airplane to Asmara, Eritrea. I hurried to the Airways headquarters. They said it was absolutely impossible to take me; the plane had been booked full for weeks. The agent showed me the manifest proving that the plane was loaded with mail, passengers, and their baggage to the last ounce permitted under British Air Ministry regulations. I insisted desperately, using every argument I could summon, especially that I had personally spent thousands of dollars with Imperial Airways and was justified in asking consideration in this emergency. Had I been dealing with any other nation than the British I should have offered a sizable bribe, but in this instance I knew better.

After an hour of hot argument the agent weakened, said he would see what he could do. He told me to go to bed, promising to awaken me at 2:30 A.M. if he found a way to take me. I left with him the sterling equivalent of $192.50, the fare to Khartoum, and went to bed, but in my anxiety tossed around without sleep.

At two-thirty he aroused me to inform me that by arbitrarily ordering the other passengers to leave behind one piece of baggage each, he had arranged to early me to Khartoum, but that I must agree in case of necessity to leave behind anywhere between Alexandria and Khartoum any part or all of my baggage. The prospect of going into the wilds of Ethiopia without equipment was highly unpleasant, but I agreed gladly.

In the motor bus to Aboukir airdrome the other passengers furiously protested leaving part of their baggage behind; fortunately they didn't know my part in the matter. A trainload of British military airplanes stood on the siding at the airdrome, for Britain was already massing her forces in the Mediterranean as a threat to Italy.

We took off at five A.M., September 25, for the 1,200-mile flight up the Nile into the Sudan. At times we followed the narrow green ribbon of astoundingly fertile earth which borders the Nile, ending abruptly in scorching desert a few miles or even a few hundred yards from the river. At other times we struck across a wild tumble of sun-baked hills, gorges, and canyons – a scene of indescribable desolation baking in temperatures of 110 to 120 with no vegetation and without an animal or human being or evidence of habitation in sight.

From a mile in the air the vital geographical fact came home to me that the Nile was Egypt and Egypt was nothing but the Nile; that the little dark green strip alongside the river provided the sole support of Egypt's millions. From the airplane I saw graphically one of the subsidiary reasons that set Italy and England at each other's throats: the question of the control of Lake Tana, one of the headwaters of the Nile. The nation that controls Lake Tana possesses the means to ruin Egypt and the Sudan by diverting water, for the rise or fall of only a few feet in the Nile means life or death to the swarming Nile valley. Any nation controlling Lake Tana can exert irresistible pressure upon England in its control of Egypt and the Sudan.

This was one, but not the most important reason I had seen seventeen British warships in Alexandria harbor, as well as hundreds of airplanes in the aircraft carriers at Aboukir. Sixteen British fighting planes were maneuvering at Cairo and air bases had been established in Egypt and the Sudan.

Shortly before midnight we landed at Khartoum, the city Kitchener laid out in the design of the British Union Jack. I retained all of my equipment. Even at midnight the heat was 100 degrees, and I slept under an electric fan after chasing grass-hoppers out of my bed. Count Ciano, to whom I had telegraphed in Asmara, had kindly arranged my passage on the Italian airs liner to Eritrea the next morning.

At dawn I took off across the wide, semi-arid uplands of the Sudan on the 700-mile flight to Asmara, the capital of Italian Eritrea, where the Northern Army had massed for the invasion of Ethiopia. At Kassala, on the edge of the eastern arable region of the Sudan, where ibis birds stalked across the air field, we lunched on sandwiches under the wing of the plane.

Just beyond Kassala rose the towering escarpment of the vast plateau upon which lay most of Ethiopia. Its stupendous wall rose abruptly over 6,000 feet from the sweeping, treeless plain, a scenic spectacle unequaled anywhere else in the world. As we climbed to surmount the escarpment I began to experience a splitting headache. Altitude produces much more severe effects on the human body in these regions near the Equator than elsewhere, for the speed of the spinning earth is greater at the Equator, throwing the air away by centrifugal force and making it thinner. My nose and gums bled, something that had not occurred in higher altitudes in the Andes, Rockies, and Himalayas.

Once beyond the edge of the escarpment we flew above barren reddish-gray mountains, which constituted the plateau section of Eritrea, formerly a part of Ethiopia, to Asmara, headquarters of the Northern Italian Army, lying in a bowl of reddish hills 7,700 feet above the sea.

At press headquarters, the Ufficio Stampa, I found Floyd Gibbons, who had arrived the day before. We were the only American or British correspondents on the ground. The little town, of about 3,000 whites and 10,000 natives, had no facilities to house the influx brought by the impending war. The press officials had constructed six corrugated iron cabins with beaverboard partitions to shelter correspondents, but the only furniture in the barren twelve-foot-square rooms consisted of cots. The meager shops in Asmara had been denuded of everything useful; it took me hours to find eight hooks upon which to hang my clothing, a month to find a table, and I never did succeed in buying a chair. I wrote my early dispatches while sitting on my cot with my typewriter on an up-ended suitcase, Circular mosquito netting entirely surrounded me to keep off the swarms of flies.

Asmara, city of "Men without Women," – Hemingway's title fitted it almost perfectly – had jumped from its sleepy, obscure provincialism into headlines throughout the world. It consisted of a feverish, bustling, sun-baked agglomeration like a frontier town in the Gold Rush days. Instead of the usual 3,000 somnolent whites, the white civilian population had jumped to 30,000 and the blacks to 20,000, not including the thousands of white and black troops that thronged the streets on their way to the front or lived in hastily built pine sheds on the sweeping, barren hills outside.

The white town had a pleasant enough outward appearance, with architecture and vegetation reminiscent of the French Riviera. Eucalyptus, tamarisk trees, coco palms, and varieties of cactus grew abundantly, and charming villas were surrounded by flowers and festooned by purple morning-glories and hibiscus. The well-paved streets had electric lights, sidewalks, and yellow flowering trees along the curbs in the residential section. There was a tall, spired, brick Catholic church and the impressive Fascist Club had been converted into press headquarters. The influx of 200,000 men into Eritrea had cleaned out the city's few score shops, and their proprietors could not obtain new stocks because all available transport had been commandeered for military purposes. Most of the stuff left was of Japanese manufacture. Prices, except on government-controlled articles, leaped dizzily, doubling and tripling within a few days after my arrival.

Laborers working at night by the light of kerosene flares hastily threw up new buildings. Columns of heavily laden motor trucks roared through the dusty streets day and night, and grimy dispatch riders on ear-splitting motorcycles filled the town.

The streets bustled with the most exotic assortment of humanity I had seen outside India. Eritrean "big shots," in white, night-gownlike shammas, wide, Stetsonlike hats, and black cloaks strode about in barefooted dignity or rode dwarf mules followed by half a dozen trotting barefooted retainers. Ebony Askaris,the native black soldiers in Italian service, wore baggy khaki pants and puttees but no shoes, and wound wide red and green cummerbunds around their waists. Their heads were topped by tall red fezzes with dangling tassels. Hindus from India wore many-colored turbans; Somali servants were dressed in tight white jodhpurs, with tunics like two shirttails fore and aft, and European vests.

Arabs, Egyptians, Hamites, and pure negroes from the Sudan wore every conceivable kind and color of clothing. The Italian officers had brilliant uniforms. Italian soldiers wore baggy khaki trousers with the seats hanging to their knees, hobnailed boots, and sun helmets. The Italian business men dressed as if they were on the Corso in Rome or the Italian Riviera. Coal-black barefooted native girls with big liquid eyes and fine, shiny white teeth padded through the streets winning glances of admiration. Their regular features were handsome by white standards. They wore their hair in twenty or thirty pencil-sized braids carried straight back from the forehead and liberally greased with stinking mutton fat, which drew a halo of flies.

The social problem created by the presence of 200,000 men without women found the solution arrived at in other campaigns, including that of General Hooker during the Civil War. A house of prostitution with twenty-six inmates was established; incidentally, opposite a church. The regulations provided for its use by enlisted men during the forenoon, price io lire; noncommissioned officers during the afternoon, price 20 lire; and officers during the evening and night, price 30 lire (the lira was worth about nine cents at the time). During the time I was in Eritrea and Ethiopia I saw only half a dozen white women on the streets; the appearance of a white woman on the streets in Asmara was such a rarity that it almost stopped traffic.

Hotel Hamasien, Eritrea's principal hotel, with thirty-two rooms and one bath, housed a spawn of war-profiteers of a dozen nationalities selling anything in any quantity, their only difficulty being delivery. Egyptians sold automobiles and trucks by the hundreds, pot-bellied Greeks marketed canned goods and tobacco, Italians, Japanese,

Germans, and Danes sold oil, gasoline, cigarettes, beer and whiskey, shoes, and everything an army required. They sold them, but ships with the deliveries aboard lay in the congested harbor at Massawa, where the temperature averaged 120 degrees. Sometimes they spent two or three months before being unloaded.

Our corrugated iron cabins stood in the back yard of the Hotel Hamasien. Typical scenes from my window: a rivulet of kitchen refuse crawling with flies; a native servant skinning the bloody carcass of a goat, which he had just killed by cutting its throat; two native women rolling from their shammas a few eggs which they had walked barefooted a dozen miles to sell; two tiny black girls clad in absurdly long cotton skirts playing under a cactus with dolls made of a small and a large stone tied in a cloth; four little black girls dancing to the tune of a boy's clapped hands a strange dance consisting of squatting on the ground and jumping exactly like frogs; four turkey gobblers fighting; goats cropping at tough weeds; a score of Italian workmen working from daylight to dark building an annex.

The native quarter adjoining the European town consisted of a sprawl of squalid, mud-brick houses roofed with corrugated iron, usually without windows and always crawling with flies and vermin. Aside from two or three streets in the market area, the divisions between the houses consisted merely of crooked trails winding up and down the hills. In the rainy season these became the paths of torrents which washed away the soil, leaving spiny outcroppings of rock exposed. There was no sanitary system; refuse of all kinds was thrown into the "street," and the stench would drive a hyena off a slaughterhouse garbage heap. A few clumps of eucalyptus trees constituted the only vegetation in the native quarter, which was continually swept by clouds of foul dust.

Here, within a few hundred yards of the European quarter, with its appurtenances of modern civilization – paving, electricity, piped water supplies, telegraphs and telephones, motor cars, shops, and two movie theatres – some 30,000 natives lived in squalor and filth, without lighting, sanitation, plumbing, or paving, lacking all the municipal improvements associated with western civilization.

In an hour's walk searching for evidences of western civilization I found only corrugated iron roofs and tin gasoline cans, which the natives used for every conceivable purpose. Down by the native market place the Italians had erected hydrants where natives came for water with their gasoline tins on their shoulders. A six-foot-six black Askari sergeant with an ox whip kept about three hundred clamoring blacks in line by lashing those who crowded out of place over the shoulders.

Also, the Italians had erected near the native market what Americans call a public comfort station, a tin structure hiding only the torso, like those on the Paris boulevards. But they forgot to tell the natives – or the natives ignored their instructions – that comfort should be obtained inside. I watched for some time, but never saw a native enter the structure. They used the outside. I wondered whether their actions were a symbolic expression of their attitude toward European civilization.

The market place occupied a flat, dusty, bare space at the edge of the native town. Hundreds of natives squatted bareheaded in the boiling sun shrilly chattering, trying to sell their meager wares: onions, tiny tomatoes no larger than marbles piled in heaps of five, potatoes the size of walnuts, double handfuls of millet, scrawny ears of corn, cheap, gaudy glass neck-laces from Japan, bits of Japanese hardware, little round mirrors and brass anklets for women, sleazy European cloth, and crude sandals made from pieces of automobile tires.

Men and women wore dirty, coarse cotton shammas which had turned to the color of weak coffee; most of them went barefooted, and their tough, scaly feet showed no evidences of washing. Women carried babies on their backs like Indian papooses, babies with eyes literally ringed with flies, so that they seemed to be wearing spectacles. Unbelievably dirty, naked children played in the dust. Loathsome lepers with stumps for fingers hobbled through the throng begging. Fierce Askari warriors threaded through the crowds holding hands. Men friends kissed upon meeting. Grunting camel caravans stalked haughtily through the squatting crowds. An overpowering stench of rancid mutton fat, with which the natives anoint their heads, filled the air. That was the characteristic odor of both Eritrea and Ethiopia, which clings to your clothes for hours.

The flies were simply beyond belief; there were literally billions of them. They crawled into your nostrils, on your lips, and into your ears. The natives were alive with them but seemed not to mind, and did not bother to brush them off; only priests and the higher natives carried goat-hair fly swishers, with which they made lazy passes. Occasionally Italian officers commanding native troops marched past, followed by an Askari carrying their swords. Children bore astonishing burdens on their heads; I saw a child of twelve carrying at least twenty-five pounds of dura or native millet.

I studied the native town of Asmara closely because it seemed to offer a fair laboratory test of whether the Italians could introduce European civilization to the natives in Ethiopia. As Eritrea had formerly been part of Ethiopia, the natives belonged to the same races, spoke the same languages, and observed the same religions and customs as the Ethiopians across the frontier. For more than a generation they had been in close contact with European civilization through the Italians. I thought perhaps their advancement or lack of it would indicate whether they were capable of absorbing this civilization.

After several visits to the native town I concluded that they either absorbed "civilization" extraordinarily slowly or hadn't been sufficiently exposed to it.

On the outskirts of Asmara natives, including Askaris, lived in tuculs, the characteristic Ethiopian circular hut, made of a ring of upright sticks calked with dried mud. They had no windows and were thatched with palm leaves. The interiors were dark, with a few mats on the dirt floor, a few sticks of rude, hand-made furniture, and some cooking utensils. The natives slept either on the floor or on low native beds of cord strung across a wooden frame. Aside from cheap trinkets, hardware, and the inevitable gasoline tin, I found it difficult to discover any object in the huts that might not have been used in the Middle Ages or even in Biblical times.

My house boy, who was about fifty-five years old, had a name that sounded like Takaley Haftamarryem. He came from this environment.

We nicknamed him "Old Creeping Death." His left eye was dead and had turned a dirty-milk color; mortification seemed to have set in on his bare feet, which were like rhinoceros hide; his clawlike hands were caked with dirt; flies covered his head, which was bald as an egg. He wore loose soiled white trousers drawn tight around the ankles like jodhpurs, a dirty white tunic whose shirttail hung out, and sometimes a European vest.

"Old Creeping Death" possessed some of the magic of the East. He could and did disappear into thin air. One moment he was squatting on the tin porch of my shack; the next moment he was nowhere to be found and remained invisible until I had done myself whatever I had wanted of him. Then he appeared salaaming and grinning and showing all his mud-colored teeth.

Next to the flies Takaley was perhaps the most annoying feature of life in the tin cabin. Besides his native Tigrina "Old Creeping Death" spoke only a few words of Italian. Whenever I tried to snatch a nap he would stick his head in the door every few minutes; he burned holes in my mosquito netting with cigarette sparks, stole my floor mat, socks, and shirts, gave the Italian workmen swigs from my pots of tea, and then disappeared just at the moment I needed him.

Whenever he got drunk, which was not infrequently, he sang in a squeaky Tigrina monotone about Major Toselli, whose name was a legend among the natives of northern Ethiopia. With the aid of other house boys I pieced together the history of "Old Creeping Death." The big event in his life was the undeniable fact that he had not accompanied the expedition commanded by Major Toselli; otherwise he would have been completely dead these many years.

When the Italian expedition under Toselli invaded Ethiopia in 1895, Takaley was the young servant of an Italian lieutenant. But when he tried to run away from his thatched hut to accompany his master, his father caught him, beat him, and tied him to a tree, thus saving his life, for Emperor Menelik's troops slaughtered the entire expedition of 1,200 men, including Toselli, at Amba Alagi. Not a man escaped. It was the Custer's last stand of East Africa. Toselli had an opportunity to get away but turned back to die with his men. His name has gone down in the heroic legends of the natives of the region despite the fact that he was a white man and led a foreign invading army. Three native songs commemorate his exploits. When "Old Creeping Death" got a bellyful of tej, the native booze made of fermented honey – the mead mentioned in the Bible – he invariably intoned one of the songs.

We feared "Old Creeping Death" was afflicted with leprosy; Floyd Gibbons solemnly affirmed he found one of his fingers in his bed. We therefore asked the Italian sergeant in command of the cabins to get us another house boy. He shifted Takaley to another cabin occupied by less squeamish correspondents.

22

ZERO HOUR

Judging by the increasingly active troop movements through Asmara, the day was approaching when the invasion of Ethiopia would commence. I wanted to form an idea from the air of the terrain over which they would advance and of the points of concentration. Gibbons and I went out to the air field to seek Mussolini's son-in-law, Count Galeazzo Ciano, commander of "The Desperate Squadron" of fliers, now Foreign Minister of Italy. We found a prepossessing, handsome young man who spoke English, French, and German fluently. He agreed to take us for a flight along the Ethiopian frontier in his tri-motored Caproni bomber.

Ciano buckled us into parachutes and explained the operation of the rip cord in case we had to jump. The bomber was stripped for action with open latticework in the floor for the bomb sights and a machine-gun placement for firing downward. With four of the crew we clung to the gadgets which filled the fuselage while the heavy plane waddled across the rough field. The rarefied atmosphere made the take-off difficult and dangerous. With the three motors thundering we rose to an altitude of 11,000 feet above sea level. Every breath caused pain in the lungs and we panted in an effort to get enough oxygen.

We saw the three principal roads between Asmara and the frontier alive with marching troops and columns of motor trucks which raised clouds of dust. Here and there lay great encampments with thousands of mules tethered in picket lines, artillery parks and tiny whippet tanks, so small that they could run under your outstretched arm.

From nearly a mile above the earth I perceived that the massed Northern Italian Army was ready for invasion. In the remarkably clear atmosphere I could see at least seventy-five miles into the grim wilderness of towering mountain ranges and gorges which confronted the Italians. Canyons thousands of feet deep intersected range after range of dark, shadowy mountains. We flew along the gorge of the Mareb River, which marks the frontier of Ethiopia, and saw the tumble of high mountains surrounding Adowa, the Italians' first objective.

Ciano invited me to sit beside him in the second pilot's seat. I climbed cautiously over the open latticework, where a misstep would have plunged me to the earth a mile below. As the roar of three motors made conversation impossible, Ciano scribbled notes from time to time indicating points of interest. Over the upper gorge of the Mareb, 2,600 feet deep, a storm was forming; Ciano penciled a note: "We'd better start back."

In an hour's time we covered about 150 miles over the great triangle in which some 200,000 men were concentrated, awaiting the word "Avanti" from Il Duce, and we had received a vivid idea of the vast Italian preparations and the terrible country that lay across the Mareb and Belesa. The end of the rainy season was approaching and I knew from what I saw from the air that the moment for the army to spring into action had almost arrived.

That night, September 27, as I typed my story on an up-ended suitcase the natives prepared for their traditional annual fete of the Meskal to celebrate the end of the rainy season. Eritreans dressed in shammas and Askaris wearing picturesque tall red fezzes, khaki shorts, and red-and-green sashes passed my cabin carrying faggots of wood for the ceremonial pyre and shouting barbaric chants that sounded like the synchronized hoots of owls. Throughout the evening the monotonous savage rhythm of tom-toms continued unceasingly hour after hour. From across the frontier in Ethiopia thunder rumbled and lightning flashed.

About nine o'clock that night several thousand Askaris defiled past General Debono's house carrying long burning brands for the ceremonial pyre. Shrieking, chanting, dancing with a curious hop, they leapt into the air to the beat of tom-toms. Filing past at a run, they soon paved the street with burning embers, upon which the Askaris trod obliviously with their leathery bare feet. Many were already drunk on tej and the excitement of throbbing tom-toms. All night the native quarter swarmed with reeling Askaris and native civilians feasting, dancing, and carousing.

Next morning saw the beginning of another phase of the celebration, which was essentially a warlike demonstration under Coptic Christian rites derived from ancient Hebrew rituals. On a big circular field below the native quarter about 10,000 natives had gathered in white shammas, washed clean for the occasion. They surrounded the rim of the field, in the centre of which stood a huge pyre of wood. At one end of the field a temporary grand stand was erected for General Debono, the members of his staff, the two Mussolini boys, Bruno and Vittorio, and various local native notables in white jodhpurs, black long coats, and broad-brimmed gray hats. After long prayers a hundred Coptic priests, clad in gaudy costumes of green, yellow, purple, blue, and cherry silks and satins embroidered in gold and silver, lighted the ceremonial fire. According to the ancient tradition, the direction in which the wind carried the smoke indicated where their enemies lay. The smoke drifted toward the grand stand where General Debono and the Mussolini boys stood. I wrote that and the censor passed it!

Bands of Askari warriors advanced and circled around the fire, dancing and leaping to the throb of tom-toms, firing rifles into the air in salvos, and vaunting their warlike courage. Each detachment danced up to the grand stand before Debono carrying banners inscribed "For Italy– for Death and Glory." One group did the famous lion dance with spears and shields simulating a fight to the death with a lion; others carrying long curved swords executed astonishingly high, graceful leaps. A detachment of Askari veterans of the Libyan wars danced and leaped with the rest; not one of them was less than sixty years old.

According to tradition, only one woman danced with the men – a handsome, stocky black female, the chief of the Asmara native prostitutes, dressed in white silk, with a richly embroidered headdress like a lampshade. Her elaborately dressed hair was thickly greased with tallow.

Throughout the ceremony the 3,000 warriors fired their rifles continually, bending to pick up the empty cartridges, which they valued highly. I estimated that they fired at least 10,000 shots; soon the field was blue with acrid gunpowder smoke, which seemed to increase the excitement of the warriors. One group carried spades, symbolizing the season for planting seeds. Dignified white-bearded priests blew weird blasts from eight-foot wooden trumpets, while a detachment of native cavalry charged across the field with drawn swords.

The priests and warriors drew up in front of the grand stand while General Debono presented diplomas and decorations to a score of native civilians – fine-looking, dignified men dressed something like Haile Selassie in his photographs. One wore a creaking pair of new patent-leather shoes; another tried insistently to kiss General Debono's hand. All carried elaborately carved fly swatters of goat's tail hair. The forest of waving hands as the crowd brushed at millions of flies made a curious spectacle. General Debono stood rigidly for an hour, not once making a pass at a fly.

At the conclusion of the ceremony General Debono made a speech. He praised the loyalty of the native troops to Italy. As he came to his dramatic conclusion, "You must seize Italy's enemies by the throat," he vehemently executed the gesture on himself. Three thousand Askaris fired salvos and shouted their curious Ethiopian ululations.

That night the native quarter throbbed again with the continuous beat of tom-toms while drunken, shouting natives filled the streets. "Old Creeping Death" was still drunk and singing about Major Toselli.

With Count di Bosdari of the press section Floyd Gibbons and I started next morning on a two-day motor trip to the Ethiopian frontier, passing through the area of troop concentration. We loaded the car with tents, cots, blankets, canned food, water, and every other necessity, for at the front the correspondents had to carry all the supplies they would need.

The area south of Asmara swarmed with troops; clusters of camouflaged pup tents, new wooden barracks, concentrations of olive-green field guns, tanks, and all the modern paraphernalia for slaughter dotted the hillsides. Roads were jammed with singing troops, regular army and Black Shirts, singing "With the whiskers of the Negus we will make a little brush to polish off the shoes of Benito Mussolini." This song reminded me strangely of another campaign I had covered nineteen years before. To the tune of "La Cucaracha," Pancho Villa's men sang exactly the same verse except that it ran: "With the whiskers of Carranza we will make a hatband for the sombrero of the valiant Pancho Villa."

We motored through Adi Ugri and Adi Quala, native towns consisting of a few hundred thatched tuculs and one or two Europeanized main streets, as we made our way to the foremost Italian position in front of Adowa. The most advanced post perched on the edge of a plateau rising 2,600 feet sheer above the valley of the Mareb, which formed the frontier. At this point stood a monument commemorating the Italian dead in the disastrous defeat at Adowa thirty-nine years before, a defeat which rankled in the hearts of Italians ever after. On the obelisk were blazoned the words: "Your example is an omen for the new Italy of its imperial destiny."

From a dugout in the lip of the plateau Captain Origoni pointed out the dark circle of peaks surrounding Adowa, including Mt. Semaiata, which reared to nearly 10,000 feet, and the broad green valley of the Mareb half a mile below us. His observation post commanded a marvellous panorama of the dark silhouette of Ethiopian mountains fifty miles ahead. The ford across the river below would be the principal crossing when the invasion commenced; Origoni's field guns niched into the brow of the escarpment were trained across the ford with the ranges plotted.

In preparation for the invasion a telegraph line with sixteen wires was in readiness to extend across the frontier. Huge dumps of grain, gasoline, canned food stuffs, and ammunition had been placed at many points near the frontier.

The Italians had surmounted the obstacles of nature in a region which lacked everything of vital military importance: water, food, shelter, communications, and roads. They had sunk hundreds of wells and I saw long trains of tank trucks and donkeys bearing big canvas water sacks that reached nearly to the ground. Heliographs winked from the mountain tops and signallers conveyed messages to airplanes with red and white strips of cloth spread on the ground. Herds of cattle had been driven toward the frontier to provide meat on the hoof when the advance commenced. At Adi Quala, Gibbons and I saw eight Ethiopians, deserters from Selassie's troops; several were former slaves, with the sores and marks of leg irons still visible.

A few miles from the Belesa River, further eastward, which was there the frontier, we visited an encampment of mounted Askaris and climbed the steep sides of a thumb-shaped rock rising two thousand feet out of the plain to lunch with the commander, Captain Albramonte. His eight-by-eight tent was perched on the half-acre top of the rock, where the entire troop had encamped; they brought their animals up out of the plain every night because of night-flying insects, whose bite would kill a mule or horse within twenty-four hours. Albramonte gave us lunch in his tent: meat from a goat killed only an hour before, spaghetti, potatoes, ash-colored bread, and canned peaches. The heat was 115 degrees in the shade and there were swarms of flies. He proudly exhibited his barbed-wire hyena trap baited with rotting meat, swore at his dog in the Tigrina language, and gave orders to the Askaris in their native languages.

While we ate under the flap of his tent, batting at flies, Captain Albramonte told us about his Askaris, who belonged to the same races and had the same religions and customs as their Ethiopian brothers.

"They are famous for their endurance," he said. "They sometimes march sixty miles a day. They eat little, mostly flinty wheat bread rolled into a round loaf the size of a muskmelon, baked with a hot stone in the middle of the loaf. Occasionally they eat meat; like the Ethiopians they prefer it raw and bloody, cut from the still warm carcass. On campaigns they sometimes carry sun-dried beef. A little millet, salt, and tea is all they want besides bread and meat. Few are under six feet tall, and I have seen some six feet six.

"As you see, they are slender, flat-bellied, and spindleshanked, without an ounce of superfluous flesh. Except on campaigns they carry their women and children with them. They are Coptic Christians or Moslems, though a few are pagans without religion. During their military duties the Copts and Moslems work together without difficulty, but insist upon observing their rites separately. For instance, animals for meat have to be killed by one of their own faith with appropriate ceremonies. They are savage, pitiless fighters but kiss one another on the cheek instead of shaking hands when they meet.

"They have a superstition that anyone who works in iron becomes a hyena at night and eats dead bodies. We have to carry a white horseshoer with each unit because they would never consent to make a horseshoe. Also, they think that anyone who blows on a metal wind-instrument becomes a hyena; we therefore have to use white buglers.

"When they have a feast they cut strips of raw beef into fringes, use them as decorations, and then eat the decorations.

"Their starting basic wage is two lire [about 160] daily, rising to about three lire as length of service increases; also, there are special allowances for war service and other special factors; thus some get as much as six lire daily. Besides, they receive a ration of eight hundred grams of flour daily for themselves, five hundred for the wife, and one hundred for each child, and some tea and salt."

I asked Albramonte about their loyalty to Italy, inasmuch as they were virtually the same peoples as the Ethiopians they were to fight. "They are loyal to those who pay them. In this part of the world there is no developed sense of nationality." By questioning several natives through interpreters at this camp and others I found Albramonte was right. "When I'm with the Italians I eat," always formed the substance of their replies.

For our benefit the captain ordered his troop of Askaris to stage a simulated attack on the plain below. We rode mules down the steep trail to watch it. Before the mock attack the Moslems chanted to inflame their courage. From our roost on the side of the rock we watched the mounted scouts advance, supported by skirmishers and followed by light machine gunners.

Finally about three hundred deployed on a broad front and charged pell-mell through the scrub thorn bush, yelling shrilly and waving curved swords and lances with pennons fluttering. After the charge the Moslems separated from the Copts and set up a monotonous chant of "There is only one God, Allah, and Mohammed is His Prophet."

Albramonte said the Askaris were excellent machine gunners and kept their weapons in fine condition. He ordered them to set up a heavy machine gun which fired five hundred rounds per minute; they had it off the mule, set up, and ready for action in twenty-five seconds. Several of them were veritable walking arsenals, carrying a lance, a revolver, and a sword in addition to a carbine. They covered their red fezzes with khaki sheaths so as not to serve as snipers' targets in the forthcoming campaign. The importance of the hat in this part of the world was emphasized by the ludicrous practice of the native corporals, who wore a European sun helmet perched on top of their tall fez; to the simple mind of the Askari the European sun helmet was a badge of rank. Despite the fact that poisonous snakes abounded, these Askaris slept on the bare ground under little tents about four feet high.

From the Askari encampment we rode across the broad, burning-hot plain of the Asamo, which is infested with jackals, hyenas, and snakes, to a Black Shirt tank encampment perched on the top of a high mountain at Mai Aini. Centurione Baldi, a bull-like, sunburned Black Shirt captain, exhibited the remarkable little whippet tanks, so small they did not quite reach a man's shoulder. They ran thirty miles an hour, carried a driver and a machine gunner, and would go almost anywhere a mule could climb. Later we visited a big military air field, some encampments of regular army and Black Shirt infantry, civilian road-makers' camps, motor-truck repair bases, and division headquarters. We also saw many other phases of a modern mechanized army. When we returned to Asmara, after motoring two days, I was convinced that it was only a matter of days before the commencement of the invasion.

I knew I possessed facts of the greatest world-wide importance regarding the inception of the war. I also realized, of course, that the military censor's chief duty was to prevent the fact of impending military movements from reaching the world and the Ethiopians. My problem was to phrase my dispatch in such a way that it would convey the all-important facts to the world but still pass the military censor.

I struggled an hour over the first few lines of the message, experimenting with various versions, considering whether they sufficiently conveyed the news but still might possibly pass the censor. Eventually I evolved a dispatch which commenced, in the original "cablese" or telegraphic form: "With Italian army on Mareb stop importantest repeat importantest developments imminent my personal impression result two-hundred-fifty mile two-day motortrip with Count Bosdari through concentration area stop area which eye traversed comprised equilateral triangle of which Asmara formed top point with base of triangle about sixty miles wide resting on Mareb River stop importantest dispositions past twenty four hours led me form purely personal judgment stop naturally exact degree imminence military secret naturally no Italian officer soldier gave me information that subject stop but basing judgment experience other campaigns eye should think have big news here or Rome before long news which world been expecting..."

Then I wrote about 2,000 words of description of what I had seen with frequently recurring vague references to the imminence of an event of importance. This dispatch I wrote on the evening of October 1. To my astonishment the censor passed it exactly as written. The congestion of wireless communications from Asmara to Europe was so heavy that the message reached New York for publication on the afternoon of 2 October, only about eighteen hours before the war actually started. Louis F. Keemle and Charles M. McCann, our cable editors in New York, thoroughly grasped and emphasized the significance of what I was trying to tell them.

23

SCOOPING THE WORLD

At five o'clock on the morning of October 2 the thunderous roar of a column of motor trucks awakened me. I rose and went down to Asmara's main street, Viale Benito Mussolini. The procession of motor trucks continued hour after hour, manned by drivers sunburned to the colour of old leather, dusty, begoggled, with their mouths and noses swathed in handkerchiefs to keep them from breathing the clouds of talcumlike dust. On some of the trucks was chalked the inscription, "Rome to Addis Ababa."

During the forenoon General Debono and his headquarters staff moved from Asmara to field headquarters, established on the top of Coatit Mountain about eight miles from the Ethiopian frontier. In my description of the passage of the motortruck columns I tried to convey the fact that General Headquarters moved toward the frontier. The censor deleted my indirect reference to it. However, he passed my mention of the general air of tension and excitement in Asmara and my appended personal message to Stewart Brown, our Rome bureau manager, in which I said, "Presume your arrangements perfected," which I hoped would tip him off that the war was about to start.

In my diary I made the following entry about nine o'clock on the night of October 2: "Church bells start ringing wildly. Searchlights crisscross sky. Darkened streets are filled by throng of excited men. Everyone seems to realize invasion of Ethiopia starts tomorrow. Governor's residence and Fascist Club floodlighted by searchlights. Impromptu band marches up street playing 'Giovinezza,' the Fascist song. Hundreds of men in ferment of emotion follow shouting, singing, chanting Il Duce, Il Duce.' They mass in front of Fascist Club, which is now press headquarters. Call repeatedly for Count Ciano, Mussolini's son-inlaw. Finally get him out, seize him, tumultuously carry him on shoulders.

"In press headquarters we implore Count di Bosdari to tell us what time war will start. About eleven P.M. Bosdari comes into press room, where Gibbons and I and several Italian and French correspondents are hastily writing description of scenes in street. We crowd around him in breathless silence. 'Advance starts at five A.M. You can go to general headquarters at one A.M.,' Bosdari said. We rush to pack duffle bags, folding cots, blankets, nettings, canned eatables, water canteens, typewriters, paper, carbons, field glasses, et cetera."

At one A.M. with Count di Bosdari and Roman Fajans, correspondent of a Warsaw newspaper, I started to General Debono's observation post on the brow on Coatit Mountain, from which we were to witness the start of the invasion of Ethiopia. It was an uncanny experience, motoring in comfort to witness the commencement at a fixed minute of a war started coldly and deliberately, to see a vast war machine grind into action at a word, to watch more than 100,000 men begin at an appointed minute the invasion of the last independent kingdom in Africa; to witness an action which would have unforeseeable repercussions. I tried to analyze my curious sensations; as nearly as I could define them they recalled somewhat the feeling of abhorrent fascination I always felt when witnessing men put to death by legal execution.

Bosdari and I were silently occupied with our own thoughts, but Fajans was excited to the verge of hysteria. He chattered continuously in French. Bosdari and I simulated sleep in an effort to shut him up, but then he talked to the driver. Finally I exploded with all the French curses I could muster and succeeded in silencing him. As we neared the front we passed long lines of motor trucks hurtling without lights along the twisting roads. I think more men were killed in accidents that night than on the first day of war.

About four A.M. we reached the stone barracks which was to be our headquarters and unloaded our gear into a bare room devoid of furniture or light. Raffaele Casertano, chief of the press section, shaved hastily by candlelight. Everyone spoke in subdued tones; some took hasty gulps of cognac. At about four-thirty we took our typewriters and set out for the observation post, a few miles away.

It occupied a flat space of about a quarter of an acre on the side of the mountain 2,600 feet above the Asamo plain. It was very dark; no lights were visible. In the low stone huts telegraph instruments clicked and officers talked on field telephones. A big table outside was covered with maps. We were introduced to several officers and then milled around smoking cigarette after cigarette, awaiting the dawn. I scribbled in my notebook as follows:

"Four-thirty-five A.M. Air quivers with suppressed excitement. Staff officer says down in Asamo plain half a mile below us General Biroli's column of about 40,000 men constituting central of three columns ready for advance. No spark of light shows in valley below although thousands of men on move.

"In the east horizon pales, showing jagged silhouette of mountains toward the Danakil, 'hell hole of creation.' Officers pace up and down, talking in undertones. Faint rose colour in east. Birds begin to sing. Now detect few glimmers light in valley below. We synchronize watches with official time.

"Press officer announces we can send only five twenty-word bulletins each over military wires. Says wires clogged with urgent military messages. Our detailed descriptions must be sent by motorcycle courier sixty miles back to wireless station at Asmara.

"Four-forty-five A.M. Sun suddenly springs up over chocolate-colored rim of mountains. General Debono, tiny, spare, goat-bearded, aged 74 but remarkably alert, drives up. Goes into consultation with staff. Light enough to see maps on table. General Gabba, Chief of Staff, explains disposition of troops–. General Santini's column of 35,000 men lies about thirty miles to our left; General Maravigna's column of about 35,000, thirty miles to our right; General Biroli's column of about 40,000, mostly Askaris, below us in the centre. Says he hears Ethiopian troops mostly withdrawn from vicinity frontier.

"Through glasses we see curtains of dust miles long in plain below.

On mountain terrace few hundred feet below, native shepherd drives out his goats to pasture–unconcerned with and probably ignorant of world-shaking event about to occur. I arrange typewriter on sand-bagged parapet on edge of plateau. Debono and Gabba pace up and down, scan plain through glasses.

"Four-fifty-five A.M. I write first of series of bulletins for release at exactly five A.M.; only six words, 'Italians commenced invasion Ethiopia five A.M.,' addressing identical messages to New York, Rome, Paris, and London marked for transmission by different cable and wireless routes. These six words will set thousands of presses spinning in forty-nine countries, spewing out extras. World will awaken to learn another war started.

"Five o'clock! War is started. Telegraph operator clicks out my messages. Through glasses I watch gray-green figures about eight miles away wade shallow Belesa River, holding rifles high over heads. Simple fact of wading that stream constitutes act which will send reverberations through world. (Later learned they sang 'Giovinezza,' cheered Mussolini; were not fired upon at any of three points where crossed frontier.)

"Had we not kept eyes on watches we should not have known from anything done or said at our observation post at five A.M. that war was officially started. General Debono and General Gabba continued slowly pacing, occasionally examining maps. No drama and no word spoken to signalize momentous act; nothing to mark difference between Ethiopia un-invaded at 4:59 and Ethiopia invaded at 5:01. I expected cheers, some gesture or word to distinguish moment when invasion commenced; there were none.

"Straddling sand-bagged parapet, Gibbons and I hammered out twenty-word bulletins, sometimes chiseling in a few extra words; the wind swirled dust eddies into typewriters and we batted at swarms of flies."

The hasty scrawls entered in my notebook from minute to minute, many now illegible, reveal that I worked under a severe strain.

At 6:03 A.M. the first airplane appeared from the direction of Asmara, apparently a scouting plane. Gabba told me that airplanes would drop proclamations in the Tigrina language announcing that civilians would be unharmed if they did not fire upon or hinder the troops. I wondered about the utility of the gesture because everyone knew that not one Ethiopian in ten thousand could read. Through glasses we saw long, serpent-like columns of dusty men, mules, and motor trucks pouring across the Belesa ford.

At 6:40 A.M. I heard the heavy drone of Caproni bombers far away to the right in the direction of Adowa, but could not pick them up with glasses. A pale rose light now bathed the fantastic saw-toothed peaks around Adowa, about forty miles away. At 8:03 A.M. I heard a series of heavy explosions from the direction of Adowa, like the clanging of huge iron doors; forty minutes later the air shook with concussions of thunderous explosions, this time from the direction of Adigrat. Both these towns lay at least forty miles away behind successive ranges of mountains but we could hear the sound of the air bombs. Within a few minutes nine huge, tri-motored Caproni bombers glistening in the early morning light droned back toward Asmara. Four days passed before I learned that the bombs had been dropped outside the cities–except for several small bombs which accidently fell within the towns–and that only a few casualties resulted.

Scrappy reports over the field telephone announced that the three columns were advancing rapidly and without resistance except on the right where, according to an official announcement, Maravigna's troops thrusting toward Adowa "overcame all resistance," but we were unable to obtain any details of the resistance. By 9:30 the sun was searing; the temperature had risen to 118 in the shade. We were exhausted from strain and lack of sleep.

Suddenly a staff officer announced that the military courier must start for Asmara within fifteen minutes and that our detailed descriptive stories must be ready or await the next courier, late in the afternoon. We pleaded for more time but the officer said the courier carried urgent military messages and must go within fifteen minutes.

Here were Gibbons and I with the biggest newspaper story since the World War–a story of sitting on top of a mountain with a grand-stand seat witnessing the beginning of a war–and we had only fifteen minutes in which to write our story. It was a reporter's nightmare. We straddled the sand bags frantically, slammed down words, trying to pack as much of the picture as possible into a few hundred words. I wrote 62o words; about a column and a half with telegraphic abbreviations expanded. The motorcycle courier roared away.

We had been eyewitnesses of the start of a war; an experience unique, I think, in the history of newspapers. Floyd Gibbons and I were the only representatives of the American press on the spot. Our competitors of a dozen nationalities, still many days away, fretted aboard the Vulcania somewhere in the Mediterranean. But we were too tired for self-congratulation; we crawled into a near-by thatched mud hut, lay on the earthen floor, and fell asleep with exhaustion when the war was less than five hours old; and I became infested with fleas.

That afternoon and night I wrote occasional bulletins on the progress of the advance. By nightfall the three columns had occupied 2,000 square miles of Ethiopian territory; Santini's army had come within five miles of Adigrat and Maravigna's column twelve miles from Adowa. In mid-afternoon planes bombed a concentration of about three hundred Ethiopian soldiers at Mai Barai near Adowa; we heard the dull explosions of the bombs. The field wireless reported the panic caused among the populations of Adowa and Adigrat, most of whom had never seen an airplane or heard an explosion louder than a rifle shot.

Next morning Gibbons and I crossed the arid plain of Asamo in a car, forded the Belesa River, and succeeded in penetrating about ten miles into Ethiopia over a trail hacked out hastily by Italian engineers in twenty-eight hours. Ours was the first automobile that had ever used the trail. We passed herds of thousands of cattle streaming forward from Eritrea to provide meat for the troops. Every few hundred yards bodies of dead mules lay beside the trail, swarming with vultures tearing out their entrails. Working parties with rifles within arm's reach wrenched stones out of the trail to make a passage for motor trucks. The picturesque Askari camel corps carried goatskins full of water to the advance positions; thousands of Black Shirt troops slogged through dust inches deep.

Late that night back at General Headquarters at Coatit I received a telegram from my New York office informing me that I had achieved a world-wide "scoop" on the beginning of the war; that my cablegram announcing the commencement of the invasion of Ethiopia arrived forty-four minutes ahead of the news from any other source; that for forty-four minutes my message was the only news in the world announcing that the war had begun. Hundreds of newspapers in the United States and in forty-two other countries which the United Press served had issued extras before the Italian government in Rome could announce the start of the war.

In the next few days I received twenty-nine cablegrams of congratulation from all over the world. I had achieved what some of my colleagues were kind enough to describe as the greatest newspaper "scoop" since the World War. It was later to win for me honourable mention for the Pulitzer Prize in Journalism.

The "scoop" did not happen by accident. Of course, I am not going to reveal the method used because the same device may be useful in the future. Suffice it to say that it came as the result of my technical knowledge of the operation of the lines of communication to Europe, knowledge absorbed during eighteen years of experience in Europe.

I had far more experience with cable transmission than any of my competitors and had learned much from my chief, Ed L. Keen, now the dean of active American correspondents in Europe. Keen knew more about transmission of news than any other foreign correspondent in Europe; during the World War he had achieved many monumental "scoops" through his knowledge of the workings of the cable systems. He had a theory that it was not enough for the correspondent to gather and write the news; that the correspondent must know his lines of communication thoroughly and be responsible for the delivery of the story to his home office. In following Keen's theory I had studied communications closely for years and had learned a number of simple devices which gave me an advantage and which sometimes enabled me to outstrip competitors in delivering to America news which we all obtained at the same moment.

24

MARCHING AS TO WAR

On the morning of October 5 Count di Bosdari, Gibbons, and I loaded food and equipment and started to Adowa, the principal objective of the first phase of the Italian advance. We crossed Eritrea toward the west to join General Maravigna's column. Near Adi Ugri we passed a column of the "April Twenty-First" Black Shirt division about ten miles long, swinging along toward the Ethiopian frontier with bands playing.

Beyond Adi Quala we spiralled down the precipice like escarpment of the Mareb valley by continuous hair-pin bends, descending 2,600 feet in half an hour. At the ford of the Mareb, on the frontier, hundreds of soldiers frantically were constructing a causeway for motor trucks. Long lines of men tossed stones from hand to hand like an old-fashioned fire-bucket brigade. Transport mules, smelling water, tore away from the columns and rushed to the river to drink. Many lay down to roll in the water with their packs on their backs and had to be unsaddled before the sweating muleteers could get them on their feet. Men ran to fill their canteens with the water made muddy by the animals. Others shucked off their sweat-heavy clothes to bathe for the first time in days.

Beyond the Mareb the trail rose, spanning wave after wave of mountain ranges. Companies of grimy men, naked to the waist, glistening with sweat, hacked at the road with picks and shovels to make it passable for motors. No wheeled vehicle had ever traversed the trail until that morning. Beside the trail lay bodies of mules upon which vultures gorged themselves, fearless of human beings. The dust was appalling; everyone swathed noses and mouths in handkerchiefs or strips torn from blankets. Officers and men had not shaved for days. Twelve miles inside

Ethiopia we hastily lunched on sardines and bread under a thorn bush while a detachment of Askari machine gunners filed past on mules.

Late in the afternoon we reached Mai Barai; it was impossible to proceed beyond on wheels; and it would take days before motor cars or trucks could proceed. At near-by division headquarters the commander refused us mules; he said he needed every ounce of transport for supplies. Bosdari agreed to go ahead to the next headquarters to try to get mules. Gibbons and I set up camp beside the trail; no tent, just cots in the open air. We had little food left, but found sufficient water from the near-by River Mesquem.

Toward evening we saw the first dead and wounded of the war returning from the battle at Passo Gashiorchi, a few miles ahead toward Adowa. An Askari at least six feet five inches tall, the white bandage at his throat showing a startling red splash of blood, limped in supported by a swarthy white Italian infantryman. He had been shot through the throat. Another Askari inert on his face, and dead or dying, was carried in by two white stretcher-bearers. Occasionally we heard scattering shots.

By following the stretcher-bearers we found a field hospital in which there were seventeen wounded, two of them dying with heart-rending groans from bullets through the stomach. On the hillside a detachment dug the grave of Lieutenant Morgantini, who had just lost his life in the same fight–the first white Italian officer to be killed in the war. From the wounded we learned that the Ethiopians had left seventeen dead on the battlefield at Passo Gashiorchi. This was actually the only appreciable resistance the Ethiopians offered in the defence of Adowa.

After dark more wounded men were carried in, and we watched surgeons operating on them in a tent by lantern light, boiling their surgical instruments over brush fires outside the tent. To our relief, because our food was nearly exhausted, the hospital commandant invited us to dinner on ammunition boxes under the stars.

The continuous passage of mule trains during the night made sleep difficult. Although the heat reached 105 in the shade during the day, the moment the sun set it became quite cold even under two blankets as we were at an altitude of about 8,000 feet. The dew was so heavy that my face and the top blanket were as wet as though it had rained.

In the morning two unarmed parties of Ethiopians numbering about twenty-five each arrived in single file to offer submission, bearing white flags and four gourds full of milk and two pullets as peace offerings. They wore grimy shammas that looked like gunny sacks. Italian soldiers laughingly tried to teach them the Fascist salute and to shout "Il Duce," which they did politely but almost unintelligibly. The Ethiopians gaped at the motor cars and artillery tractors, as they had never seen machines before.

Two Ethiopian prisoners believed to be from Ras Siyoum's army arrived under guard and were put to work unloading trucks. Their awkwardness and unfamiliarity with manual labour were somewhat ludicrous. At 9:30 A.M. seventeen Caproni bombers droned overhead in the direction of Aksum. We listened for the sound of bombing but could hear nothing over the noise of passing mule trains.

Bosdari had not returned and we could still obtain no mules. After consultation we made a compact that I would proceed to Adowa on foot while he would return to Asmara to telegraph the material we had already gathered; in exchange for his sending my messages, I agreed to give Gibbons whatever news I obtained in Adowa.

Floyd's heart was affected by the altitude; he felt that he was not physically able to make the arduous march to Adowa over mountain ranges rising to eight and nine thousand feet. He gave me all our remaining food—two boiled eggs and a triangle of cheese about the size of three postage stamps—and his two-quart felt-padded water canteen. Estimates of the distance to Adowa varied between twenty and thirty-five miles. The temperature was 108 in the shade. With my coat and overcoat wrapped into a roll I set out alone for Adowa. I marched all that afternoon over unbelievably rough trails that wound up and down over the successive waves of mountains, and waded rivers seven times that afternoon. The few isolated native huts along the trail were abandoned; often I marched entirely alone, but at intervals detachments of the Gavinana Division overtook me. Although the soldiers carried three or four times as much weight I could not keep up with them.

Toward nightfall I fell in with the Eighty-third Company of the Gavinana and found a corporal who spoke French, and he introduced me to his captain, who strongly advised me to stay with them. "It would be extremely dangerous to go ahead tonight. There is sniping between here and Adowa and you cannot sleep outside alone because of wild animals. In the darkness you might lose the trail."

I decided to march with his company and at dusk we went into camp. They posted sentries on the surrounding hills and quickly erected tiny pup tents, but built no fires and prepared no hot food. I crawled into a little pup tent with my corporal friend and five soldiers and we ate flinty hard-tack and cold corned beef pried out of the can with a bayonet blade. One of my boiled eggs had smashed in my pocket–in those altitudes you cannot hard-boil an egg because water boils at such a low temperature–but I divided my one remaining egg and triangle of cheese with the corporal. Then we scratched away the pebbles on the bare ground, covered ourselves with blankets and coats and lay down to sleep without undressing or removing our boots.

Many of the men were in a state of exhaustion. Their uniforms were soggy with sweat and caked with dust, and sharp rocks had torn through the soles of their shoes. I saw several who had wrapped their feet in strips from their blankets through which dried blood showed. Before we fell asleep we heard the hideous yelping of hyenas and the barking of jackals, common in this region.

At dawn a bugle awakened us, the 180 men crawled out, rapidly struck camp, and set off at six o'clock without food or coffee. By noon I could not keep up with them any longer. The trail was simply a mountain mule track always steeply ascending or descending. At places the defile was too narrow for pack mules to pass through and the men had to unload the packs, lead the mules through the defile, carry the packs, and reload the mules.

I dropped out under a thorn bush while the company pushed on. After three or four short marches alone with no troops in sight I became exhausted. When I tried to resume the march I found that I could not rise to my feet. This frightened me because I feared I should fall asleep and that vultures might pluck out my eyes while I slept. The Italian soldiers had been warned that if they fell out of column in exhaustion or if they were wounded they must lie on their faces with arms encircling their heads because the vultures would pluck the eyes out of living men while they lay asleep or helpless from wounds. My water was getting so low that I drank only a swallow now and then, holding it in my mouth for minutes before swallowing it in driblets. I spent a thoroughly miserable hour under a thorn bush repeatedly attempting to get on my feet.

Eventually a detachment of soldiers appeared. The commanding officer, Lieutenant Vaccari Odoardo, of the 24th Compagnia Trasmissioni, halted them and came over to me. When he learned that I was an American correspondent he was extremely kind. He gave me swigs of cognac and cold coffee but said he had no food. He urged me to accompany his detachment and strapped my pack on his heavily loaded mule.

His presence and the cognac revived me sufficiently so that I was able to get up and march. My feet were so badly blistered that every step was painful. We marched all the rest of the afternoon and reached the outskirts of Adowa just before dusk; the town had been occupied at ten o'clock that morning. Italian troops swarmed like ants in the mountain-rimmed bowl in which Adowa lay.

Headquarters of General Maravigna, commander of the column, were established in the ramshackle Italian consulate a couple of miles outside Adowa. I went to see Maravigna; he was distinctly displeased by my presence; told me gruffly that I could not go into Adowa that night and that they had no food or blankets to spare. He told me that I was the first correspondent of any nationality to reach Adowa. He saw that I was on the verge of collapse from exhaustion and finally said I might sleep in an outhouse which he indicated. I dropped on a pallet on the floor and slept without food and without undressing; I did not dare to remove my boots because I knew I could not get them on again.

Next morning, still without food, I went to General Villa Santa, commander of the Gavinana Division, which had occupied Adowa. He informed me he was just starting to take formal possession of the town; that I could go with him and he would provide a horse.

With Villa Santa and his staff I rode into the town, which I expected to find lying in ruins. To my astonishment I found no evidence of bombing during the three hours I rode about. Villa Santa said that the bombs had been dropped outside the town to frighten the people.

Adowa, one of the principal towns in Ethiopia, consisted of only a few hundred acres of squalid thatched huts in baked-mud compounds, perhaps a dozen buildings with corrugated iron roofs, a Coptic church, and Ras Siyoum's so-called "palace" on one of the two ridges upon which the town perched. There were a few score eucalyptus trees, narrow, crooked streets, and a mud-and-stone wall around part of the town. Most of the four or five thousand inhabitants had fled when the bombing started.

As we clattered up the steep, rocky streets the inhabitants humbly bowed their foreheads to the ground. We rode to the Coptic church, a circular, corrugated, iron-roofed structure within a mud-walled compound. Priests came out dressed in gaudily coloured robes and the peculiar loaflike headdress of the Copts. Advancing to where we sat on our horses, they tendered a gilt cross for us to kiss. General Villa Santa and his staff leaned forward, inclined their lips toward the cross, and saluted. The cross was brought to me twice, but none of us actually kissed it after glimpsing the filthy hands of the priests and the grimy religious symbol. After the simulation of kissing the cross the half-dozen priests gathered on the steps of the church. From his saddle General Villa Santa made a speech, which was translated to the priests. When he told them that their religion would be respected, the group emitted the curious shrill ululation which is the Ethiopian version of a cheer. Villa Santa then received a delegation of merchants led by one who was apparently more important than the rest because he wore patent-leather shoes, the first shoes I had seen in Ethiopia. The general asked them to inform their people that there would be no more bombing; that the inhabitants who fled should return; that Italy would protect their property.

We rode through streets only five feet wide up the dry stony torrent bed which constituted the main street to the "palace" of Ras Siyoum. He was the most important man in northern Ethiopia and had married Haile Selassie's daughter. After his brief resistance at Passo Gashiorchi, Siyoum abandoned his "palace" and withdrew with his army. Although his residence was the most elaborate structure in town, it consisted of only half a dozen low, tin-roofed, whitewashed stone buildings surrounded by a stockade. Italian soldiers dug a grave in the courtyard for a corpse lying under a sheet swarming with flies; this was the body of the only Ethiopian killed in the fighting in Adowa. Five Ethiopians in Siyoum's "palace" had fired upon the advancing Italians and killed one Askari; the ensuing exchange of shots killed one Ethiopian, while the other four escaped.

After General Villa Santa raised the Italian flag, thus taking formal possession of the town, we visited Siyoum's "palace," which swarmed with flies. The floors were covered with straw and carpeted with rough rush mattings, and there were only a few pieces of furniture – three or four rickety chairs, a rude, wooden, canopied throne, and an old brass bed. The walls displayed childishly painted pictures of the Lion of Judah with moustaches and a crown, a coloured chromo of the Crucifixion, and some crude native paintings of African animals. Empty wine bottles were scattered everywhere. Villa Santa said Siyoum looted the Italian consulate of its furniture and wine after the Italian consul departed and before the war began.

Across the cobblestoned courtyard stood an open thatched shed with terraced stone seats covered with bamboo matting. It was the tribunal where Siyoum heard court cases. Torn handwritten documents in the Tigrina language were scattered about the shed; adjoining was Siyoum's prayer house in which a dog abandoned by Siyoum howled. An Italian officer found among Siyoum's documents a gilt-edged parchment in English. Under date of July 8, 1924, it granted "the dignity of an Honorary Knight Commander of the Civil Division of the Order of the British Empire" to Ras Siyoum and bore the autograph of King George and the Prince of Wales. General Villa Santa gave me a few pieces of Siyoum's printed notepaper and envelopes bearing his curious crest with crown. Besides the parchment, these were the only printed papers found in the "palace."

As our party rode back to Villa Santa's headquarters, past the ruins of the old palace of Emperor John, grandfather of Siyoum, we saw parties of Ethiopians streaming back to Adowa in single file carrying white flags; all were barefooted and bareheaded, clad in dirty ash-Colored shammas.

Villa Santa invited me to luncheon, and it was the first food I had eaten for forty-two hours. Owing to excitement and strain, I had not felt much hunger at any time, and even Villa Santa's passable luncheon of soup, fresh beef, spaghetti, and white bread, served in what was once the consulate stable, did not find me ravenous.

Several Italian and French correspondents had arrived. We explained to General Villa Santa the importance of informing the world of the fact that Adowa was not bombed to the ground and swimming in blood. For the Ethiopian government was telling the world that the bombing of Adowa had resulted in 1,700 dead and wounded.

Villa Santa promised to transmit not more than twenty-five words for each of us over the military wire which had been strung on the ground and over thorn bushes as the column advanced. He said there was so much vital military communication that he could not send more. We wrote the messages, but learned two days later that they never reached the outside world.

To enable us to reach Asmara to telegraph our detailed stories, Villa Santa lent each of us a mule and assigned us three riflemen as guards. He had no saddle mules, so we had to ride perched on top of the pack harness—an arrangement of parallel wooden slats attached to an iron frame buckled under the mule's belly. Pack harnesses were definitely not constructed for human transportation.

We set off at four P.M. to get our story of the Italians' capture of Adowa out to the world. With my French and Italian colleagues I rode seven hours continuously, and it proved one of the most painful ordeals I had ever undergone. My feet, on which the blisters had repeatedly broken, were in such a condition that I could not dismount occasionally and walk to relieve the cramps and pain caused by the wooden slats.

Hour after hour our mules clambered up and down the rocky trails. At night it was dangerous because the mules often stumbled (I'll never again believe that myth about the sure-footedness of mules) while overhanging thorn bushes tore at our faces. There were times during that unforgettable night when I thought I could no longer endure the pain in my cramped legs and seriously considered dropping out, although there were no habitations or camps.

About eleven P.M. we reached the point where road gangs had hacked out a trail over which motor trucks could pass. Lieutenant Colonel Riccardi, bless his soul, the commandant of the road gang, rolled out of his blankets, ordered food prepared for us, brought us red wine, and promised us a motor truck to take us as far back as necessary.

At midnight we set out in Riccardi's truck along with several empty gasoline drums. The road was atrocious; the truck threw us about like dice as we dodged the rolling gasoline drums. One drum struck my galvanized iron water canteen and smashed it flat. After an hour we reached a point where we borrowed an automobile. From one A.M. to seven A.M. we jolted over the trail, crossed the Mareb, climbed the escarpment, snatched some coffee at a field hospital at Adi Quala, then rode until mid-afternoon, arriving in Asmara after nearly twenty-four hours of constant travelling.

I reached my corrugated iron cabin in a state close to physical collapse. I had eaten only three times in seventy hours, had not bathed, shaved, or removed my boots or clothes for four days. Gibbons and our native servant pulled off my boots; the socks were worn to bloody rags which stuck to blistered patches the size of dollars, which had broken and bled repeatedly. They soaked my feet in salt water and bound them with antiseptic adhesive tape. The scars still showed six months later. After I gave Gibbons details of what I had seen in Adowa, I sat down to write the first eyewitness story of Adowa, which no other American correspondent reached until seven days later. Then I slept for sixteen hours.

25

THE ROAD OF
1,500 TURNINGS

With John Whitaker, of the New York Herald-Tribune, and W. W. Chaplin, of Universal Service, I started a few days later to Adigrat, the second of the towns captured in the first phase of the advance. It lay in the line of march of General Santini's army on the left wing.

To reach Adigrat we traversed one of the most remarkable mountain roads in the world, close to Adi Caieh in Eritrea. Coney Island never invented a ride with so many thrills per yard. It had 1,500 hairpin bends in thirty-one miles and traversed some of the most impressive mountain scenery in the world – a mixture of the Grand Canyon, the Dakota Bad Lands, and the buttes and mesas of New Mexico. In those thirty-one miles the road clung to the mountainside with sheer drops of from 50 to 2,000 feet into gorges, canyons, and chasms. The mountains had fantastic forms and colouring, ranging from red and brown to mauve and dark green. Double lines of motor trucks threw talcumlike dust into the air until it was like a London pea-soup fog. A quarter-inch layer of dust coated all our faces and clothes and made our nostrils and lips the colour of putty. I wound eight thicknesses of cheesecloth around my nose and mouth, but still tasted the acrid dust. Every day many trucks plunged over the precipices, usually killing everyone aboard. I counted wrecks of seventeen trucks which had dropped hundreds of feet. Often truck drivers fainted from exhaustion after making this "journey of death"; others became hysterical from the strain. Italy has so comparatively few motor cars that not enough experienced drivers could be found. Many of these truck drivers had had no experience before coming to Africa.

Our native Eritrean chauffeur drove a new popular-priced American car. Its power intoxicated him, though he knew little of its mechanics. He tried repeatedly to pass motor trucks on hairpin bends, disregarding our pleas of "più lento" (more slow). We narrowly escaped serious accidents several times. In desperation I leaned over and hit him on the ear, which slowed him down for a few minutes.

Suddenly we reached a scene that sobered him. A motor truck had just plunged over a precipice and dropped 150 feet. The mangled remains of the driver lay in the road. He was a tall, handsome young fellow with horrible gashes on his head and broken arms and legs, and he was dying. An officer excitedly commandeered our car to take him to a hospital. While we were unloading our equipment, an empty car drew up and was taken instead of ours.

At night many of the motor trucks ran without lights as the rough roads jolted their lighting systems out of order. Each of the four times I traversed these thirty-one miles of road I sat tense with fright during the hour and a half or two hours which it usually took to negotiate the 1,500 hairpin bends. Over this road every ounce of supplies for Santini's army had to pass. I had traversed mountain roads in the Rockies, Alps, Andes, and Himalayas, but never any so dangerous as this road. After our first passage I detected in my moustache eleven new gray hairs, some of which I attributed to that ride.

Across the frontier the Ethiopian natives worked tranquilly in their fields of dura and corn, quite oblivious of the invasion. They threshed grain as in Biblical times by driving oxen over the grain and tossing the chaff into the air for the wind to blow away. Groups of Ethiopian children, the youngest stark naked, fearlessly watched Italian workmen labouring on the roads and sometimes performed native dances for them.

When you saw the name "Adigrat," one of Ethiopia's fairly important towns, in big letters on the newspaper war maps you probably imagined it bore some resemblance to a city. Actually it consisted of a squalid huddle of rude, one-story, flat-roofed, mud-plastered stone huts covering about forty acres and housing about 3,000 miserable, bareheaded, barefooted ebony human beings clad in dirty, nightgownlike shammas, their greasy heads crawling with flies and fleas. Half-starved dogs, scrawny chickens, bleating goats, and half-naked, spindle-shanked children filled the narrow, stony streets.

We happened to arrive on the first market day after the Italian occupation. A bare, dusty space at the edge of the village swarmed with about five hundred villagers and country folk shrilly chaffering over eggs, goats, tiny baskets of grain, and squawking chickens suspended head downward on sticks. One merchant's stock consisted of only one egg, which he was still vociferously trying to sell when we left. Most of the menfolk carried rifles, which the Italians had permitted the civilians to retain. Although most of them were from thirty to fifty years old, the natives kept them brightly polished; in fact, the rifle seemed to be the only object the Ethiopians we saw in the north kept clean.

The arrival of our automobile almost disrupted the market. Crowds surrounded us, staring and touching the automobile. A Coptic priest dressed like the others except that he wore a loaf-shaped turban strode around the market carrying a hammered iron Byzantine cross which the villagers knelt to kiss.

We visited the principal building in Adigrat – the circular, thatched, stone-and-mud Coptic church, about a hundred feet in diameter, more like a cow shed than a church. Inside the church ran two narrow concentric corridors floored with straw and corn husks and covered with bird manure. In the inner concentric ring were painted scores of crude religious pictures depicting Biblical scenes in raw, primary colours. The artist had a particular liking for bloody incidents and kept showing heads being hacked off with swords. He represented St. Paul being hanged head downward with a stone tied to his neck. They did not let us enter the centre of the church, as that part was reserved for the priests. The church was alive with fleas. Both John Whitaker and I became infested, and after we emerged 'Whitaker spent half an hour "reading his shirt."

This squalid village lay cupped in a lovely mountain-rimmed valley surrounded by green fields of corn and millet, dotted with herds of humped African cattle, donkeys, and goats. A little stream in which hundreds of naked Italian soldiers were bathing ran through it. General Santini's camp, quartering twenty or thirty thousand men, spread across the valley and smoke rose from hundreds of campfires.

At one end of the village in a two-story, mud-plastered building and compound lounged about a thousand Ethiopian soldiers who had deserted Haile Selassie and come over to the Italians with their chieftain, Ras Haile Selassie Gugsa. They wore ragged khaki tunics and bandoleers. They carried an assortment of Japanese, French, German, Belgian, and Czechoslovak rifles dating back as far as 1870. Few had ammunition that fitted their guns. They were being fed and re-armed by the Italians. We found no evidence that bombs had fallen in Adigrat. As at Adowa, they had been dropped around outside the village. The French Catholic missionary at Adigrat assured us that the total casualties consisted of two natives wounded and five oxen killed.

After lunch with General Santini in his headquarters' tent, word arrived that an Ethiopian who served with the Italians in the Battle of Adowa in 1895 had come through the Italian lines and wished to pay his respects to the general.

Santini took us to witness the scene. The Ethiopian, a white-whiskered man of about sixty, in dirty shamma, hobbled up on a wooden leg made from thorn bush. His right arm and left leg had been amputated. He knelt and kissed Santini's boot. Then he stated through an interpreter: "My name is Adera Chidanu and I live in Hausien. It has taken me four days to walk forty miles from Hausien. I was with the Italian army in 1895. After the defeat at Adowa I was captured with about 1,200 other natives of the Tigré province. As a punishment for fighting for the white man, Emperor Menelik ordered that the right arm and left leg of each of us be cut off. Menelik's men held me and cut off my arm and leg with a sword, then plunged the stumps into boiling mutton fat. They did this to 1,200 men in one day at Adowa. I heard that more than half of the men bled to death. When I heard that the Italians were in Ethiopia I wanted to join them again, so I came here to join your army."

He dropped to the ground again and kissed Santini's boot. Santini then asked the Askari interpreter to explain to Chidanu that he was too old to join the army but that the Italians would see to it that he was taken care of. Later I learned that seven of the men dismembered after the Battle of Adowa in 1895 bled to death in the outhouse of the Italian consulate where I slept in Adowa.

With the permission of General Santini, Whitaker, Chaplin and I next day visited the most advanced front lines beyond Adigrat. Our automobile was the first to penetrate that far. Although the trail had been in use by caravans for centuries, the natives had never seen an automobile. They fled in terror into their thatched mud huts when we entered the hamlet of Edaga Hamus. After a time they emerged cautiously and finally gathered around our car, touching the fenders and tires and chattering shrilly about the strange contraption.

To reach Edaga Hamus, our destination, we ascended to 9,100 feet over twisting, precipitous rocky trails which had never before borne wheeled vehicles. Often we progressed less than five miles in an hour, frequently getting out to push the car or to roll boulders out of the trail. Groups of men, women, and children were returning to Adigrat, from which they had fled during the bombing, their scant possessions loaded on the backs of donkeys. Upon our approach they fled in terror into the thorn bushes. Most of the men were carrying their rifles, which the Italians surprisingly permitted them to retain.

General Somma, commander of a Black Shirt division, accompanied us in person to a marvellous observation post on the edge of a rocky precipice overlooking the Ogoro plain toward Makale, which was the next objective. His post commanded a view extending fifty miles ahead to the south and to the edge of the escarpment on our left, over which lay the famous Danakil Depression, aptly called "the hell hole of creation," which shimmered in the intense heat.

The Danakil is one of the least known spots in the inhabited world. Europeans have traversed it from south to north only once in history. On that occasion the Nesbitt Expedition, during weeks of danger and hardship, recorded the highest temperature known in the world – 161° in the shade. The inhabitants are savages who still make fire by rubbing sticks together; they kill strangers upon sight and still fight with spears. Several expeditions attempting to explore the Danakil had been massacred. Santini's army skirted the western edge of the waste of sun-scorched Danakil, which lay at or below sea level; Santini was on the plateau 7,000 feet higher.

Back in Asmara two days later I accidentally met Ras Haile Selassie Gugsa, governor of Eastern Tigré, the region around Makale. This worthy man had voluntarily submitted to the Italians with his army of about 1,200 men when the Italians promised to make him chief of the whole Tigré Province, which included all the territory lying adjacent to the northern frontier. Gugsa announced that he joined the Italians because he was a "partisan of European civilization." In reality he was an enemy of Ras Siyoum, the governor of Western Tigré. Knowing that the Italians would occupy the Tigré, he hoped to displace Siyoum as puppet governor. Gugsa had married one of Haile Selassie's daughters who had died a few years previously of pneumonia because their "palace" had no window glass and she caught cold. Haile Selassie wanted to send a European doctor, but Gugsa insisted that she be treated by the native witch doctors.

After Gugsa's submission the Italians brought him to Asmara to indulge in some of the advantages of European civilization as exemplified in Asmara. I met him in the local barber shop. He was about twenty-seven, over six feet tall with bulky hips, negroid features, and thick, frizzy hair. The Italians gave him a European-style khaki uniform, with wide red stripes on the trousers, a Sam Browne belt, high laced boots, and an elaborate wrist watch fitted with every modern attachment, including stop-watch device. Obviously the watch filled him with inordinate pride, but he couldn't tell the time because he could not read the numerals.

I saw Gugsa on a shopping splurge at the barber shop's cosmetic counter, accompanied by his "prime minister" and an Italian officer. He made Signor Mariella, proprietor of the shop, remove the stoppers from every bottle of his meagre stock of perfumery. He sniffed each one and then chose those that pleased him. He had already selected three large bottles of Houbigant perfume, half a dozen little silk-and-gilt perfume atomizers, and several gold-plated safety razors. Gugsa grinned expansively and enjoyed his taste of European civilization, especially riding around the streets in an automobile. I learned he had been in an automobile only once before in his life, when he visited Addis Ababa, the only other trip outside his own territory. He spoke no language except his native Tigrina. The Italian officer refused to let me try to talk with him through his interpreter, but I interviewed him later in Makale.

Next day the first European who knew about conditions inside Ethiopia reached Asmara. He was Fernand Bietry, a Swiss engineer employed for four years by Haile Selassie's department of public works to build a road from Addis Ababa northward beyond Lake Aschangi. Selassie had assigned him a bodyguard of 250 troops who deserted him when the war started. Bietry walked 120 miles to the Italian lines because he feared the natives would kill him.

He told me: "Haile Selassie has practically no authority in the northern regions. I believe other tribes will join the Italians. The Imperial troops acting as my bodyguard had not been paid for three months. They pillaged the countryside, stealing cattle, telling the natives they were for me.

"The people in the regions where I was working distrusted the Emperor and complained that he made no effort to protect them from his own troops or from the local irregulars. These local irregulars were poorly armed and so hard up for ammunition that they tried to make cartridges by filling the empties with match heads as explosive."

Two days before the second phase of the invasion commenced – the push to capture Makale and attain the line of the Takkaze River– I learned the exact time when the movement would begin. Naturally the censorship would delete any reference to the impending drive; in fact, the chief censor notified us that no reference to it would be permitted until after the "zero hour."

I tried to devise phraseology which would convey the news through the censorship. I wrote a routine story about the work of consolidation of positions reached during the first phase, prefacing it as follows: "Soldiers front line singing tonight stop singing Italian equivalent of song Americans used sing in France quote where do we go from here boys where do we go from here unquote."

As I had hoped the censor apparently considered the sentences a flattering mention of the Italian morale and passed the message. Our New York cable editors, as I had hoped, noticed that the two sentences bore no relation to the rest of the dispatch; that they were not the "lead" of the story, and guessed that they had special significance. They issued a note to editors pointing out that apparently the phraseology was devised to intimate that the soldiers in the front lines were going somewhere, that another movement was imminent.

On November 12 Henri Gris, a Latvian correspondent, Chaplin, and I left Asmara to try to reach Makale, although we were told the road beyond Dolo was impassable to wheeled traffic. We made another passage over the "road of the 1,500 turnings." Clouds of choking dust hung stationary for minutes at a time in the narrow defiles, forcing the motor trucks to spread out at hundred-yard intervals. Although I could easily withhold my admiration from many phases of the campaign, it was impossible not to admire the spirit of these motor-truck drivers, who had probably the hardest job in the army. They were a grim-looking lot, dirty, unshaven, their faces sunburned brick-red and etched by lines of strain.

Outside Adigrat we sighted a huge concentration of camels. Captain Venzio Ramacci, the commandant, sunburned to the colour of chocolate, told us he had 1,200 camels in the detachment, the first of 10,000 camels which were being concentrated to carry supplies southward. His detachment had just arrived from Keren in western Eritrea, having covered 175 miles in eleven days. His Askari camel drivers squatted among the kneeling camels, making native bread from flour and water, wrapping the dough around hot stones to bake it. Ramacci served us hot tea flavoured with cayenne pepper such as his Askaris drank. That night we slept in our tents at Adigrat without undressing.

In my notebook I find the following entries covering our trip to Makale:

"November 13. – Up before sunrise. Black coffee from thermos bottle; nothing else. No water to wash or shave in. Leave 6:15 A.M. for Makale. Climb tortuous road to Edaga Hamus at 9,100 feet. Radiator boiling; at this altitude near the Equator water boils when it's scarcely hot enough to burn your fingers.

"While awaiting push toward Makale soldiers here built broad boulevardlike road, set out cactus plants alongside, erected carved stone mileposts inscribed: '105 kilometres to Makale.' Towering ocher-red mountain ramparts 1,000 feet high overlook plain. Down in plain we pass Sila division of regular army on march—about 18,000 men stretching as far as eye can reach across broad valley. They trudge along under burning sun-by eight A.M. it's scorching although water freezes at night at Edaga Hamus. One totes a huge bass drum.

"Tremendous ambas or solitary rocks shaped like human thumbs rise 500 feet from valley floor – a distinctive feature of Ethiopian landscape. Huge eagles sit on rocks beside road within twenty feet of our car, fearless of humans. Also birds the size of sparrows with two-feathered tail two feet long – so long and heavy they fly with great difficulty in short arcs.

"While driver repairing car watched millions of ants about half an inch long building anthill ten feet high. They leave trails which kill vegetation, even faintly mark rocks over which they pass. Speculate how many billions times their tiny feet must touch rocks to wear such trail. Rather terrifying to watch their frantic activity.

"Pass slow, swinging camel caravans southward bound; some ten miles long, tied tail to nose, in single file.

"Reach beginning of bad trail. At Adigrat they said we'd never reach Makale in automobile. Believe it now. At times advance only three miles in hour. At least twenty-five times get out to push, roll big stones from trail. Estimate I move at least half-ton during afternoon. All fenders smashed, top torn by thorn trees, one door handle falls off, another door damaged – won't stay shut. Two hub caps badly dented by rocks. Twice convinced crankcase broken. When we started it was new car only 1,272 miles on mileage indicator. Now look at it.

"Rocky trail twists and rises sometimes 45 degrees. Passage of Nagasc Pass is nightmare. In whole day didn't find more than total dozen miles level ground. Aside from few fertile, watered valleys, entire region semi-arid, covered by leaf cactus, candelabra cactus, euphorbia and thorn trees blistering in heat.

"Just before nightfall we reach edge of steep escarpment with fertile plain of Makale below. Except for twenty minutes' lunch beside trail took eleven hours make 78 miles – average about seven miles per hour.

"From plateau 600 feet above town had first view of Makale in setting sun. Lies in saucerlike plain perhaps ten miles circumference, ringed by flat-topped buttes five to six hundred feet high. Fertile plain dotted with small, putty-colored villages surrounded by irregular dura, corn, and rye patches with grazing herds of humped cattle, goats, and donkeys.

"Our car lurches down rocky camel and mule trail over which only four other automobiles ever passed-those of General Debono and his staff, who were half an hour ahead of us. Had much difficulty finding passable street through which car could advance. Once or twice seems car will capsize in dry torrent beds forming main street. We get out to prop it up. Natives stare in amazement at automobiles, which never before seen in Makale.

"Makale most considerable town I yet seen in Ethiopia; normally about 5,000 people. Houses built of rough, natural flat stones, crudely cemented with mud, tops of houses flat, covered with earth and straw stacks, streets narrow, winding, unpaved, and dusty.

"Principal building, King John's old abandoned palace, a medieval-looking, rectangular structure with square towers, crenelated battlements, surrounded by two concentric, irregular, oval stone walls about twenty feet high. Makale's main square, which fronts palace, is large open space intersected by deep, rocky, dry torrent bed beside which lie dead mules. Narrow streets swarm with white-shcmzmaed natives, red-fezzed Askaris, donkey and camel caravans, with scarcely a white man in sight.

"Local dignitaries ride through streets on mules surrounded

by corteges of retainers ranging from two to twenty, according to importance of dignitary. Corteges trot barefooted around rider, each carrying rifle, some old flintlock muskets. One dignitary has only one old man and one ten-year-old boy staggering under heavy musket.

"Native jet-black belles stand timidly within doors. Some really handsome, with fine features, large liquid eyes, and good complexions. Invariably dressed in dust-coloured shammas wearing cheap, brightly coloured beads and anklets of Japanese manufacture.

"Besides King John's palace there only four or five two-story buildings in town. On hill dominating town stands octagonal stone Coptic Christian church, surrounded by two well-built concentric stone walls; church about 150 feet diameter roofed with corrugated iron; bell-tower separate from church about 100 feet away.

"Obtain permission of Captain Salvietti, commander of tank corps, to erect our tent in tank camp beside church wall."

Salvietti, a broad, jovial officer, invited us to dine with him. He said he had little to eat as supplies had not yet arrived, so we contributed canned goods and ate with him on top of ammunition boxes under an open flapping canvas by lantern light.

The captain amused himself by getting his monkey, "Arcu," drunk on cognac. It lapped cognac out of a saucer avidly, then squeaked, staggered, and leaped with every evidence of intoxication, provoking roars of laughter from Salvietti.

Late that evening Salvietti told us that Ras Siyoum's men were expected to attack Makale during the night; the camp was on the alert and sentries doubled and tripled. Salvietti made frequent inspections of his outposts and his whippet tanks, which were in readiness for an attack. At two A.M. there were still no indications of an attack so we crawled into our tent with Salvietti's promise to awaken us the moment firing commenced. Hyenas howled and fought over the bodies of dead mules in the town square, but no attack developed that night.

At nine-thirty the next morning ten Caproni bombers roared over Makale, headed southward. The natives were terrified by the thunder of the motors. Shortly afterward we heard faint thuds of bomb explosions from the direction of Scelicot. Almost simultaneously artillery in Fort Galliano, an old, round stone fort on the hill about 600 feet above the town, opened fire. The shells were directed over the rim of hills to the northwest.

From the churchyard we watched with glasses the flashes of guns and counted the seconds before we heard the roar of shell explosions. We heard the greasy slither of three-inch and five-inch shells through the air and the dull explosions of shells about fifteen seconds later. Firing continued sporadically, sometimes in salvos of three, during about twenty-five minutes. We could get no details of the reasons for the bombardment. Some three-inch shells fell in the valley below us. Through glasses we watched the jetlike columns of dust thrown up by the explosions. At 11:15 A.M. there was another outburst of firing for a few minutes. Several officers told us the firing was for "range-finding purposes and the moral effect."

That afternoon General Debono and his staff, escorted by Ras Gugsa, who had been named puppet governor of Tigré Province, visited the tomb of Gugsa's father and the Coptic church. Gugsa arrived dressed in his European uniform and sun helmet, riding a yellow-caparisoned mule with richly embroidered, scarlet velvet saddlecloth and gold-and-silver-embroidered bridle. On each side of the mule loped four barefooted soldiers with light machine guns, presented to Gugsa by the Italians. A trotting barefooted rabble of about 200 shammaed, armed men without semblance of military formation encircled Gugsa. Debono and his staff arrived on horses.

Ras Gugsa grinned and bowed deferentially as he showed Debono the fifteen-foot-square stone tomb of his father, which was inscribed in Tigrina: "Descendant of Solomon." He tried to open the ironwork door of the tomb, but it was locked. Debono removed his cap and saluted the tomb.

As we emerged from the churchyard Gugsa's mule, evidently more patriotic than his master, tried to kick General Debono. Although Debono was seventy-four years old, the leap he executed probably set a record for septuagenarians.

Late in the afternoon we visited Ras Gugsa's residence, one of the few two-story structures in town. It was built of rough stone set in a stony courtyard crowded with the rabble of his troops. We elbowed our way through them into the Ras's "palace," which consisted of only four rooms. Gugsa was not at home but we examined the place unhindered. His "throne room" was a dark chamber about twenty feet square with one glassless window. The floor was covered with straw. In one corner a native rug was thrown over the straw and on it stood the "throne"– an ordinary wicker porch chair. The only other article of furniture was a wooden kitchen chair. Gugsa's bedroom had a pallet on the floor and two or three suitcases and some boxes. We were told that Gugsa slept with a machine gunner manning a machine gun on each side of his pallet.

About dark Gugsa arrived on his caparisoned mule accompanied by his "prime minister" and retainers. He came into the throne room, grinned, and stood beside the wicker chair with his hand thrust into his tunic a la Napoleon. His "prime minister" could speak a few words of French, and two words of English which he interjected now and then. They were "good night."

I asked Gugsa what elements of European civilization he wished to introduce into the Tigré. "That's a matter for the Italians to decide," he said. We knew that already. I asked him what he knew about America. "I've heard of it," he said and grinned. "When I was at Addis Ababa I rode in an American automobile. I'd like to have one." That was all I could get from him about his knowledge of America.

He told us he intended to make Makale the capital of the Tigré and live in King John's old palace. General Debono had previously told us that he was not going to live in King John's palace and that Adowa or Aksum would probably be the capital of the Tigré.

Gugsa proudly exhibited his marvellous wrist watch, then sent his "prime minister" to bring two little cardboard boxes. He ceremoniously extracted from them a little envelope and a cheaply printed calling card on which his name was inscribed in Tigrina and Italian and presented them to us with a bow. He had had them printed in Asmara. Inasmuch as he had nobody to call on in Makale, he apparently decided to give them to persons who called on him. We perceived no evidences of the perfume he bought in Asmara; one smell only permeated his "palace," and that was the characteristic Ethiopian odour of rancid mutton fat, unwashed human bodies, and dust.

We visited the native market place where squatting natives and Askaris haggled over chickens and goats in the dust. Chickens sold for nine lire – about forty-five cents. Adjoining the market was Lepers Lane, where about a dozen hideously loathsome lepers with fingers and toes missing begged. One Ethiopian stood five minutes looking at himself in a tiny hand mirror on sale by one of the vendors; undoubtedly he had never before seen a mirror. Another native traded a chicken for two boxes of matches then stood and lighted them one after another; we learned that most of the natives in this region had never seen matches. A grave, dignified, white-bearded Coptic bishop wearing white tennis shoes and white socks rode through on a mule. As I rode across the square on a mule lent me by an Italian officer, I was nearly thrown when the stolid animal suddenly leaped like a jack rabbit and ran, pursued by my Askari escorts. He had sighted a dead mule, and I had learned that the only object an Ethiopian mule fears is a dead mule.

Henri Gris, the Latvian correspondent, joined us at the market place. He had lost his notepaper, could obtain no paper anywhere, and had been making notes with his fountain pen on his finger-nails, which he transcribed to paper we loaned him.

Next morning we set out on a 210-mile journey back to Asmara to file our dispatches, as the Italians would accept no press material for transmission over the inadequate signal-corps wire. Captain Salvietti gave us some American gasoline which Ras Siyoum had abandoned.

It took us two full days of steady driving to reach Asmara, halting overnight at Adigrat on November 15. We had not shaved, bathed, or removed our clothes for four days when we reached Adigrat and had eaten only meagerly from our limited supply of canned goods.

After writing my dispatches I underwent a physical collapse from the effects of two months' physical and mental strain. In altitudes of 8,000 to 9,000 feet, intensified by our proximity to the Equator, we suffered curious mental effects: extreme irritability, deep melancholia, hysteria, and intense susceptibility to noise, which penetrated our eardrums like a stiletto because the air was so thin that it did not muffle sounds. Floyd Gibbons had collapsed weeks previously and had gone to bed with spells of delirium and weeping that lasted five days before we could get him into an airplane for the Sudan. John Whitaker's nerves were frazzled, which led to an amusing interlude.

Roman Fajans, the Polish correspondent who talked too much, lived in our cabin. He had an annoying habit of occupying the only toilet half an hour every morning. Whitaker paced up and down one morning, ready to start to the front. Finally, he summoned the Pole to the door of the toilet and expostulated with him. After a heated colloquy in broken French, Whitaker lost his Southern temper, shoved the Pole in the face, slammed the door, locked it, and threw the key into the yard, shouting: "That's where you belong." Fajans screamed bloody murder, but nobody would release him until the Italian sergeant in charge of the building combed the yard and found the key.

On my second day in bed, while William W. Chaplin of Universal Service was in my cabin talking with me, I commenced weeping for no particular reason and could not stop, except at intervals, all the afternoon. Whitaker and Chaplin brought an Italian army doctor, who said that I must get into a lower altitude immediately. All the eleven cars in the press section were in the repair shop, including the new one in which we had just returned from Makale. I could not get aboard an airplane for the Sudan because the planes were carrying only military couriers and mail. Whitaker and Chaplin used rather high-handed methods with Casertano, chief of the press section, to induce him to lend his own car and driver to take Herbert Matthews, of the New York Times, suffering exhaustion after his difficult trip across the edge of the Danakil, and me to Kassala on the Sudanese frontier.

We left early next morning for the trip across the Eritrean plateau toward the Sudan. Our native driver, named Haile Selassie, drove barefoot, and he had such big feet that when he pushed the brake he sometimes hit the accelerator simultaneously.

We descended from the plateau 6,600 feet over a road nearly as contorted and dangerous as that of the famous "journey of death." Hour after hour Selassie whipped the little car around hundreds of hairpin bends.

All afternoon we wound across the sweeping hot plains of the "Bassopiano Occidentale," dim mountains shimmering on the horizon. After nightfall we were lost several times but finally reached Tessenei, a small native village on the Eritrean-Sudanese frontier, where only eleven white men lived. Here we succeeded in getting a native woven-rope bed, in a tin-and-matting hut; and after fourteen hours of hard travel it felt comfortable. Outside hyenas, baboons, and jackals made the night hideous.

Early the next day we started to Kassala over flat plains thickly covered with coarse grass higher than the car. Nothing demarcated the frontier except a couple of sticks erected as barriers between half a dozen grass huts that Askari frontier guards occupied. Since they could not read our written permission to cross the frontier, we had to take the sergeant back ten miles to the nearest telephone so that he could assure himself verbally that we had permission. Upon our return the sticks were formally lowered. It was rather ludicrous, because there was nothing for hundreds of miles in either direction to prevent a car from crossing the imaginary line denoting the frontier.

As we entered Kassala our car stuck in the deep sand and we had to finish our trip on foot across a strip of burning sand where thousands of camels were massed for sale to the Italian army.

After great difficulty, because we could find no native who knew any language we spoke, we located the residence of the British District Commissioner, T. R. Blackley. Seeing I was near collapse, Blackley took me into his house and immediately put me to bed. As no train ran to Khartoum for four days, Blackley arranged with the Italian air line to take me there the next day. Since Kassala was a mile and a quarter lower than Asmara, the plane could lift a heavier load there.

At Khartoum, where the Blue and White Nile join, I spent five days in bed in an excellent hotel and six days more convalescing, enjoying the luxury of fresh vegetables, clean sheets, baths, and quiet. Lieutenant Colonel Whitby, a British army doctor, strongly advised me not to return to the high altitudes of Ethiopia. Also Dr. George Crile of Cleveland, passing through on a scientific mission to Tanganyika, advised against returning. He said my blood was full of fatigue toxins and that I must refrain from exertion for a considerable time. When I had recovered sufficiently, I flew down the Nile to Cairo, remained there a couple of weeks resting, then flew across the Mediterranean to Europe and London.

26

THE CASE FOR THE AGGRESSOR

What I had learned about Ethiopia and the Ethiopians diluted my original bitterness toward the Italian invasion. I still did not condone the deliberate aggression and violations of treaties, which further shook international confidence in written instruments between nations, already weakened by Japan's violations in Manchuria, the Allies' infractions of debt contracts, Germany's violations of the Treaty of Versailles, and other breaches of international agreements. Such violations had struck paralyzing blows at the whole network of treaties erected since the war for the purpose of preventing another great European war.

But after studying the history of the partition of Africa by European powers I felt that the Italian invasion was in fact no less and no more reprehensible than the series of unprovoked aggressions and land grabs by which England, France, Belgium, Spain, Portugal, and Germany had gobbled up the entire continent of Africa, excepting Ethiopia and Liberia, previous to the World War. There did not seem to be much difference between these aggressions and Italy's, except that hers had been committed after the World War, which was presumed to have ended aggression, but hadn't.

I hated the idea of bombing and gassing practically defenceless people from the air. But in Morocco ten years before I had seen the Spaniards bomb the Riffs, who were armed only with rifles; and only five years before I had watched the British on the Northwestern Frontier of India bombing the Afridi tribesmen, who were virtually defenceless against airplanes. Nineteen years before in London I had seen eleven German air raids slaughter and maim hundreds of unarmed civilians, including women and children. I knew that in the next great war the use of air bombs and gas would be absolutely merciless, that noncombatants would be slaughtered indiscriminately.

I also knew that what primarily impelled England's bitter opposition to the Italian invasion was her natural fear of having a powerful, aggressive nation obtain a foothold directly athwart her line of communication with her Empire in the East – her Imperial jugular vein; and her fear that this would eventually menace her domination of the Mediterranean and the sea route to India and Australia. I saw France play a slippery double game in the Ethiopian affair, motivated largely by her fear of Germany. For the French tried simultaneously to placate England, maintain their friendship with Italy, and prevent a rapprochement of either country with Germany.

I had seen how the other Allies after the World War cheated Italy out of her share of the territorial war loot. And I knew, as other European nations admitted, that Italy needed territorial expansion to care for her rapidly increasing population, whose previous outlets by emigration had been cut off by immigration restrictions of the United States and the South American republics. I also realized that Italy needed access to raw materials more urgently than any other major European nation. These considerations, and what I saw and learned in Ethiopia, contributed to alter considerably the preconceived ideas I took to the war.

Of all the populous areas in the world, I found Ethiopia the most savage, uncivilized, and unknown. Its social fabric rested upon the institution of slavery; the Abuna, or "Pope," of the Coptic Church owned the largest number of slaves; war was the national industry and men were honoured by the number of people they had slaughtered. Not one person in ten thousand could read or write; intertribal wars and criminal punishments involved cruel mutilations; unchecked disease was rapidly killing off the population, and the vast majority lived in filth, poverty, and degradation. The lowest estimate of the syphilis rate is eighty-five per cent.

I learned that roughly two-thirds of the population were already conquered peoples under the military domination of the alien Amharas, who differed from the subdued tribes in race, customs, and often religion, and maintained dominion by frequent wars that threw all the prisoners into slavery. Even the Emperor had usurped the throne. I found that the country was not homogeneous. The people spoke more than seventy languages and two hundred dialects. National patriotism in the Western sense was almost nonexistent; only hatred of the white man united the people for war. Only a handful read or wrote the languages (Amharic, the principal language, contained over two hundred syllable signs) and priests tried to prevent dissemination of knowledge of reading and writing.

I found that the Italian staff maps bore large white spaces marked simply "unexplored territory," and nobody knows even the population of Ethiopia's 350,000 square miles, estimates ranging from 4,000,000 to 13,000,000. Fernand Bietry, the Swiss engineer who spent four years in the country, told me the infant mortality was so high and the races were dying out so rapidly that he believed the population might be as low as 3,000,000.

The mass of people know nothing whatever of the outside world. Bietry, who spoke Tigrina, said that few Ethiopians had ever heard of the continent of America or the World War. They seldom travelled more than a few dozen miles and lived almost as their ancestors did one or two thousand years ago.

The Ethiopians seemed to me to be at about the same stage of culture that the American Indians reached after the white man came. They had adopted the rifle and the steel knife, but had taken over little else from the culture of the white man. I perceived many analogies between the manner of living and fighting and the culture of the Ethiopians and the American Indians. But from what I knew of the American Indians I thought their moral and physical development before the white man came had reached a much higher stage than that of the Ethiopians.

Although the use of the wheel is considered one of the greatest advances in civilization, I found that most Ethiopians knew nothing about it. I never saw a single native wheeled vehicle or implement in the two months I spent in Ethiopia, although I visited the principal towns of the north: Adowa, Adigrat, and Makale.

Roads passable on wheels virtually did not exist in most of the country. Transportation was by muleback over rocky trails that the feet of animals had worn through centuries. Communications with the interior were so primitive that weeks after the invasion commenced caravans reached the Italian lines not knowing that war had begun. I heard that the "mayor" of Dessie, later the Emperor's headquarters, did not know until a month afterward that Adowa had fallen.

Another vital factor that prevented the Ethiopians from achieving progress in the modern sense lay in their superstition that anyone who worked in iron became a hyena at night and ate dead bodies. Only one small tribe, the Falashas or "Black Jews," who practiced the ancient Judaic religion, worked in iron, and for that reason the other tribes detested and feared them. Even the tips of the primitive wooden instruments used for cultivation were not shod with iron; the ploughs were merely crooked sticks.

Ethiopians used iron instruments manufactured abroad; in fact, the rifle is the national implement. Every grown man who can obtain a gun of any kind carries it every moment, usually placing it lengthwise across both shoulders and grasping it with both hands by the muzzle and butt. The rifle is virtually a symbol of manhood and indicates the man's position in the community.

An absolute autocracy based on a loose feudal system governed the country. Each chieftain bore responsibility only to the chieftain next above him, hence the fealty of the mass to the Emperor amounted to little.

Local chieftains and Rases received no salaries; they existed by extracting everything possible from their subjects. The basic tax averaged one-tenth of a man's foodstuffs and animals paid in kind and one day of labour out of every four for his overlord; also, supplies of food to the overlord's troops or guests in the area, in addition to further levies in money or kind. These exactions left the mass of people barely above the subsistence level; the main preoccupation of the great majority was to get enough food to live on. The Rases paid to the Emperor a share of the silver and commodities which they had collected from their underlords.

From what I saw, heard, and read, I became convinced that the Ethiopian version of the Coptic Church, a primitive form of Christianity deeply overlaid by paganism and rank superstition and little resembling the Western forms of Christianity, constituted the most backward and obnoxious influence in the country.

The Coptic Church owned about one-third of the country outright, and the ignorant, parasitical priests and deacons comprised about one-quarter of the male population. They did no work, were exempt from military service, and lived off exactions from the people. Payment of about five dollars and no further qualification enabled a man to become a deacon and to live on his fellows. Few could read or write; in personal filth and dress they resembled the mass of people.

The Church bitterly opposed progress or innovation and wielded wide influence upon the governing class. Neutral foreign observers told me that the Church exerted little influence on the morals of the people and that houses of prostitution and drinking dens flourished without opposition. In Adowa and Makale I saw a number of foul huts flying a dirty cloth marked with a red cross – the symbol of a brothel in Ethiopia. Although Haile Selassie made an honest effort to abolish the slave trade– he once estimated that the task would take twenty years – the head of the Coptic Church, as the largest slaveholder, consistently opposed reform. Priests of the Church were served by domestic slaves.

The marriage customs of the people were extraordinarily lax; usually the man and woman simply lived together until one or the other decided to leave. If they did have a formal marriage, they went before the "mayor" and entered into a contract specifying their respective properties, which were equally divided upon divorcement. Either party could divorce the other by a simple statement. Since girl babies were unwelcome, they were often abandoned for the hyenas to eat. Ethiopians of the Coptic religion maintained only one wife at a time but "remarried" frequently, often a dozen times. Among the Galla tribes, the largest section of the population, men kept two or three wives simultaneously. They were Mohammedans and more devout religiously than the Coptics.

The mass of people practiced gross superstition. Criminals were sometimes "detected" by drugging a young boy and sending him around the huts to "smell out" the criminal. Witch doctors or priests sometimes treated disease by simply writing – or pretending to write – the name of the sick person upon a piece of paper or a tree, and charging a fat sum. The people strongly believed in the "evil eye" and were convinced that evil spirits inhabited certain places.

Administration of criminal justice rested upon the ancient Mosaic law of "an eye for an eye." In cases of manslaughter or murder the relatives, unless they agreed to accept blood money, could demand that the criminal be killed by the same means. Punishment for repeated theft involved severance of an arm or leg in public, and the bleeding stumps were plunged into boiling mutton fat. Debtors and creditors were chained together until the debt was paid.

In my stories of Adowa, Adigrat, and Makale I have already described the wretched conditions in which the great mass of people live.

Conversations with neutral foreign engineers long familiar with portions of the country convinced me that the Italians could develop Ethiopia to their own, and eventually to the natives', advantage. Indisputably, the country contains great agricultural resources, now only sketchily exploited with prehistoric implements. The broad watered valleys of the interior in Goj jam, and around Lake Tana, contain tens of millions of acres of rich land. Owing to the exactions of overlords, the Ethiopians had little incentive to work the land more than enough for their own foodstuffs and taxes in kind. Like the American Indians, the Ethiopians usually farmed only patches large enough for their own needs.

Excellent coffee and passable tobacco and rice grow wild. Wheat, oats, flax, and corn flourish abundantly in many parts of the central region. Great tracts of fine grazing land support herds of cattle, which could be greatly increased without interfering with the natives. Rich forest tracts exist.

Whether minerals exist on an exploitable scale remains problematical. Engineers told me that gold, platinum, and other valuable minerals were known to exist, but the Ethiopians' suspicion of the white man had prevented much prospecting. The Galla tribes extracted alluvial gold in small quantities from the Wollega and Shangalla regions. Traces of oil had been found in various districts, but the extent of the deposits remained unknown. Two foreign engineers told me they were convinced that iron, copper, and coal existed in profitable quantities. Naturally the Ethiopians had never made an effort to discover and exploit any of these mineral resources.

Contrary to the general belief abroad, I learned that the Ethiopian plateau is quite suitable for white habitation. It lies at an average altitude of six or seven thousand feet, is not much hotter than the Middle West in summer, and is always delightfully cool at night. Anyone not afflicted with a weak heart or lungs becomes acclimated fairly quickly.

Although the invasion was doubtless morally indefensible, I felt after I came to know more about actual conditions that perhaps domination of the country by the white man was less reprehensible than it at first seemed. I felt that if any of the "civilizing missions" carried out by white nations among alien races had any justification, the Italian invasion of Ethiopia had no less. I concluded that the mass of people would undoubtedly be no worse off and probably much better off under white rulers and that the world in general would be likely to benefit, politically and economically, from the modern development of the country.

As had happened in India and elsewhere, my preconceived ideals were reluctantly shouldered aside by less high-minded practical considerations.

27

TWO 27-HOUR DAYS

I spent Christmas week of 1935 in London and then sailed to New York to go on a lecture tour. During two and a half months I travelled all over the United States, spoke fifty-one times in forty cities on my Ethiopian experiences, and travelled about 15,000 miles, chiefly by airplane. I had almost no experience in public speaking, which I found a severe ordeal, and always felt like a damp dish rag when I finished.

Late in April, 1936, I sailed on the Bremen to Germany to make the first transatlantic flight in the Zeppelin Hindenburg, inaugurating the first regular passenger service by air across the North Atlantic.

Although I had travelled about 150,000 miles by airplane in America, Europe, Africa, and Asia, this was to be my first experience aboard a lighter-than-air craft. The United Press insured my life at Lloyd's in London; the one-per-cent premium was comparatively low; they had paid seven per cent for my flight to India five years before.

The little town of Friedrichshafen, beside the placid Lake of Constance, close to where Austria, Switzerland, and Germany meet, seethed with excitement. The German nation regarded the inauguration of air service to the United States with justifiable national pride, for it had definitely gained supremacy in passenger, mail, and freight service to both North and South America by air. Only seventeen years before, the Treaty of Versailles had virtually swept Germany's shipping from the seas when the Allied Powers had seized her merchant marine and also crippled her air development by the treaty. Now the German flag had returned to the seven seas; the Bremen and Europa were two of the fastest and largest liners in the world, and the airship Graf Zeppelin was making her 107th crossing of the South Atlantic to South America. She had safely carried more than 12,000 passengers in her career and travelled nearly a million miles. The first flight of the Hindenburg would clinch German predominance in transoceanic air traffic, and a sister ship for the Atlantic services was under construction. Germany rejoiced.

As darkness fell on May 6 buses took the fifty-one passengers and about a ton of baggage to the vast Zeppelin hangar. Fifty pounds of baggage could be carried free; excess weight cost about seventy-five cents a pound.

After we passed through the customs and passport control and were warned against carrying matches aboard, we mounted into the bottom of the craft by a retractable stairway. A band played, hundreds scurried around under the ship shouting farewells, the passengers craned out of the open windows, Herr Arthur Voigt, a Danzig millionaire, unbuckled his wrist watch and tossed it out as a farewell present to a relative. There was as much tension and excitement as at the sailing of an ocean liner.

About a quarter past eight the two hundred men of the ground crew hauled at cables and briskly walked the craft, which was attached to a movable mooring mast, out into the field.

At a word from Commander Ernst Lehmann, the cables were thrown off. The huge ship, nearly one-sixth of a mile long and as high as a thirteen-story building, weighing 236 tons with its load of fuel, mail, freight, foodstuffs, water, passengers, and crew, lifted gently as thistledown. One hundred and six persons were aboard, the largest number ever to embark on a transoceanic flight.

As the huge bulk drifted upward silently and slowly we looked down into the upturned faces of thousands of frantically cheering townsfolk, spotlighted by the downward beams of two searchlights in the belly of the ship. The waving forest of arms gradually receded. Signal bells jangled in the engine gondolas and the four 1,100-horse-power motors roared. It was 8:27 P.M.; we were off on the 4,300-mile flight to America, suspended in air by 6,710,000 cubic feet of inflammable hydrogen gas.

From the slanting windows of the passengers' promenade deck, we glimpsed the snow-covered mountains of Switzerland and Austria and the gleaming surface of the Lake of Constance beneath. The Hindenburg headed down the Rhine toward the English Channel – a detour of hundreds of miles because France refused to permit the ship to cross her territory. Stewards with wireless telegrams paged the passengers and distributed a passenger list like that of an ocean liner. They announced that smoking was prohibited until an hour after sailing, and then it must be done in the hermetically sealed smoking room.

After the excitement of the take-off subsided, passengers inspected their accommodations, which comprised about 4,500 square feet entirely enclosed within the belly of the craft. On each side of the twenty-five two-bedded cabins ran a promenade forty-six feet in length flanked by slanting windows permitting a view outward and downward. Alongside the starboard promenade were a salon and a writing room furnished with duralumin chairs, writing desks, and piano. The dining room, forty-six feet long, with two tables seating fifty persons, adjoined the port promenade. The rooms were tastefully decorated. Each small, comfortable cabin had a wash basin with hot and cold water, a tiny desk, a clothes closet, and an electric light.

The deck below the cabins housed the shower baths, the kitchens with electric cooking apparatus and refrigeration, the toilets, and the smoking room. Inasmuch as the hydrogen gas in the sixteen bags that supported the craft was highly inflammable, extraordinary precautions had to be taken with the smoking room. You passed through a special entrance constructed like two leaves of a revolving door, and this locked the air in the room. Air pressure was maintained higher inside than outside in order to prevent gas from entering even if leaks should accidentally develop. The ash receivers automatically closed airtight to extinguish the lighted butts. Drinks were served from a small bar adjoining.

Within an hour after the take-off the passengers settled down to a routine of life similar to that on shipboard, playing cards, writing postcards, drinking beer, and eating sandwiches. Professor Franz Wagner, a celebrated European musician, played the piano; Pauline Charteris, wife of the British novelist, and Lady Wilkins, wife of Sir Hubert Wilkins, danced with several of the passengers. Others strolled to the promenade and hung out of the open windows to see the Rhine gleaming in the moonlight a thousand feet below.

I had difficulty convincing myself that we were actually making a historic flight, the first regular passenger service to North America. We slipped through the air with velvety smoothness and almost no vibration. The ship did not sway or buck, the motors hummed but faintly. It was only when you thrust a hand out of the open window into the eighty-miles-an-hour wind that you had any idea of our speed.

At 10:20 P.M. the lights of Mannheim slipped beneath us, and at 11:15 we slid over the millions of lights of the great city of Cologne. Except for the initial take-off, that provided about the only thrill of the evening. After passing Cologne most of the passengers adjourned to the smoking room and toasted Commander Eckener and Captain Lehmann. Others went to bed, leaving their shoes out in the corridor as on shipboard. Newspaper correspondents aboard set up their typewriters in the salon and typed occasional bulletins, which were wirelessed direct to the United States.

Before daylight we reached the mouth of the Rhine, coasted down the English Channel, and caught a glimpse of the white cliffs at Dover. As the British objected to the Hindenburg's flying over England, it kept about a dozen miles out at sea.

As we slipped along the south coast of England at eighty miles an hour the rising sun silhouetted the South Downs like a relief map. The sea was calm and the passengers all slept, except the newspaper correspondents. Shortly after six I leaned out the promenade windows and watched the last land we were to see for 3,000 miles slowly slide away from us – or so it seemed. That was the jutting point of Land's End, the southwesterly tip of England; its white houses, red cliffs, and fresh green fields glistened in the early morning sun.

As the rocky finger of Land's End faded from sight and we started across 3,000 miles of rolling water, the full realization of the romance and adventure of the flight came home to me. During the forenoon we flew for hours a few hundred feet above a vast sea of dense, cottony clouds so white that it was almost impossible to look at them in the blindingly brilliant sunlight. The sharp black cigar-shaped outline of the Hindenburg flashed along across the snow-white floor, sometimes surrounded by three concentric circles of brilliantly glowing rainbows.

At 8:30 A.M. the passengers assembled for a breakfast of fruit, sausages, jam, toast, and coffee. The tables bore vases of fresh flowers and exquisite blue-and-white china. Presently we sighted the liner Staatendam, which saluted us with blasts of her siren; passengers crowded the decks waving handkerchiefs. Throughout our crossing we saw only half a dozen vessels although we were on the regular steamship track part of the time.

That day Sir Hubert Wilkins, the famous Arctic explorer, worked on his plans for a submarine in which he intended within a year to go to the North Pole under the ice. "I shall have a special submarine constructed," he said, "which will carry us from Europe to America under the ice of the Arctic region. I plan to start from Spitzbergen, off the coast of Norway, and travel twenty-two hundred miles under the ice to Point Barrow in Alaska, by way of the North Pole, at an average speed of about sixty miles a day. I proved by my previous experiments under the ice near Spitzbergen that it is perfectly feasible. We would come up through the ice once daily to make scientific and meteorological observations, transmit wireless messages, and recharge our batteries.

"My previous experience in the Arctic and Antarctic has shown that there are seldom more than twenty-five miles without great rifts in the ice, through which we could rise. If we find no rifts when we want to come up, we shall drill through the ice. I have invented a special thermal drilling device which will enable us to drill through ice up to eighteen feet in thickness, at the rate of a foot a minute. We could emerge through these holes.

"I am convinced that we shall find near the North Pole the greatest depths of water yet found on the globe. We shall take soundings cont uously. I believe that the earth is shaped slightly like an apple with a great depression at the top in the North Pole region. I am going to make the trip in connection with my scheme for a world-wide meteorological organization; in these days of air travel such an organization is necessary.

The weather of the world is greatly influenced by vast air currents originating in the Arctic regions. Eventually it will be necessary to have permanent meteorological posts in the Arctic. This, I believe, can be done only by means of relays of submarines."

Captain Ernst Lehmann conducted me through the interior of the craft. I reminded him that nineteen years before he had commanded a Zeppelin which bombed London. "I was two miles below you dodging your bombs," I said. He laughed: "Well, that was a long time ago."

On a foot-wide catwalk a few inches above the fabric of the belly of the ship, we threaded our way from the stem down into the immense tail fin of the Hindenburg. Sixteen great hydrogen bags filled most of the interior. They contained nearly seven million cubic feet of gas ten times as light as air and so inflammable that one spark would explode the craft in an instant. The huge rings of aluminium alloy which formed the Zeppelin's outline were braced by an intricate system of strong "Swiss cheese" girders and finger-thick wires. On either side of the catwalk lay great tanks carrying 143,000 pounds of Diesel oil, water tanks, bays for food supplies, freight, and mail, and officers' and crew's quarters.

As I trod the narrow runway I clutched nervously at struts and girders, fearing that a misstep would plunge me through the thin fabric into the ocean half a mile below. "You needn't be so concerned," Lehmann said, noticing my expression. "That fabric is strong enough to bear the weight of a man. You wouldn't go through if you slipped off on it." He perceived my incredulous look. "Here, I'll show you." He jumped off the catwalk on to the fabric, only a fraction of an inch thick. It bore him easily, although it was not attached to the body structure anywhere within eight feet. He explained that the fabric was unbelievably strong, having been manufactured at great expense for this particular duty.

Lehmann took me down into the control cabin, suspended under the belly of the ship, whence the Zeppelin was navigated. From there we viewed a marvelous panorama of ocean in every direction, with the immense bulk of the Hindenburg above and behind us. Dials, gauges, meteorological and navigating instruments filled the cabin. He showed me the operation of devices which valved out gas or water ballast to lower or raise the ship, a duplicate steering apparatus, and signal telegraph and telephone to every vital part of the ship. He explained the weather charts, which were revised every few hours on the basis of wireless reports from ships at sea.

With Fritz Sturm, chief engineer, I visited one of the engine gondolas, suspended on struts fifteen feet in space outside the envelope of the craft. That was an experience I do not want to repeat, and when I asked Lehmann's permission I did not know what it entailed.

To reach the gondola I climbed out over empty space on a collapsible ladder a foot wide slanting down from an opening in the envelope into the egg-shaped gondola. Before starting Sturm tied a helmet to my head, told me to leave my overcoat behind, and then showed me how to clutch the frail ladder on two sides, crooking my elbow around it to the windward and clutching the other edge with my fingers. This precaution was necessary to prevent the eighty-miles-an-hour wind from tearing me bodily off the ladder. I found it a ticklish, frightening business; each time I raised a foot the wind wrenched it away from the ladder rung and flung it back toward the stern of the ship. Nothing in the world could save you if the hurricanelike wind tore you off the ladder. Nothing but yawning space spread out on either side, and the ocean lay half a mile below. After a few steps down the slanting ladder I wished I hadn't conceived the foolhardy idea of visiting the gondola.

Inside the gondola a narrow passage ran alongside the 1,100-horsepower diesel engine, which drove a huge nineteen-foot propeller that deafened me with its thunder in spite of my padded helmet. Only a few struts the size of an ankle fastened this power plant to the craft, which loomed gigantically beside us. Once inside the gondola, Sturm closed the collapsible ladder. Empty space surrounded us on every side; we felt as if we were being shot through the air inside a huge artillery shell with open windows. An engineer remained continually on duty inside each of the four gondolas, shifts being changed every few hours.

Next morning, from an altitude of about three-quarters of a mile, I actually detected the curvature of the globe with the naked eye. From that height we could see scores of miles; the atmosphere was remarkably clear and the horizon sharp as a knife. By following the horizon closely I perceived, or thought I did, the slight bend of the earth's surface. That provided one of the greatest thrills of the trip; I had always known that the earth was round, but it was deeply stirring actually to see an infinitesimal section of its rotundity. Once before I had felt that same awesome sensation – when I stood one night on the edge of the chasm of the Grand Canyon and watched the opposite lip of the abyss wheel up toward the stars. I saw the turning of the earth as the rim of the Canyon rose, covering star after star; I imagined I even felt the world whirling under my feet.

About one o'clock Friday morning, in mid-Atlantic, the Hindenburg ran head on into a severe storm. In inky darkness as black as the inside of a black cat, the vast bulk of the Hindenburg swayed and bucked; hail and torrents of rain lashed at the windows of the promenade decks. With a few passengers I gazed down at the fascinating spectacle of the heaving ocean 2,000 feet below, one round area in the blackness illuminated by the spotlight in the belly of the craft. The downpour of rain and gale-force wind buffeted the craft about half an hour. This was the first time we had felt any deviation from the velvety motion of the ship.

So far as I could tell, none of us watching the storm felt any trepidation or appreciable sense of danger. The passengers already asleep were not awakened, vases of sweet peas and carnations on the writing and dining tables did not turn over. In my cabin not a drop spilled from a full glass of water. But at last you realized you were flying the Atlantic and were out here alone and helpless, 1,500 miles from land, fighting the elements and beating them.

Dr. Hugo Eckener, his deeply lined, weather-beaten face calm and composed, lumbered up from the control car. "This is really a severe storm," he said, "but I am pleased by the behavior of the ship. As you see, the motion is gentle. We have collected in special tanks five tons of water from the storm to replace many tons of weight lost by consumption of fuel oil. That will be useful to us in landing. With that additional weight we shall not have to valve out so much gas to get her down at Lakehurst. Sometimes when we sight a rain storm on the horizon we go over and run through it for the purpose of collecting water ballast. Unless we collect water from rain storms during a flight, we sometimes have to valve out as much as one-third of our gas. That is expensive; it has to be replaced before we commence another flight. We collect in tanks all of the water used by the passengers for toilet and bathing purposes during the trip and use it for ballast."

In the morning I saw a lone white bird 900 miles from land; he tried to follow us for awhile but gave it up, and we left him out there alone. I'll wager he doesn't go home to roost very often. Some 500 miles off Sable Island we passed over several glittering icebergs, one about an acre in extent, and watched three whales spouting.

Father Paul Schulte, of Aix-la-Chapelle, known as the "flying padre," celebrated the first mass in the air, for which the Pope had granted special permission. Schulte erected an altar in the salon, where all the passengers gathered. The candles were not lighted because of danger of explosion.

That night stewards served a five-course gala dinner, including fresh trout from the Black Forest. Many of the passengers wore evening clothes for the occasion. After dinner we made a broadcast to the United States including a piano recital by Professor Wagner, songs by Lady Wilkins, and speeches by Dr. Eckener and several of the passengers, including myself. After the broadcast, passengers gathered in the smoking room and bar to celebrate with many toasts and songs our approach to the American continent. Pauline Charteris introduced a song she had picked up in Nassau which ran: "Mamma don't want no gin, because it makes her sin." We discussed a suitable name for the first child conceived in mid-air aboard a Zeppelin – a possibility nowadays. I suggested Helium, if it were a boy, and Shelium, if a girl. That idea was adopted. The hilarious party continued most of the night.

In the morning before dawn we caught the first glimpse of the American continent. At 4:12 A.M. we sighted on our right a necklace-like string of lights miles long – the coast of Long Island. Passengers crowded to the promenade windows. At 4: 35 we came over Long Island and cruised toward Brooklyn while passengers gathered in the dining salon for a light breakfast of sliced sausages, coffee, toast, and jam. The sleeping millions a thousand feet below seemed unaware of our passage.

At exactly five A.M. the Hindenburg slid over the Battery. Dawn was just breaking. Suddenly a great pandemonium of hundreds of whistles from steamers and liners rose to greet us. We saw white jets of steam from the whistles of boats in the Hudson and East rivers. Passengers craned from the windows in excitement, chattering in several languages. Lights in the promenades were turned out to afford a better view.

We cruised up past the Empire State Building at reduced speed, passing only a few hundred feet above it. The sight brought exclamations of wonder from Europeans aboard who had never seen New York.

About the centre of Central Park the Hindenburg swerved toward the Hudson and flew over Germany's other symbol of re-emergence in world commerce – the liner Bremen, which directed two powerful searchlights upon us. Her deep-throated whistle bellowed. Our German passengers waved handkerchiefs from the windows in a fever of patriotic excitement.

The continued shrieking and bellowing of steamship whistles awakened thousands below. We saw people running from buildings and pointing and staring upward. Then, as the sun rose the airship turned down the Hudson and flew directly over the Statue of Liberty toward Lakehurst. I hastily wrote a description of our passage over New York and dropped it out of the window to one of our men when we hovered over the Lakehurst field.

The gigantic bulk of the craft settled gently at Lakehurst sixty-one hours and thirty-eight minutes after leaving middle Europe, a flight of 4,381 miles. We had eaten only two luncheons, two dinners, and three breakfasts aboard. We had spanned the ocean so rapidly that we had difficulty keeping track of the time on board because our days were twenty-seven hours long. This led to constant confusion between Greenwich time, Central European time, ship's time – which roughly corresponded with our position on the globe – Eastern Standard time, and Eastern Daylight time; and a prankster who frequently set back the clock in the bar so he could celebrate longer introduced still another factor. Even the airship officers sometimes seemed a little uncertain about Eastern Standard and Eastern Daylight time and their relation to ship's time and Greenwich time.

This rapid translation from continent to continent across 3,000 miles of ocean left in me an uncanny sense of confusion. The mind had not been able to keep pace with the body. Less than sixty-two hours before I had been in middle Europe. In that time 106 of us had been transported across one-fourth of the globe and my body, so it seemed, had left my mind behind. It took another day before I became orientated and fully grasped the idea that I was back in America.

28

THE EDUCATION OF
A NEWSPAPER MAN

During twenty-four years I have had a grand-stand seat at the most momentous show in history. From there I have witnessed the decline and fall of empires, the birth of new nations, the rise of new philosophies of government and the disappearance of old ones. I have seen the map of the world redrawn and come to know men and women of fifty-one nationalities and of a dozen creeds and religions. I have made friends with presidents, premiers, dictators, generals, soldiers, common workers, murderers, thieves, pimps, panders, and prostitutes.

The most important thing I learned professionally was that the truth about anything is difficult to obtain; that the more I studied the various aspects of any particular subject, the more qualified, the less definite and clear-cut my opinions became. Twenty centuries ago Greek philosophers discovered there is no exact truth except in mathematics.

Even when I witnessed an event myself I saw it differently from others. When I questioned eyewitnesses, persons who had no reason to distort the truth, each told a somewhat different story. I had to strike an average of their stories and temper this with my judgment of the circumstances and interests involved to come somewhere near the truth. I found that even when people with the best will in the world tried to tell the truth and nothing but the truth they could not do it. Each one saw something different. Every man's imagination unwittingly distorted what his eyes saw.

I encountered the most recent example while flying the Atlantic on the Hindenburg. A trained observer describing the mass celebrated on board by Father Schulte wrote: "Then the candles were lighted." The feature of the mass was the fact that candles were not lighted because of the danger of explosion. That observer knew that lighted candles were always used at mass and his imagination supplied what his eyes did not see and unconsciously falsified an interesting point of the story.

When the persons involved had a direct interest in distorting, magnifying, or concealing facts, as happens in a large proportion of the daily news, the task of arriving somewhere near the truth was greatly increased. Fortunately human beings are imbued with an almost irresistible desire to talk to someone.

I learned that the great majority of reporters and newspapers want to print the whole truth if they can get it. They are mortified and humiliated when they fall or are led into error. I found that, despite the haste in the production of a newspaper, the standard of accuracy is really astonishingly high when dealing with concrete facts, that is, facts obtainable without conscious or unconscious distortion.

Every market page prints thousands of concrete facts. Before they reach it they pass through the hands of five or six persons humanly prone to err. The number of errors in news of this kind is miraculously small. I found that the ordinary reader has not the slightest conception of the care and attention devoted to the attainment of accuracy in newspapers.

The establishment of censorships during and after the World War has made the attainment of truth even more difficult than under normal conditions. Following the rise of dictatorial governments, under which censorship became a fundamental rule, about four-fifths of the world's area has fallen under some form of censorship. Hundreds of millions of persons in the greater part of the world know only what their ruling cliques want them to know. By terrorism and control of communications these rulers attempt to prevent the outside world from knowing anything about their countries except what they desire. Adolf Hitler threw an army into the Rhineland before his own people or the world had an inkling of it. Mussolini moved an army to the Austrian frontier in secrecy. Never has the truth in foreign affairs been so difficult to obtain. Yet, considering all the circumstances, comparatively little of vital, world-wide importance escapes newspapers for long.

I have come to believe that the most significant development during my generation, not even excluding the World War, is the sudden burst in the advancement of science and machinery. It has introduced into the lives of the people of the world, into individual and international relations, imponderable forces which can make for their unprecedented material happiness or destruction; forces the effects of which are as yet little understood.

I believe that these mysterious economic, financial, and political forces released by machinery and science are destined to affect the lives, liberties, and relations of peoples and nations more than any other development of the age. And I believe that the most vital task before the world is experimentation with these forces to harness them for the welfare instead of the destruction of human beings.

I have concluded that the price the world must pay – and is already paying – for the material advantages of the modern machine is increasingly greater curtailment and restriction of the personal liberty of people. Already I have seen the machine infringe upon personal liberty in a multitude of ways. For instance, you cannot walk or drive when and how you please, and this is an interference with the fundamental liberty of movement. Owing to the advent of the automobile, you have to cross streets at prescribed places and times, halt and start your automobile at the winking of lights.

It seems to me that this principle on a wider scale is being and will have to be increasingly applied to many phases of human life and government. I think that the rise of dictatorial or authoritarian forms of governments was basically impelled by these forces.

Call it collectivism, regimentation, New Dealism, Fascism, Social-ism, Communism, or what you will, it is all of a piece – a general move-ment inevitable sooner or later as a result of the astonishing development of machinery and science. It has come more rapidly or more slowly in various countries, depending upon local conditions, economic advancement or backwardness, the temperament and training of the people, their geographical position and natural resources.

It seems to me that two separate governments, economic and political, cannot continue to exist in their old forms in parliamentary democracies under the impact of the vast forces generated by the machine. I think that the "economic government" which prescribes indirectly how much a man shall eat, how he shall live and clothe himself, the amount of work he shall do or not do – that is, capitalism, business, or the employer-will have to come more and more under the control of the political government which prescribes how much taxes a man must pay, the uses to which they will be put, and other political functions inextricably intertwined with and dependent upon the economic life of the people.

I have not been drawn to these conclusions by any attraction for those forms of government. As an American brought up in the democratic tradition, I detest the authoritarian or regimented forms of governments and do not want to live under them. I even resent restrictions upon when and where I shall cross a street. But I reflect that within my memory, under pressure of crises, the United States twice submitted temporarily to mild, voluntary forms of authoritarian government: during the World War and for a brief period during the banking crisis. In the modern Machine Age old-fashioned pure democracy seems too unwieldy at a critical juncture. I hope that the United States, with its heritage of liberty and great natural advantages over Old World countries, will make the necessary economic and political readjustments gradually and without conflict, but I am not convinced that this will happen.

In travelling about the world I have perceived that economic and political systems are badly out of kilter and urgently require fundamental readjustment. Machines possess the potentiality of easily providing sufficient food, shelter, and clothing for every human being on earth. But I have visited country after country in which the foremost preoccupation of tens of millions is to obtain enough food each day to sustain life, in which they live in hovels unfit for domestic animals, with standards little above those of the Dark Ages.

I have travelled through or flown over millions upon millions of acres of fallow land capable of feeding multitudes. I have seen millions jammed in cities living in poverty and degradation; elsewhere I have seen crops rotting in the fields and fruit dropping unpicked from trees because there was no market for the food.

There must be some system, I should think, of bringing the capacities of production and the requirements of consumption together so that the whole world can enjoy the advantages made available by the machine. Science and machinery have solved many more intricate problems.

I have seen that relations between nations are essentially similar to relations between individuals. They are subject in the main to the same instincts of self-preservation, fear, ambition, and avarice. From my reading of history and from watching it in the making, I believe that the fundamentals of human nature have not changed through the ages. The advent of the machine has changed the relations between nations and made them more interdependent, which ought to make for peace. But under authoritarian governments in which one man virtually sways the destinies of his country, nations are more than ever moved by the same emotions, instincts, and interests as the single individual.

It is conceivable that a dictator awakening one morning with a bellyache might throw his country into a war which might never have happened if he had taken a cathartic the night before. Rigid internal and external censorships make it perfectly feasible for an authoritarian government to be at war before the people of that country, or the country attacked, know anything about it. The Japanese did not declare war upon Manchuria, nor did Mussolini upon Ethiopia. That is undoubtedly the way the next war will start.

And I am convinced that the Old World is being rushed toward destruction and annihilation by the very same forces that could make for its unparalleled material happiness and well being. Instead of being used to provide adequate food, shelter, and clothing – the components of material happiness –and leisure – which could make for mental happiness,–the power of the machine is being more and more concentrated upon manufacture of means of destruction and slaughter.

I have seen the major nations of the Old World plunging headlong toward another great war. The only thing in the European situation that I feel absolutely certain about in my own mind is that another great war cannot be avoided. None of the masses of people want it. They seem like a person afflicted with vertigo who casts himself from a high place to destruction despite his will to live. Which nations will be in the war, when it will start, where and why, I cannot guess; neither can the rulers nor peoples. But they, also, know it is coming and are frantically preparing for it.

I have seen the whole edifice erected to maintain peace after the World War undermined. All of it is tottering, and sections of it have crashed in ruins. The League of Nations failed lamentably in the four vital tests which it faced: disarmament, revision of the Treaty of Versailles, Japanese aggression in Manchuria, and Italian aggression in Ethiopia. The Locarno Treaty, the Kellogg-Briand Pacts, the pacts outlawing war, the limitation of–armaments treaties, and the network of treaties of friendship and arbitration have all been vitiated by violations and defections. Nations no longer place any confidence in written instruments but put their trust only in instruments of slaughter and military alliances for war.

I have watched Europe slump back into a situation far more critical than that of 1914, or any other period in history. A desperate, world-wide armament race is now in progress, while the nations pick sides for the next war. They have more men under arms than ever before; they possess more destructive machines for slaughter. Everywhere "economic wars" go forward, and the authoritarian and parliamentary-democratic systems of government become increasingly hostile. Meantime, the plows of peasants turn up rotted corpses from the last war, and tens of thousands of pitiful wrecks of men drag out hopeless lives in wheel chairs in military hospitals.

If any one cause could be assigned as mainly responsible for the fantastic and loathsome plight into which Europe has again sunk, that cause is fear, one of the primary human instincts. The United States stayed out of the League of Nations because it feared European entanglements, France refused to disarm because she feared a re-awakening Germany,

Russia armed because she feared the enemies of Communism, Germany re-armed because she feared France and Russia, Poland armed because she feared Russia and Germany, England re-armed because she feared Germany, the United States armed because the others did, and so on. Each nation lives in mortal terror like a man under an anonymous threat of death, not knowing exactly where the danger lies. And fear begets fear.

Ever since the War some of the world's best minds have applied themselves to finding methods of banishing fear from the relations of nations, but they have failed. Fear seems as deeply impregnated in the instincts of nations as it is in the instincts of human beings.

I have had unusual opportunities during two decades for observation of world history and contact with the men who made it. I have read hundreds of history books, books on the origins of the World War and other wars, biographies and autobiographies of men who directed the destinies of wars and of nations. Far more than the average man, I felt I should form definite opinions about the fundamental problems of the world, about right and wrong in international relations. But I must confess that generally I have not succeeded; I am no less confused and uncertain than the men who direct the currents of international affairs. I have learned that the only way to retain a firm, clear-cut opinion about anything is to know little or nothing about it.

I have been gradually forced to the conclusion that right and wrong in international affairs are seldom static. Paul Henri Spaak, Foreign Minister of Belgium, expressed this idea in courageous words: "Right is a concept of the mind which is always disputable. . . . Is it not a mistake to found the principles of foreign policy solely on right, which is in perpetual evolution, and to risk the fate of men and of future civilization itself upon what is, after all, only momentary?"

Twenty-four years of newspaper work, nineteen of them spent in foreign countries, have altered me greatly inwardly and outwardly from the timid, awkward, colorless country lad who went from the farm to Chicago in 1912. By deliberate effort I have succeeded in beating down most of the inhibitions which made my work difficult for many years.

Using self-made methods not unlike those of Dr. Coué – although when I started practicing them I had never heard of him or his ideas – I mastered my backwardness in human contacts and even attained a certain proficiency in that direction.

Before starting to interview an important personage or working on a big story, I have often convinced myself that I was adequate for the task by telling myself repeatedly: "You have interviewed so-and-so and so-and-so, you have covered such-and-such big stories and you can do this." By keeping in mind my successes and forgetting my failures as soon as possible, I achieved a considerable measure of personal and professional self-confidence.

I deliberately sought the company of women and eventually conquered my long-standing diffidence in their presence. I found that Charles Erbstein's rule applied to women even more than to men – that if you liked them they almost invariably liked you. And upon acquaintance with most women I found that I liked them. (Publisher: "Were there no women in your life?" Me: "Yes, but that is another and much more interesting story.")

I have built up by premeditated effort a personality very different from the one which heredity and early environment shaped for me. I can give a passable imitation of a man of the world, know which forks to use at a state dinner, know the best champagne vintages, can eat caviar, and can kiss the hand of a princess without feeling too uncomfortable. I have educated myself by books so that I feel confidence and little constraint in any company.

I retain my liking for occasional solitude and whenever possible go away for a couple of days' walking alone. During these trips I speak to almost nobody. This solitude serves as a useful mental astringent.

I have clung to the philosophy of Thoreau, which still gives me mental comfort, although I realize it is impractical as a rule of life. That makes no difference; all that matters is that I have faith and draw serenity from it.

Often I wish I could find the peace which Walden represents to me . . . but now I am starting back to Europe to cover the next war.